The Red Mirror

The Red Mirror

Putin's Leadership and Russia's Insecure Identity

GULNAZ SHARAFUTDINOVA

OXFORD
UNIVERSITY PRESS

Oxford University Press is a department of the University of Oxford. It furthers
the University's objective of excellence in research, scholarship, and education
by publishing worldwide. Oxford is a registered trade mark of Oxford University
Press in the UK and certain other countries.

Published in the United States of America by Oxford University Press
198 Madison Avenue, New York, NY 10016, United States of America.

© Oxford University Press 2020

CIP data is on file at the Library of Congress
ISBN 978–0–19–750294–5 (pbk.)
ISBN 978–0–19–750293–8 (hbk.)

I dedicate this book to my parents, Gulia Kh. Sharafutdinova (1947–2011) and Chulpan Z. Sharafutdinov (b. 1948).

Contents

Preface

VLADIMIR PUTIN IS not the president of my choice. However, he is a president by virtue of the choices made by people I care about. My brother is proud of Putin. My father respects his foreign policy. My cousin voted for him, fearing instability and not seeing any viable alternatives. Educated as a political scientist, I understand the institutional mechanisms and policies in place for removing viable political alternatives and making Putin seem the only choice. Yet it is hard to deny that the degree of genuine support for Putin in Russian society goes beyond the fact that people find themselves choosing in the absence of alternatives. Soviet politics also lacked alternatives, but was far from producing pride about the Communist leaders. Putin's appeal to many Russians has been real, and the analysts need to take this reality seriously, and to explore its nature and sources, its meaning and implications.

Needless to say, Putin's appeal varies across the time of his outsized presidential tenure. The puzzle this book is motivated by applies best to the window of time between 2014 and 2018—the moment that could be referred to as a prolonged post-Crimean syndrome, or even "high Putinism."[1] This moment was ruptured to an extent by the effects of the unpopular pension reforms announced in the summer of 2018. Still, the significance of this moment and the meanings shared in Russian society in regard to Putin's leadership are likely to be more lasting.

This book is motivated primarily by a personal urge to understand the gap between how many of my schoolmates, friends, and family "back home" perceive Putin's leadership, and how I perceive it. It is a gap in thinking about Russian politics that might not have existed if I had continued to live my life in the place I was born. It is a gap in perceptions that draws attention to the fact that our thinking is a product of the social environment. I have to take it seriously. I cannot treat these differences casually and do not believe—as some observers do—that they result from brainwashing and propaganda, or originate in the cultural preferences for a strong hand, or even moral bankruptcy and the inability of Russian people to distinguish right from wrong.

The new Russia was born in the Soviet Union—a country with a great ambition to change human nature and create a new "Soviet man." This new species—an idealized Soviet person—was supposed to love work and sacrifice her individual desires and motivations for the benefit of the collective, her motherland, and the future of Communism and the coming generations. Brought up under a strong influence of my father—a product of Soviet social mobility of the 1960s who moved from a poor rural background to a position of political and social dominance in one of the regions in the Republic of Tatarstan—I was as close to an ideal Soviet girl as one could probably get, and I absorbed the ideas of self-sacrifice and work for the common good early on. More than two and a half decades after the fall of the Soviet Union, I find myself on the other side of the newly rising "curtain"—a Soviet girl who tended to ducklings growing up in the village turned into an American-educated political scientist. Meanwhile, some respected Russian sociologists proclaim that the Soviet man is back and that the personality features given rise by the Soviet system are being expressed in the younger generations. The Soviet era that produced a special Soviet personality mold is gone. How could it be reproduced in the present conditions?

The analysis advanced in this book is not neutral. It is biased toward understanding the Russian predicament and empathizing with the Russian population, rather than pointing to where it went wrong. It is biased toward attributing the blame on the historical circumstances in which the agents acted, rather than on their inherent qualities. It is driven by the urge to share responsibility among individuals and actors in power positions, rather than the Russian masses. I believe in the value of such an approach to research. A completely neutral political analysis is hardly possible to begin with, since the very choice of the research question and even the specialization in a field or discipline are connected to the researcher's preexisting proclivities, opinions, interests, and biases. Awareness and recognition of such biases is the first step needed in any research endeavor.

We know that empathy and emotional intelligence are powerful tools in interpersonal understanding. Shouldn't we strive for an emotionally intelligent understanding of international relations and collective processes? Shouldn't empathy be seen as an essential epistemological tool and a unique route to knowledge linked to *Verstehen?* Scholars have approached this tool as "experiential understanding" that provides the observer with knowledge of another person's thoughts, feelings, and behavior.[2] In individual psychology, empathy is an essential tool for empowering the individual in need of transforming her actions and reactions. The role of empathic understanding in social and group psychology is as constructive and transformative as it is in individual psychology. American social psychologist Daniel Batson has long argued about the moral significance of empathy based on the understanding of the other's perspective.[3] Dylan Marron, an American writer and performer, has argued that "[e]mpathy is not an endorsement. Empathizing with someone you profoundly disagree with does not compromise your own deeply held beliefs and endorse theirs. It just means acknowledging the humanity of someone who was raised to think differently."[4]

We have entered a new, post-globalization era, characterized by a global backlash against liberalism, multiculturalism, and globalization and defined by more particularistic, group-driven politics of recognition. The current domestic politics and leaderships in Russia and the United States, Great Britain's decision to leave the European Union, and populist tendencies in Poland, Hungary, Italy, Austria, and other countries around the world all signify the arrival of new times. Francis Fukuyama, a Stanford-based professor and a perceptive observer of our times, has declared identity politics to be "a master concept that explains much of what is going on in global affairs."[5] This book is also about identity politics—national-level identity politics in Russia.

Russia and the United States have often played each other's "external other," using the images of one another to construct their own identities. For someone like myself, born and raised in the Soviet Union and Russia and spending my adult years mostly in the United States, this perspective of the "other" is, in reality, the perspective that is also my "own." My ultimate hope for this book is that it can serve as a contribution to enhancing the understanding of Russia, Russian society, and Russian citizens in the West. The logic of conflict might make it hard to reach out to the outer concentric circle of our identities and to perceive the ultimate commonality of all humans, whatever their nation and culture. For the West, it is all too easy to fit into the "old shoes" and reconstruct the old, Cold War–era views about Russia, just as it has been easy to promote anti-Americanism and anti-Westernism in the past two decades in Russia. It is too easy to succumb to the confrontational dynamics of inter-group relations in international politics, driven by simplified political and media representations of Russia and the United States. The collective drive—normally shared by and expressed through the group members—to view their own group (or a nation) as morally and culturally superior to the other is hard to resist.

The social dimension of thinking and feeling is a boutique sphere of knowledge. Cognitive sciences and the study of various thinking processes such as perceiving, attending, classifying, signifying, timing, and remembering most often focus on either the individual or universal aspects of these psychological processes. It is the scholars who are interested in the understanding of social groups and cultures who have brought attention to the social aspects of cognition, developing entire subdisciplines such as cognitive sociology, social psychology, and cultural and cognitive anthropology that try to explain how and why thinking differs across societies and groups. In political science, cognition is a variable central to the subdiscipline of political psychology. However, most political psychologists (especially in the US tradition) are predisposed toward looking at the individual-level mechanisms that are expected to be universal across cultures (when studying voting behavior, for example). Except for scholars who rely on social identity theory and those who study group-based phenomena such as nationalism or identity politics, the importance of the social aspect of human cognition appears to have been underappreciated. Within political science, constructivist scholars in the field of international relations have long argued about the importance of social-cognitive structures for international political outcomes. It is a good time for comparativists also to recognize that thinking and believing are sometimes done in groups and are shaped by the historical and social context that varies across groups' boundaries. Engaging with these issues in the Russian domestic context, I believe, is promising, both analytically and politically.

You cannot step twice into the same river—a classic saying. Or can you? Do our senses force us to see the familiar, the known, the expected, and dismiss the unfamiliar, the strange, the unknown? How can we use the insights in social psychology to arrive at a less biased understanding and give credit and the blame where they are due? Russian society is a diverse mix. One can always find in there what she or he is looking for. Along with the revival of the Soviet person, you can find a *civic person*, organizing to fight the fires and the floods, defending parks and forests, opening new stores and businesses, fundraising for worthy causes. You can find a *religious person* attending a church or a mosque, praying and fasting, walking in sacred processions, and traveling to Mecca for the Hajj. You can find an *ethnic entrepreneur*—a man or a woman—who uses the market forces to revive ethnic customs and rituals, folklore clothes, dance, and holidays. You can find *bandits* and *criminals*, *crooks* and *charlatans*. But you can also find *heroes* and *visionaries*, those who dedicate their lives to public causes, pursue an idea, fight injustice, and help others. You can find activists who want to revive Stalin's cult in Russia, but you can also find those who invest their lives and limited resources into discovering and commemorating the victims of political and social repressions that took place during the Soviet era. Recognizing this diversity is important. Making any of these groups and categories of people a focus of research is likely to result in a different vision of Russia, to point to different challenges that the country faces, to highlight different social and political trends, achievements, and failures, and to have different implications for understanding the country's past, present, and future.

A focus on the Soviet legacy and Russia's present-day collective, national identity comes at the cost of ignoring and smoothing out other markers of social difference in present-day Russia that are as real and consequential as the issues attended to in this book. However, what is gained in return is valuable—for me personally and, hopefully, for the reader—for making sense of some of the psychological conundrums that have emerged in the social and political realities of Russia of the 2010s.

Acknowledgments

I WOULD LIKE to thank Venelin Ganev, Rosa Magnusdottir, Olga Irisova, Natasha Rostova, Ted Hopf, and Jevgenijs Steinbuks for reading and commenting on draft versions of this book. Stephen Norris, Neringa Klumbyte, Zara Torlone, Scott Kenworthy, Ben Sutcliff, Ted Gerber, Brian Taylor, and Sam Greene provided useful comments on separate chapters and papers related to this project. The Kennan Institute has been a great place to germinate this project in the summer of 2017. I am thankful to Kennan Institute staff for their help and to William Pomerantz and the participants of the Kennan Institute seminar for encouragement and useful comments on the ideas and approaches that became the basis of this book. Maria Grigor'eva was instrumental in organizing focus-group interviews in Samara. My college friends, Larisa, Luiza, Il'mira, Murat, and El'vira, made focus groups possible in Kazan. Stepan Goncharov from the Levada Center helped with organizing the survey in November 2017. I am thankful to Elizabeth Woods, Marsha Olive McGraw, Sergei Oushakine, Regina Smyth, and Henry Hale for their generous moral support, encouragement, and advice in the process of writing and producing this book. I am thankful to Sam Greene, Adnan Vatansever, Marc Berenson, Alexander Kupatadze, and Gregory Asmolov—my colleagues at King's Russia Institute—for their continuous support and for being a constructive part of the workplace I value and thrive in. I am indebted to Elena Larukhina, Tolkyn Mukhangalikyzy, and Elena Kazakova for their friendship and generosity with helping my family when I am absent. David McBride, Senior Editor at Oxford University Press, provided necessary support throughout the publishing process; I am thankful to him and his team including Holly Mitchell for their professionalism and positive energy in relation to my project. My biggest gratitude is to Jevgenijs Steinbuks, my life partner. Without his moral and intellectual support, this book would not have been written.

PART ONE

Of Leaders and Followers

People like simple explanations. When it comes to Russia and its predicament, some observers see Russia under Putin as returning to its Soviet past; others refer to resurgent nationalism and even fascism. When trying to explain these unwanted developments, some observers blame Putin or "collective Putin"; others blame *homo sovieticus* and draw attention to cultural and psychological imprint of the past. In Part 1 I engage with these views and explanations and provide my own, based on social identity theory and on understanding the Russian nation and Russian society as a group, as a community that wants to value itself, and the role played by Putin's leadership in making this happen, if temporarily.

I

The Return of the "Soviet" through the "National" in Post-Soviet Russia

*No quality of human nature is more remarkable, both in
itself and in its consequences, than that propensity we have
to sympathize with others, and to receive by communication
their inclinations and sentiments, however different from, or
even contrary to our own.*

—DAVID HUME, *A Treatise of Human Nature*, 2007, 206

*Many of the things happening now are the remains of the
Soviet past [. . .]. The Soviet past was not buried in the 1990s
and it has now resuscitated in a mutated and a half-rotten
way. We have to live now with this monster reawakened by
those who knew its physiology, neural centers and who inserted
needles in specific spots. A form of a domestic voodoo . . . I am
afraid this experiment will have catastrophic consequences.*[1]

—VLADIMIR SOROKIN, 2015

ON DECEMBER 10, 2011, as the big crowds of "angry urbanites" gathered on the
streets of Moscow, *The Economist* ran a puzzling headline on "The Long Life of
Homo Sovieticus." While many Moscovites demanded honest elections marking
a new era of greater political engagement in the Russian society, some Russian
sociologists associated with the Levada Center, a respected polling agency,
proclaimed the return of the Soviet man. Deservedly, the "angry urbanites" in
Moscow received more media attention at the time than the purportedly regen-
erated "Soviet man." After all, they were more vocal, visible, politically active,
and centrally located. Enthused by these developments, I, for one, wrote about
the hope for Russian progressivism, recounting the lessons of the American "progressive era."[2] Alas, the political and social developments in Russia after these
promising events of 2011–2012 turned backward very rapidly.[3] The promise of

The Red Mirror. Gulnaz Sharafutdinova, Oxford University Press (2020). © Oxford University Press.
DOI: 10.1093/oso/9780197502938.001.0001.

progressivism was replaced by the consolidation of conservatism and the assertion of traditional values promoted as the new, moral foundation of the Kremlin-
led politics. The country underwent a wave of national consolidation in support
of the 2014 Crimea annexation. The subsequent international sanctions against
Russia and the continuing crisis in Eastern Ukraine created a new status quo
characterized by polarization and a tense standoff between Russia and the West.
Russia of 2011 and Russia of post-2014 seem like two different countries, belonging to different historical eras and separated not merely by a few years but by
decades, if not centuries.

 This abrupt turnaround in the political and social landscape in Russia war-
rants a closer look at the category of the "Soviet man" suggested by the Russian
sociologists. Understanding the nature and meaning of the alleged "return" of
the Soviet person a quarter-century after the Soviet system itself collapsed might
provide a clue to understanding present-day Russian politics. Many other signs
point to the increasing trend of the "return of the Soviet" in Russia. Over the
last years, the Levada Center has been observing a growing sympathy toward
Joseph Stalin. Thus, the number of respondents who expressed sympathy toward
Stalin—as one of the revolutionary leaders—has tripled from 8% in 1990 to 24%
in 2017.[4] Furthermore, the number of respondents who expressed their respect,
sympathy, and admiration of Stalin—as one of the historical figures—reached
a record 51% in April 2019, spurring heated debates on social media and online
blogs about the symbolic meaning of Stalin in the Russian society, as well as the
interpretation of polling results.[5] Among the Soviet-era leaders, only Leonid
Brezhnev—associated with the stability and relative domestic calm of the late
Soviet Union—received a similarly high level of support among Russian citizens.
In 2017, 47% of respondents expressed positive views about Brezhnev.[6] The same
poll placed support for Russia's current president, Vladimir Putin, at 83%.[7]

 Many Russians mourn the collapse of the Soviet Union. According to Levada
polls, 66% of respondents in December 2018 confessed to regretting the Soviet
collapse, and 60% believed that it could have been saved.[8] In 2000, the number of
those who were uneasy about the Soviet collapse was even larger, reaching 75% of
all respondents and viewed by sociologists as the peak of Soviet nostalgia. But in
the past few years, the numbers were growing again, setting a new trend.[9]

 For Westerners who had witnessed the Cold War rivalry and were condi-
tioned by anti-communist propaganda, and even for those who were born later
and might have studied communism from history books, such Soviet nostalgia
and, even more menacingly, the rising support for Joseph Stalin—a historical figure frequently placed side by side with Adolph Hitler—are understandably very
alarming and perplexing. Stalinism, with its mass murder of the Soviet people,
is not a system to be nostalgic about. But only a select few in Russia think about

mass murder when they talk about Stalin today. Many Russian people credit him with Soviet economic expansion and industrialization, contrasting these achievements to Russia's current economic decline and over-dependence on energy and other natural resources. They associate Stalin with the "holy" victory in the Great Patriotic War, as well as with the patriotism and national consolidation that accompanied the war efforts. They see in Stalin a leader who built a country that was strong, powerful, and admired by others. Meanwhile, the murderous aspects of Stalinism are downplayed or even explained away with reference to "the brutalities of the times."[10] These other parts of history are often disregarded and forgotten, as if they are an aberration unrelated to what the regime stood for.

The mythologization of Stalin's figure in Russia has not been occurring by chance. This process appears to be preordained by the evolutionary logic of Russia's political system under Vladimir Putin. The image of the leader who built the Soviet Union and led it to the "holy victory" more than half a century ago today resonates with the image of Vladimir Putin, who is credited with saving Russia from the chaos and fragmentation of the 1990s. The two myths that recognize the outstanding role of these "strong" leaders in Russia's national history prop each other up and perpetuate popular convictions that in some historical situations "it is necessary to concentrate all power in one man's hands."[11]

The changing attitudes toward Stalin in Russia and the shift of dispositions from a vigilant "never again" to the patriotic "we can repeat it again" (*my mozhem povtorit'*) have baffled observers within and outside of Russia. Some pundits wrote about the moral impotence of the Russians, viewed as being unable to face the collective guilt for the crimes of the Soviet regime. David Satter, an American journalist and Russia observer, complained that the Russians are too passive and unable to pass moral judgments; they do not value individual life and prefer nationalist delusions.[12] Even earlier, Dina Khapaeva, a Russian-educated literary and cultural studies scholar, argued that "post-Soviet society is seriously ill with a partial amnesia that makes historical memory strangely selective."[13] She developed a conception of "gothic morality" propagating the "striking equality of Good and Evil," a cult of force, and a preoccupation with personal interests to capture the societal consequences of this collective amnesia.[14]

Other commentators took a more sanguine posture and noted that the very recognition of "who the victims are" under Stalinism is a challenging and arbitrary process. The existence of the large "gray zone" formed by the blurred lines between the victims and perpetrators under Stalinism made it hard to apply the concepts and ethics from the transitional justice paradigm used, for example, in the German case of "overcoming the past."[15] Arseny Roginsky, a historian and one of the founders of "Memorial" human rights and historical preservation society, argued,

In the memory of the terror, we are unable to assign the main roles, unable to put in their rightful place the pronouns "we" and "they." This impossibility of disassociation from evil is effectively the main obstacle for the development of fully-fledged social memory of the terror.[16]

Antony Kalashnikov, a historian who inquired into different normative perspectives that opposing narratives on Stalinism build on, also called for more analytical nuance and attention to the Russian context in the study of the collective memory of Stalinism in Russia.[17]

The moral repentance and atonement for the mass crimes in Soviet society did start in the Soviet Union during the *glasnost* period. Leon Aron wrote about the profound shift in values that drove the Russian Revolution of 1987–1991.[18] He brought attention to the "troubadours of truth"—the journalists, writers, and activists who were in the avant-garde of the ongoing moral restoration. Aron's book came out at a promising moment of widespread protests in Russia, when thousands of people took to the streets with demands for dignity, honest elections, and accountable government. It was a moment that allowed Aron to link the value shift of the late 1980s to the demands of protesters in 2011–2012. But the moment was a fleeting one.

The political and social developments in post-2012 and, particularly, "post-Crimea-annexation" Russia brought into relief the fact that the discussed moral restoration of the late 1980s that was supposed to bring Russian society face to face with its past—to avoid its repetition in the future—did not last. The consolidation that Russian society underwent in the aftermath of the Crimea annexation in 2014, the rising popularity of Stalin and Brezhnev, the Kremlin's success in propagating anti-Americanism and anti-Westernism—all point to the unfinished character of the attempt at "collective repentance" and learning "history's lessons" associated with the perestroika years. Judging from what is being discussed on Russia's main TV channels, the opposite trend—a belligerent defensiveness and resentful nationalism—seem to dominate collective feelings in Russia today. How and why did Russian society reach this point? Have the decades of post-communist transformation in Russia all gone to waste, if such uncritical appreciation of the Soviet system has made a comeback? What does the Soviet past have to do with the current Russian condition?

It is hard to deny that Russia's historical trajectory under Vladimir Putin increasingly bears Soviet markers. Slowly but surely, we witness the return of practices and institutions, symbols, and rhetoric invented and used by the Soviet regime. It started with the rewritten Soviet anthem in 2000 and was reflected, among other things, in a slow transformation of the United Russia, the current party of power in Russia, into an institution that increasingly resembles—in its style and practices—the Soviet-era Communist Party of the Soviet Union. "Do they smoke something Soviet?" asked jokingly Danila Galperovich, a journalist from the Voice of America, in the aftermath of the 18th Congress of the United Russia held on December 7–8, 2018.[19] The revival of Soviet-like party congresses and party schools, of humanitarian aid to Syria and Donbass (Ukraine), of Soviet-era rhetoric about "foreign agents," of foreign wars fought by the military but not officially recognized by the state, of patriotic organizations for engaging and educating youth in the spirit of defending their motherland, of censorship and self-censorship in the media, of increasing repression and other Soviet-era governance practices, institutions, and attitudes—all signify Putin's Russia. These reinvented "remains of the past" coexist with the new communication technologies, in the atmosphere shaped by Instagram, Twitter, YouTube, Facebook, and its more important Russian equivalent, VKontakte. This list has been expanding in the past few years. Russian interference in electoral processes in foreign countries is also not a new phenomenon, but a revival of the menu of "active measures" associated with Soviet intelligence services, such as the Main Intelligence Directorate (GRU) activities during the Cold War.[20]

These developments are hardly accidental. But it would be a mistake to treat them as if they have been predetermined by Russia's history, culture, or type of "human material," better known today under the label of the "Soviet man." Such arguments, which have become quite popular, even among the Russian intelligentsia, convey hopelessness and resignation and, at times, simple Russophobia. Many Russian intellectuals, who knew better than to join the new "patriotic consensus" forged in the aftermath of the Crimea annexation, found themselves marginalized by the Kremlin's new identity politics. Many critically oriented journalists, writers, editors, business people, and others have left Russia or are looking for an exit, preferring to live in Kyiv, Prague, London, Riga, and other foreign countries and cities. Their deep sense of disappointment and hopelessness, reflected in their choice to leave the country, their feelings of loss, and the challenges of creating new lives and new careers in a new environment are all understandable. Some analysts estimate that up to two million people have left Russia since 2000. The emigration flow has sped up since 2012, driven by Russians leaving the country for political and human rights–related reasons.[21] The disappointment and even resentment of those who had to flee, finding their life in Russia unbearable, are understandable. Yet their occasional "retreat" into blaming "sovok" (a slang for a Soviet person) is misplaced and reflects, arguably, their own sense of powerlessness in the face of the external circumstances they could not change. After all, researchers of political contention dynamics in Russia suggest that there is more social and economic activism in Russia than is commonly acknowledged.[22] It is localized and less visible than public protests in Moscow and other big cities, but is, nonetheless, important.

In this book, I argue that Russia's present and unenviable condition is a result of political choices made by the Kremlin under the leadership of President Vladimir Putin. Putin took the helm of the Russian government at a critical moment. Faced with the traumatic social dislocation caused by the transition and hit by the 1998 economic crisis, the country began the path to economic recovery in 1999. More than a decade into reforms, Russia's identity issues have not been resolved.[23] There was neither external anchor motivating Russian elites to persevere on the path of the democratic choice made in 1991, nor internal consensus supporting that choice given the social and economic outcomes of the reforms. The political landscape, long characterized by a split into two big camps—pro- and anti-reform—was structured differently by the late 1990s. Many influential regional leaders came together in a powerful electoral coalition, Fatherland-All Russia (OVR), challenging the Kremlin in 1999 parliamentary elections and eyeing the subsequent presidential elections as the ultimate goal.[24] The Kremlin won that contest, bringing Putin to power.

Putin started his tenure with reforms that clearly revealed his political goals. The Kremlin's policy initiatives—in relation to regional leaders and institutions, Russia's powerful oligarchs, and media—all signaled the desire and will for political control. The concepts of "managed democracy" and "managed pluralism" advanced in the first decade of the 2000s by Russia watchers captured this trend toward management and control of the political system.[25] The Kremlin supported these policies by referring to the order and stability sorely missed by the Russian public.[26]

The early Putin was an economic liberal who continued the "second generation" market reforms, including the introduction of a flat income tax of 13%. The state of the Russian economy, which was picking up from 1999, conceivably gave the Kremlin a chance to build on the reforms of the 1990s and to argue that the commitment to reforms pays off and that the reforms conducted by the Yeltsin government had been vindicated by the Russian "economic miracle" of the 2000s. After all, the Russian economy was expanding until 2007. This trajectory of the Russian development, however, was closed in 2003, when the Yukos affair started a wave of re-nationalization and Putin's preoccupation with the control over strategic industries revealed his statist, anti-liberal ideological leanings.

The 2011–2012 protests in Moscow and other cities in Russia revealed the limits of the Kremlin's political control and necessitated a new political strategy. Since the beginning of Putin's third presidential term in 2012, the legitimation strategy pursued by the Kremlin turned squarely toward collective identity politics. The Kremlin officials placed the issues of traditional Russian values and Russian exceptionalism—presumably revealed through its millennial history and cultural achievements—at the forefront of public debates. Furthermore, the Kremlin-led political and cultural discourse constructed and elevated the idea of Vladimir Putin *securing* and *strengthening* Russia. To infuse this frame with additional clout, the Kremlin-controlled media and state officials presented pre-Putin Russia using the frame of the turbulent 1990s (*likhie devianostye*). The top-down propagation of this frame that was available from the 1990s (but was then used by the anti-reform political forces) resonated strongly in Russian society. The public resonance of this frame was instrumental and critical for the success of the reverse frame presenting Putin as the leader who had secured and strengthened Russia. The annexation of Crimea—the emotions and the meanings associated with it—became the sealant of this identity politics that elevated Putin's image of an undisputable national leader.

Putin's leadership—especially as it evolved from his third term in power—could be seen as a case of successful leadership from the perspective of group analysis. The Kremlin's political choices worked to consolidate the Russian nation in the sense of infusing Russian citizens with a sense of belonging and a sense of pride, patriotism, and faith in their country. This success, which was evident specifically during 2014–2018, is, however, momentary and tenuous. It is personally tied to Putin's leadership and is unsustainable from the perspective of Russia's future. In fact, this strategy has turned Russia away from its future and toward its Soviet past. Responding to the challenge of constructing a shared collective identity that could unite and become a foundation for the Russian political community, Vladimir Putin relied on the mechanisms and ideas that were used successfully by the Soviet government, combining them with the modern means of political communication and political persuasion.

The Soviet project of constructing a new breed—a Soviet man—was utopian from the start. But the Soviet project of constructing a Soviet society and instilling it with a widely shared collective identity succeeded. Soviet citizens shared ideas and beliefs about themselves as a collective body—as a group. Some of these beliefs were internalized to the extent that they were taken for granted. These beliefs underlaid the sense of community and the sense of national belonging in the Soviet Union. In this book, I discuss two core ideas that underpinned the sense of collective identity of the Soviet people, shaping their perceptions of themselves and the world around them. Specifically, I refer to the sense of Soviet exceptionalism and the role played by external conflict and the image of an enemy in consolidating the Soviet nation. And I argue that Vladimir Putin's leadership phenomenon derives from the resuscitation of these ideas to forge the new Russian collective identity and his own image as a great leader of the Russian nation.

Understanding the Russian nation and Russian society as a group, as a community that wants to value itself, and the role played by Putin's leadership in making this happen, is one of the central aims of this book. This task is different from understanding Russia as a collection of individual Russians with specific personality traits and value preferences. The prominent social psychologist Solomon Asch (1952) pointed out long ago that

> group consciousness, group purpose, and group values have an existence in individuals, and in them alone. But they cease to be "merely" individual facts by virtue of their reference to others. It follows that a group process is neither the sum of individual activity nor a fact added to the activities of individuals. (p. 252, cited in Bar-Tal, p. 156)

Even earlier, already in 1929, Karl Mannheim noted that

> [t]here is no such metaphysical entity as a group mind which thinks over and above the heads of individuals, or whose ideas the individual merely reproduces. Nevertheless it would be false to deduce from this that all the ideas and sentiments which motivate an individual have their origin in him alone, and can be adequately explained solely on the basis of his own life-experience. (Mannheim 2013, p. 2)

That individual views and preferences form under the direct influence of the community that an individual sees herself as part of is widely recognized in political science scholarship.[27] The importance of national identity—as one of the collective identities available to an individual—is normally captured through studying the commonly accepted values and ideas of patriotism and nationalism.

Nationalism and the ongoing processes of constructing, contesting, and negotiating collective identities related to the national group are politically significant everywhere. Contemporary sociologists argue that "nationalism in settled times" is as important (if less visible) or maybe even more so than such fleeting "rallying around the flag" phenomenon that occurs in the aftermath of specific events that concern a national community.[28] We know that varying views about homeland shape American politics in the late twentieth and early twenty-first centuries."[29] If that is true in the state that has securely maintained its statehood for the last 200-plus years, how could it not motivate political action and political attitudes in the political community that faced an abrupt ending of its previous state structures in its recent past?

Many analysts of Putin-era Russian politics have recognized the importance of Russian nationalism. Marlene Laruelle has long investigated various strains of nationalist ideas circulating in the Russian public space during the 1990s and the first decade of the 2000s and their significance for Putinism.[30] Veljko Vujacic, another scholar of Russian nationalism, has noted the complicated legacies of Soviet nation-building during Stalin's rule for Russia's modern political and national development.[31] The topic of Russian nationalism received a particular attention boost after the 2014 Crimea annexation that incited fears of revanchist Russia among Russia's neighbors. The nationalist aspects of the Kremin's actions in Crimea are debated.[32] On the one hand, there is an understanding that Putin's political strategy since 2012 has developed as a response to the rising nationalist political challenge to the Kremlin.[33] On the other hand, empirical studies of public opinion in Russia before and after the Crimea annexation find that the post-Crimea patriotic euphoria could be better characterized as rallying around the leader, as opposed to rallying around the flag. Mikhail Alexseev and Henry Hale established that such feelings as ethnic pride and other indicators of ethnic nationalism in Russia have not changed in the aftermath of the annexation.[34] Meanwhile, pride in Russia as a multiethnic state has risen.[35] Furthermore, and rather surprisingly, Russia's ethnic minorities have supported the territorial expansion that was couched in terms of aiding an ethnic majority group (Russians in Crimea).[36] This was a direct challenge to theories that would emphasize inter-group dynamics and the effects of rising threat perceptions among minority ethnic groups confronted by the prospects of an increasing majority ethnocentrism.[37] While it might seem obvious why ethnic Russians supported the annexation of Crimea, the same degree of enthusiasm and support for this action among the Tatars, Bashkirs, Chechens, and other ethnic non-Russians is puzzling indeed. Similarly, how do we make sense of a surprising drop in support of the nationalist slogan "Russia for Russians" that occurred after the annexation of Crimea?[38] References to growing nationalism in Russia, at least of an ethnonational variety, are of little help here.

This book attends to these issues from a different angle. I rely on a sociopsychological conception of collective identity and "the new psychology of leadership" that views leadership processes from the social identity perspective. I analyze Putin's politics as national identity-driven politics to inquire into such issues as (1) how national (state-level) identity was brought into political salience and how it is kept elevated in everyday life; (2) what specific ideas and symbolic constructions mattered for achieving post-Crimean social consensus; and (3) why these ideas resonated so intensely with the Russian public. The focus on the nexus of political leadership and historical context and on Putin's leadership as defined by the nature of his response to the challenges confronting Russia's national identity is crucial for making sense of contemporary Russian politics. Putin's popularity rests on his contribution toward the individual perceptions that many

Russians carry in relation to their understanding of Russia as a community and a nation, and themselves as part of that community. Putin's long-term political consultant Gleb Pavlovsky formulated Putin's main political achievement in the following way:

> Putin made the Russian people accustomed to the idea that they live in Russia. Prior to 2000, and this is confirmed by many sociological surveys, people thought they lived in some type of a transient formation, waiting for it to end and some type of a new state to come into being, as it happened in 1991. If I remember correctly, half of the population did not recognize Russia's borders, and a similar proportion did not recognize the Russian Federation as a state. Putin made people accept this reality, and his personal role was significant because he was able to get into the position of an average person, and he used the language of an average person. [...] He made people believe in Russia.[39]

The challenge of articulating new ideas that could define and orient Russia has existed since the 1990s. Keeping with this lasting tradition, Russia's cultural and literary elites vocalized this problem long before its articulation in the political sphere. A character in Viktor Pelevin's *Generation P* (1999) expressed it most lucidly (if somewhat crudely, as he was a thug) in the following passage:

> I will briefly explain the whole thing to you, on my fingers, Vovchik said. Our national business is going onto the international arena where you could find the money from all over the place: Chechen, American, Columbian, and so on. If you look at them simply as money, they are all the same. In reality, each of these monies has some national idea behind it. Long ago we had Orthodoxy, autocracy and nationality. We then switched to communism. But now, once it ended, we do not have such idea except for the money. But money cannot stand behind money, you know? Because then you do not know why some are ahead and others are behind ... [...] We lack national i-den-ti-ty. ... You see? Chechens have it but we don't. That's why everyone looks at us as shit. What we need is ... a simple and clearly articulated Russian idea, so that we could explain, to any bitch from any type of Harvard: [what we are about]. ... So that they, bitches, feel such spirituality, as in 1945 under Stalingrad, you see?[40]

Pelevin made the post-Soviet Russian identity problem central to his other masterpiece, *Chapaev i Pustota* (Chapaev and the Void, 2000). Edith Clowes, an American professor of Slavic languages and literatures, investigated Pelevin's and other Russian writers' works on Russia's "imagined geographies," seen as important arenas for constructing and contesting Russia's collective identity.[41] She highlighted that the writings produced in the late Soviet Union and Russia of the 1990s and early 2000s brought forward the image and metaphor of the periphery as "the crucial problem for post-Soviet Russian identity."[42]

This topic was central to Russian cinematography as well. Alexei Balabanov's cult movie, *Brat 2* (2000), was focused on the assertion of Russia's authentic identity, represented to be superior to that of the West. The clash with the West was played out in the film through the main storyline, which involved the central character of the movie, Danila, traveling to the United States to avenge his friend and resolve the troubles of his friend's brother in Chicago. Danila's brief exchange with his own brother about the source of human strength ("*V chem sila brat?*") was very revealing and became one of the most quoted lines of this film. Reflecting on the answer given by his brother that the source of strength is in money and its amount, Danila says, "I think that the source of strength is in truth. Whoever has the truth is a stronger one." Implicit in the movie, and clearly shared by Russian viewers, was the association of the primacy of money with capitalism and the West, whereas the primacy of truth ("Pravda") was associated with Russian values, albeit missed in the Russia of the 1990s that had turned toward capitalism.[43] Nonetheless, the film asserted the superiority of the Russian way of thinking and living, reflecting a deep longing for a bigger idea of what the "Russian way," with which people could proudly identify, was.[44]

Why is recognizing the "group aspect" of Russian society and the collective aspect of the individual self in Russia so important today? What do we gain from an approach that places group values and group beliefs in the driver's seat when explaining contemporary Russia? The simple answer is: because they matter. They matter intensely in Russia's specific post-Soviet historical context, brought to prominence by Putin's leadership and the political choices made in the Kremlin.

I argue that the approach followed in this book helps in unraveling a few of the paradoxes that have marred Russian politics. The *first paradox* is Vladimir Putin's unwavering popularity—domestic as well as worldwide. From a person largely unknown to the Russian public and the foreign audience in 1999, Russia's second president turned into a highly popular leader who was able to maintain remarkably high support ratings at home and, later, developed much sway abroad. He topped the list of the man of the year in Russia for 15 consecutive years (2000–2014). Yes, initially his presidency was associated with the years of economic growth and growing prosperity for many Russians, driven by record energy prices. Not surprisingly, political analysts have argued that presidential popularity is a function of the economic situation.[45] Many others contemplated that it was a matter of time for it to go down, as economic realities worsened after the 2008 economic crisis and especially with the economic slowdown since 2013. Indeed, Putin's popularity was on a downward trend since 2008.[46] Yet ultimately, it not only withstood the economic downturn but rose to new heights after the Crimea annexation in 2014 and has remained high despite growing economic pain and insecurity. The Russians' faith in the direction of their country had dropped in 2016. Their sense of economic stability and well-being had plummeted. Yet Putin's popularity was not affected.[47] It changed only in 2018, when the Kremlin decided to go forward with pension reform, interpreted by most Russians as a direct personal rip-off that invalidated individual and family-based hopes and aspirations.

After the Crimea annexation, Putin's leadership acquired a charismatic quality. Russia's famous singer Joseph Kobzon made headlines in 2015 when he suggested that he knows whom Vladimir Putin married for the second time.[48] He suggested that Putin is married to Russia, and added, "what can you do, if no one else exists for him besides Russia."[49] Even earlier, in 2014, Kremlin's deputy chief of staff Vyacheslav Volodin made another headline, suggesting at the 11th Valdai Club that "there is no Russia today if there is no Putin."[50] Many Russians indeed do not see Russia without Putin. A July 2019 poll by the Levada Center found that more than half of Russians want to see Putin as Russia's president beyond 2024, making him, potentially, serve as a leader of the country longer than Josef Stalin, who stayed at the helm of the Soviet Union for almost three decades.[51] The constitutional reform initiated by the Kremlin in January 2020 enables Putin to realize such scenario and stay in power beyond 2024.[52]

It is also evident that Putin's constituency extends far beyond Russia's borders.[53] His international influence was recognized by various Western magazine rankings, including the *Times* ranking "A Man of the Year," which Putin topped in 2008 and 2014. He was also deemed the most influential person of the year in 2015 and the most powerful person of the year in the *Forbes* ranking of 2014. Putin has strong allies in the West among right-wing nationalist populists. He has reintroduced Russia as a global player in the Middle East. Under his leadership, Russia has been associated with attempts to influence the outcomes of the 2016 US presidential election, as well as elections in other countries. Putin has systematically built influence in Russia's neighboring countries with Russian-speaking minorities.[54] No wonder that foreign policy is deemed to be Putin's strongest suit by the public at home, especially during Putin's third and fourth terms in power.[55] Various media commentators have reintroduced the label of Russia as another superpower; this is certainly not a small feat from Putin's own perspective, as well as from the perspective of the Russian citizens.[56]

The *second paradox* is related to contradictions and vacillations in societal preferences revealed through opinion polls. In the last few years, Russian citizens' preferences have fluctuated between desiring stability, order, and economic prosperity domestically, on the one hand, and longing for Russia's "great power" status and international recognition, on the other.[57] Thus, popular support for Putin during his first two presidential terms was frequently suggested to be a function of his role in bringing order and stability to the country after the tumultuous (*likhie*) 1990s. Some measure of economic well-being as the Russian economy experienced eight consecutive years of economic growth, the systematic increases in salaries and pensions, and increasing living standards—all these improvements in the material aspects of life were undoubtedly credited to Putin's government.[58] However, support for the Russian president did not drop as the economy started stagnating in 2013 and then tumbled after the 2014 Crimea annexation and the Western economic response. Putin's foreign policy actions have affected Russia not only economically. The public opinion polls have revealed that many Russians fear a new confrontation with the West and the United States.[59] So the sense of order, stability, and rising welfare associated with Putin's first terms in power had given way to renewed fears of international confrontation and social stagnation and economic retrenchment. Yet Putin's political legitimacy seems to have only risen, and Russian citizens now credit him with successful foreign policy and restoring Russia's rightful place in the world.

A seeming turn away from the long-preferred European values and modernity—instilled by the Soviet system and reasserted after the Soviet collapse—is also surprising. It appears as if a big part of Russian society has gone through an overnight transformation and turned toward traditionalist conservatism, anti-Westernism, and anti-modernism. The conservative ideas and values—supported by the Russian Orthodox Church and other state religions in Russia—are promoted at the level of the Kremlin's political discourse and have had serious legal and social repercussions, whether in terms of the treatment of women's rights, the LGBT community, or anyone on the liberal side of the cultural spectrum, including artists and performers, looked at by the regime guardians with increased suspicion. The heated debates about the film *Matilda*, directed by Alexei Uchitel and released in 2017, the ban on Armando Ianucci's satirical film *Death of Stalin* (2017), denounced in Russia as sacrilegious, the arrest of film director Kirill Serebrennikov, the wave of cancellation of popular rap concerts throughout the country, attempts to close Russia's best universities in the field of humanities (EUSPb and Shaninka)—all these events reflect the state-prompted cultural and political swing toward conservative values in Russia.[60]

The gradual rehabilitation of Stalin in Russian society and the new monuments being erected to the Soviet leader around the country pose another challenge for our understanding. The 2007 opinion poll in Russia suggested that 92% of Russians knew about repressions and the scale of terror under Stalin. The same poll revealed that 80% of Russians thought that "Russians have every right to be proud of their history," and two-thirds did not place any responsibility on the Russian people for the crimes committed under the Soviet regime.[61] As discussed earlier, it is clear that the significance of the mass terror is heavily discounted in Russia today. How does such a thing become possible, and what are the motivating factors behind such selective forgetting and mis-remembering?

The Russian people's tendency to say things no one believes in is yet another, relatively new, and fascinating phenomenon observed by Russian sociologists. "Our public opinion," says Alexei Levinson of the Levada Center, "now follows the language of our state diplomacy. People say things they don't expect anyone to believe!" For example, although Russian propaganda says there are no Russian troops in Ukraine, Russians are well aware of the opposite being true. "But as it is in Russia's interests to say that these forces aren't present in Ukraine, people are OK to deny it."[62]

Russian sociologist Leontii Byzov suggested that there were two main views about the post-Crimean state of Russian society: an optimistic one, which emphasizes the solidarity and national consolidation forged in 2014, and another, more pessimistic one, based on the view that the short-lived mobilization of national identity in 2014 would bring an inevitable painful "withdrawal syndrome." Even while sharing a more pessimistic view, Byzov noted that by 2018, the number of Russians that feel a personal responsibility for what is going on in their localities and in the country has increased noticeably. Levada polls demonstrate that the number of such conscientious citizens in Russia has grown in the last year from 9% to 28%.[63] Other respected scholars also inquire into the issue of grassroots-based modernization in Russia and its meaning and implications in the context of a conservative, authoritarian regime.[64] These observations point to the dynamic nature of Russian society and to an ever-present possibility for social change. While recognizing such dynamism and hoping for its potential to play a progressive role in shaping Russia's future, my goal in this book is to explain the main ingredients, the concoction of factors that gave rise to the current societal condition that many observers describe using the clichés of the Soviet man, and post-imperial and/or post-traumatic syndrome.

Other commentators trying to make sense of these contradictions are split between the "party of refrigerator" and the "party of television." Some scholars have expected that political support for the regime will decline with the growing economic stagnation and falling living standards—the so-called "refrigerator challenge."[65] Other analysts—"the party of television"—have emphasized the importance of political propaganda and the Kremlin's control over information channels as the key factor behind regime support.[66] The conception of the individual in both of these viewpoints is, however, rather simplistic and one-dimensional. The Russian citizen is either a rational self-maximizer who cares about his material needs and evaluates authorities based on the satisfaction of these needs. Or, as the alternative view posits, the Russians are victims of state-waged propaganda and duping, administered through the state-controlled TV channels and social media and conditioning the Russian population to think in the directions suggested by the Kremlin's political technologists.

In reality, we are all—ethnicity, religion, and economic background notwithstanding—much more nuanced than what these views allow for. The individual self is composed of not only personal but also numerous social selves. Both of these logics—the personal, driven by individual material circumstances and individual realization and advancement, and social, driven by social and community recognition—are important, and their relative importance might differ depending on the social context. Community-wide shared ideas and perspectives that are seen as meaningful and valuable from the citizens' perspective shape their attitudes toward the regime and the country's political leadership. Under specific historical conditions, these ideas and values might play a bigger role than in "normal times," and the political authorities, especially in authoritarian systems, have the media-based mechanisms to propagate and perpetuate the salience and centrality of these ideas and values in their societies.

This perspective recognizes the significance of social and national identity issues as a crucial factor in forming individual attitudes and preferences. It posits that each individual cares not only about his/her personal pocket and personal well-being. Individual preference structure and viewpoint are shaped by a membership in a group, even if the salience of different group memberships can vary.[67] Each individual tends to hold perceived group interests as his/her own, especially when the group membership is valued. In short, collective identity and, related to that identity, normative, cognitive, and affective structures shape what people think about their leaders and about their country. Understanding Putin's Russia, with all its contradictions and paradoxes, is only possible if we capture the important nuances of the historical, social, and political context shared by the majority of Russians and if we do not impose our own ideological and normative preferences and biases onto Russian society and Russia's complex and tortuous history. Is there a country with a simple history?

Calling for more nuance in evaluating the Soviet and Russia's more recent past, Russian poet Lev Rubinstein shared in his blog in 2015:

The epochs we personally lived and felt through can be neither rehabilitated nor vindicated. The only adequate view is through the double optics: subjective and objective. My parents, for example, who experienced their youth in the 1930s, remembered these years as frightening and

happy at the same time. You know why they were frightening. But they
were also happy because they met and fell in love in those years, because
my eldest brother was born in those years, because of Tairov's theater, of
the comedy "Jolly Fellows," of the ice cream at the All-Union Agricultural
Exhibit. Yes, they were lucky: none of their closest people were turned
into the Gulag dust. And if they sincerely felt that they were happy then,
it does not mean that they glorified or justified the cult of personality.
I never heard from them that "there was order under Stalin." I just heard
that for them personally those years were happy. I believe them.

If I say that the seventies brought the height of creativity, dazzling
artistic ideas, years of love, friendship and happy midnight parties, it does
not mean that I wholeheartedly approve and support the party congress
decisions, the international support to the brotherly Afghan people, and
that I express my excitement about the high artistic achievements of the
outstanding literary work "Malaya Zemlia} [Brezhnev's memoir] or that
I am indifferent towards the persecution of dissidents. [. . .]

History, live history, is a sum and a complex interaction of concrete
real individual lives, some happy, some tragic, and all very different.
A country's and humanity's history is a history of individuals, very different and all autonomous.[68]

The Argument

The core argument advanced in the book treats the two paradoxes discussed
in the preceding section as parts of one story. Vladimir Putin, Russia's second
president, has been successful in promoting his image as an embodiment of the
shared national identity of Russian citizens. He has articulated the shared collective perspective and has built a social consensus by tapping into powerful
group emotions of shame and humiliation, derived from the painful experience
of the transition in the 1990s. He was able to turn these emotions into pride
and patriotism by activating two central pillars of the Soviet collective identity,
including a sense of exceptionalism that the Soviet regime promoted to consolidate the Soviet nation, and a sense of a foreign threat to the state and its people,
foundational to the Soviet Union. Putin's assertive foreign policy decisions—
culminating in the Crimean annexation—appeared to have secured, in the eyes
of the Russian citizens, their insecure national identity.[69] The top-down leadership and bottom-up collective identity-driven processes coalesced to produce a
newly revanchist Russia, with its current leader perceived by many citizens to be
irreplaceable.

What we witness in post-Crimea Russia is not the return of the Soviet man, the Soviet system, or the Soviet identity. We have witnessed a *moment* of consolidation, emergence, and the coming together of a post-Soviet collective identity envisioned through the central symbolic pillars of the Soviet identity and the integration of Russia's pre-Soviet, Soviet, and post-Soviet historical trajectory into a single vision of "holy Russia." Vladimir Putin—in the eyes of many Russian citizens—has pursued the systematic reclamation and strengthening of the Russian nationals' sense of collective identity, and this has become arguably the most crucial, socially and politically significant, achievement of his leadership. This is the key accomplishment that the Russian citizens support him for. This accomplishment has been recognized not only by the Russians in Russia, but also by many members of the Russian-speaking diaspora in the new post-Soviet states adjacent to Russia, who have also experienced a recovered sense of collective identity and pride of being Russian.[70]

Given the transient nature of identity politics, this is a work in progress for the Kremlin. The *moment of emergence* sealed by Crimea is just that—a fleeting moment. Russian citizens, confronted with worsening economic conditions, social degradation, crumbling health care, corrupt state officials, and many other problems, are by no means free of the growing concerns and frustrations arising in their daily lives. The 2020 pandemic amplifies all these concerns, creating yet another moment of political uncertainty and threatening to shatter the shared meanings linking Russia's positively construed national identity to Putin's leadership. Nonetheless, Putin's leadership might still be lasting. It is important to recognize the foundational elements on which this politics relied at its prime time.

Vladimir Putin's politics of collective identity reclamation has rested on the following important objectives and mechanisms: (1) making sense of the experience that Russian society went through in the 1990s in a way that resonated with ordinary Russians; (2) reconstructing the Russian national identity by emphasizing the positive aspects of the Soviet and pre-Soviet experience and by playing into the core cognitive structures that made up the Soviet collective identity; and (3) working to instill a sense of pride and positive distinction associated with belonging to the Russian nation. The Kremlin achieved these objectives by politicizing the Russians' collective identity and by transferring the political cleavages away from the domestic political landscape into the international context.

Many Russian citizens recognize Putin's successes in foreign policy to be greater than those in the domestic sphere. Yet his popularity is immune to the rational assessments of the balance between his domestic and foreign achievements precisely because the appeal of his leadership in the eyes of the Russian population (at least since 2014) lies not in his contribution to Russia's economic prosperity, but in his contribution to the Russians' sense of national identity and collective purpose that Russian citizens relate to and value. The economic growth of the first decade of the 2000s in Russia undoubtedly played into Putin's popularity and helped his reputation as a successful national leader. But by the mid-2010s, the relationship between many Russian citizens and President Putin had long lost its economic basis, and it has not been underpinned by citizens' rational calculation based on their personal preferences.[71] Although the 2018 pension reform that raised the pension age for Russian citizens quite significantly (by five years for men and eight years for women)[72] damaged Putin's unquestioned symbolic authority and highlighted the importance of economic issues again, the basis of the post-Crimean consensus in Russia was still largely intact by the beginning of 2020.

Although individuals might rationalize their vote for Vladimir Putin during the elections, in essence, their vote represents an expression of support for the new collective frame of belonging that Putin has been able to provide. Voting for Putin in Russia has acquired a meaning of voting for the Russian nation— a nation that was proclaimed to be morally superior and stronger compared to many others. Voting for Putin turned into expressing support for the leader who successfully reclaimed the lost identity of "great Russia," and has recovered the sense of belonging to a nation that matters; a nation that can stand up for its principles and interests and make a difference in the world; a nation that can defend its own (and related) kin against the enemies.

Vladimir Putin advanced his identity politics in response to an acute symbolic crisis and normative disorientation experienced by Russian citizens after the Soviet collapse. The structures of meaning making up Soviet citizens' worldview—about who they were, what was the nature of the community they were part of, what were the social goals and purposes of this community—were all shattered in the late 1980s and early 1990s. A sense of belonging to a community that people could be proud of, that had a special meaning, purpose, and efficacy had vanished, being replaced by the sense of belonging to a community that had collapsed, fragmenting along the imperial lines drawn by force and manipulation; dragged into social and economic chaos and hardship by incompetent politicians; marginalized and snubbed geopolitically. The damaging economic and social consequences of liberal reforms, accompanied by electoral politics that worked to publicize cronyism and corruption among the elites, worked to discredit the reformist elites and democratic institutions. Public opinion in Russia grew increasingly uneasy about competitive elections (especially at the regional level).[73] The August 1998 financial crisis and the growing political influence of Evgeny Primakov, nominated by Yeltsin as Russia's prime minister in the aftermath of the crisis, signaled a growing demand for a new type of politics in Russia.[74] Vladimir Putin responded to that demand, "going into power like a hot knife through butter" and acquiring by 2014 an image of Russia's savior.[75]

The identity politics initiated by the Kremlin under Putin's leadership has evolved. Putin's first two presidential terms relied on the political super-majority incorporating the views of the reform winners as well as the interests of those who have lost as a result of these reforms. Gleb Pavlovsky, the architect of this early paradigm, and a long-term Putin's political advisor (until a political fallout with the Kremlin during 2011–2012) referred to this group as a "pro-Putin majority." At that moment, the Kremlin's political strategy combined the pursuit of order, stability, and strengthening of the state with maintaining Russia's liberal economy, closely integrated into the global markets.

Such "hybrid" politics that combined the pursuit of a strong state with the overall liberal economic orientation did produce support for Putin's presidency. Many people craved the proclaimed goals of order and stability and appreciated the growing economy and increasing pensions and salaries of Putin's first two terms in power. But the proclaimed goals were still ambiguous in terms of their identity implications for the Russian national community. If anything, at that moment Russia found itself in a classic "catch-up" position vis-à-vis the West. In 1999 Putin famously articulated the goal of Russia catching up with Portugal in terms of GDP, and this debate about catching up with Portugal continued throughout the first decade of the 2000s. The mass electorate recognized that Russia stands unfavorably when compared to many other countries. Russia's dependence on the Western model of economic development and integration into the global markets, driven mostly by the export of energy resources, was also evident and not flattering. These hybrid politics, therefore, did not evoke intense emotions on the part of the population and followed a more rational understanding of Russia's priorities.

Putin's third term began with a sea change in the Kremlin's political orientation. From hybrid politics combining issues of sovereignty and a strong state with the Western model of development, Kremlin shifted toward proclaiming Russia's unique developmental path, justifying it by the country's millennial history and civilization, its Christian values, and traditional family orientations. The economic goals of development and modernization took a back seat as the Kremlin's new conservatively oriented discourse aimed at building a social consensus based on the losers of liberal economic reforms in the 1990s. From 2012 the defensive views about the liberal economic and political order and globalization became predominant.

The advancement of the Kremlin's new symbolic, morality-driven politics was enabled by the preceding years during which the state-controlled media promoted the vision of the 1990s as a traumatic period in Russia's history. This victimhood frame that presented Russia being ripped apart by greedy capitalists—foreign and domestic alike—resonated deeply with the Russian public. It politicized the Russians' collective identity, prompting a search for perpetrators—Russia's enemies abroad and inside the country. It is in this political momentum—of politicized collective identity and the country's perceived victimized status—that the annexation of Crimea became such a powerful inspirational moment and produced collective euphoria in Russia. Vladimir Putin's charisma and popularity skyrocketed, along with the identity boost experienced by the Russian population.

The Crimean annexation worked to cement the Kremlin's new ideological turn that started in 2012. The new, morality-driven political agenda and defensive orientation became particularly relevant as Russia faced Western sanctions and rising anti-Russian rhetoric abroad. The economy stagnated slowly since 2013, but people had time to adjust to worsening conditions. Meanwhile, the identity boost and the national consolidation behind Vladimir Putin—the main national hero, who, at long last, asserted Russia's agency at the international level—was powerful and lasted until the summer of 2018, when the government-initiated pension reform curbed the euphoria, returning Putin's popularity ratings to the pre-Crimea period.

The identity boost spurred by the Crimean annexation lasted longer than expected by many observers. I associate the lasting quality of this identity effect with the revival of the key elements of the Soviet collective identity in Russia in the past few years. Since 2012, the Kremlin has resuscitated the idea of Russia's national exceptionalism and relied heavily on the paradigm of Russia as a "beseiged fortress" surrounded by enemies. These ideas were familiar to many Russians. They were constitutive for the Soviet collective identity and, arguably, had been deeply missed in the atmosphere of a generalized Soviet nostalgia in Russia. The recognition of the degree to which collective identification was central to Soviet individuals—their self-esteem and their perceptions of in-group and out-group members—helps in appreciating (1) the traumatic impact on the sense of collective identity experienced by the society as a result of the collapse of the Soviet Union; and (2) the crucial importance of Putin's efforts to reclaim the lost identity of "great Russia."

The emotional reaction to these returning paradigms cannot be explained simply by their historical familiarity. The reinstatement of the collective identity of the Russian citizens, in these rather jingoistic terms, happened in the context of the Kremlin-propagated victimhood politics mentioned earlier. These politics emphasized Russia's shattered national identity, humiliating events, and economic, social, and political distress resulting from the Soviet collapse. The social consensus was first built and promoted around the meaning of the 1990s and, specifically, around the collective trauma associated with the 1990s. The "chosen trauma" of the 1990s around which the Kremlin built its new policies became one of the crucial pillars of Vladimir Putin's new legitimation strategy. This potent tool allowed the Russian leadership to revive the national consolidation mechanisms used by the Soviet state. It allowed the Kremlin to harness collective emotions and to build a powerful image of the leadership securing Russia's insecure collective identity.

Undertaking such a political strategy required massive communication resources. The state-controlled media in Russia was and still remains arguably the most important tool used by the Kremlin to control domestic political sentiments and orientations. Modern political communication technologies and skillful anchors are employed every day to promote the Kremlin's messages through television programming. Confronted with the expansion and the growing role of social media, especially among the younger generations, the Kremlin has also invested massive resources to dominate virtual media. Besides political communication, the Kremlin places a heavy emphasis on cultural production and youth education in Russia. Control over the sphere of cultural production has increased significantly since 2012. But even in the first decade of the 2000s, Russia's film industry, in particular, dependent on state financing, played into the state's hands, producing films propagating state patriotism.[76]

The media is central to the operation of the political system in Russia and is one of the Kremlin's main assets, just like the control over the country's fossil fuels. Vladimir Putin recognized as much when he suggested in one of his meetings that an information confrontation is a form of competitive struggle, just as "the struggle for mineral resources."[77] The emphasis on the media highlights the role of propaganda and implicates the audience in being brainwashed and manipulable. But the crux of my argument is not merely about the effects of propaganda. I seek to uncover the psychological appeal of specific messages promoted through media sources. I reveal why and how specific messages were used to build social consensus in Russia. I illustrate how the anger and outrage-based programming and the political talk show industry controlled by the Kremlin works to provoke emotional responses in the audience, seeking to instill shared meanings and to consolidate the viewers' opinions on the burning issues of the day. I argue that such consolidation of the views about "today" becomes possible only when the audience shares the vision of Russia "yesterday," i.e., Russia of the 1990s. Building social consensus about the 1990s was a stepping stone for reaching the political cohesion in Russia today.

The analysis presented in this book illustrates the centrality of political choices made by the Kremlin in the specific historical context in which Russia found itself. Many people in Russia embraced the Kremlin's position and reacted with an enthusiastic approval to Russia's newfound assertive stance in the international arena. Such reaction was expected and logical, given the propagated and

widely shared vision of the "wounded," insecure collective identity in Russia, and
the promotion—through these new policies—of the new image of a more secure,
stronger Russia.

To use a metaphor from Hans Christian Andersen's "Snow Queen" story: collective identity could be seen as a big mirror that group members look into and
recognize themselves as part of the bigger community. The shattered Soviet identity went flying around—as fragments of a broken mirror—resonating especially
strongly in the eyes of those hurt by the transition, distorting their view and making them fall under the spell of the Kremlin-orchestrated messages tailored to
capture those lost souls. The nostalgia for that collective mirror, the shame associated with the new, post-Soviet mirror, and, finally, the "collective effervescence"
experienced by the society in the state of recognition of the familiar reflection in
the mirror—given the leadership's attempt to reinstate it—is at the core of "the
Putin phenomenon" and is the central pillar in the societal base of Putinism as we
know it since 2014.[78]

The Approach

I rely on the social identity theory from the field of social psychology to address
the puzzle of Putinism. Henry Tajfel and John Turner originally developed this
theory in the late 1970s to study group behavior.[79] The theory builds on an observation by Aristotle that human beings are social animals; they live in groups. An
individual self incorporates two parts: the personal (what makes one unique vis-
à-vis other individuals) and the social (what marks our differences from other
groups). The social aspect of one's identity is experienced as something intensely
important and personal. But it cannot be reduced to an individual. It is a historical and cultural construct incorporated at the individual level. Each individual's social identities are multiple. One can be a Democrat, an American, and a
Catholic at the same time (and many other things, too, for that matter). But the
relevance and salience of being a Democrat might be more pronounced during
the elections; being an American might be more important on foreign ground,
if the United States wages war (or is under attack); and being a Catholic might
be more relevant during religious holidays. The salience of different identities
depends on the social and political context. The process of constructing such
identities is interwoven with the process of group formation, and the mobilization of collective identities is one of the most important drivers of collective
action in different societies around the world.

This theory was developed in the process of exploring inter-group behavior
and conflict. The theory's basic premise is that groups provide individuals with a
sense of belonging, pride, and self-esteem. Given such psychological value derived

from groups, group members seek to determine the meaning and standing of the group by making social comparisons between their in-group and relevant out-groups. They also seek to define their group favorably by differentiating it positively from relevant out-groups along the dimensions that matter.[80] This process of seeking positive distinction plays out differently in different social contexts and sometimes involves discriminating against and devaluing the out-groups.

Under specific circumstances, selected forms of social identity can become more salient and can lead individuals in the direction of assuming that "group/collective" perspective as their primary and actively mobilized social identity. Groups have higher-order emergent properties that can transform individuals; they also allow individuals to engage in group processes that are capable of transforming the world around them.[81] Charles Taylor (1994) used this insight to craft the notion of the politics of recognition, and the politics of difference in relation to the social struggles of minorities (whether sexuality-, gender-, or race-based) in pursuit of dignity, equal rights, and entitlements. Individuals are not preformed, insisted Taylor. They are constituted by recognition, in interaction with others. Axel Honneth (1996) further developed these ideas, linking the imperative of recognition to deep emotional needs and demonstrating its strength as a basis of collective action in response to perceived injustice associated with non-recognition.

The politics of recognition conducted by states at the international level is different from the politics of recognition in the domestic sphere. The main form of collective action on the international level is normally top-down and state-centered, while domestically, the type of minority politics referenced by Charles Taylor is often grassroots-driven. The forum of such action—international versus domestic political system—is also radically different in terms of the presence of the rule of law, democratic institutions, and law enforcement. Finally, and perhaps most importantly, the ways in which recognition is granted differ. In domestic politics, recognition is granted first and foremost in legal changes that recognize equal rights and responsibilities of particular groups (i.e., voting rights, marriage rights, rights to equal pay, etc.). International recognition is often symbolic in nature. While it can be expressed in institutional changes (e.g., membership in the G20, G8, or UN Security Council, etc.), it is driven by status considerations. If the side that seeks recognition is insecure (or unstable) in its self-identity, the external recognition might never suffice because the insecurity of one's identity will always play a destabilizing role, resulting in a continuing search for more recognition. Hence, the politics of recognition can turn into a vicious circle whereby the side that is insecure about its identity seeks external verification but, due to its internal insecurity, never gets enough of it. Furthermore, external recognition could be used by political leaders and governments for domestic legitimation purposes, and this aspect of the *raison d'être*

of such politics is another element that makes it different from the politics of
recognition on the domestic level.[82]

Constructivist theorists in the field of international relations recognize the
significance of recognition by others as a central motivator and driver of state
behavior. Swedish scholar Erik Ringmar, for example, advanced the analysis of
relations between Soviet Russia and the West as driven by the identity-based
model of external recognition. Soviet leaders, according to Ringmar, throughout Soviet history sought out Western recognition of Soviet Russia: first as a
"legitimate state," then as a "great power," and, after World War II, as a "superpower." Such politics of recognition is the driving force, according to Ringmar,
behind Bolshevik diplomatic activities after 1921, Stalin turning to Hitler prior
to World War II, and the arms race during the Cold War.[83] Viacheslav Morozov,
professor of EU-Russia studies at the University of Tartu (Estonia), also has long
applied a relational approach to Russia's national identity, illustrating that Russia
traditionally played the role of "the other" to Europe (2012, 2009). These discursive practices created the structural conditions that prevented Russia's integration into European structures, according to Morozov. In his important account
of identity discourses in post-Soviet Russia, he also highlighted Russia's own
inability to construct a new historical narrative that would delink Russia's new
image from its imperial past. Assuming a role as the main successor of the Soviet
Union, Russia, according to Morozov, predestined itself for a "neo-imperial
restoration."[84]

Besides "recognition games," constructivist international relations (IR) scholars have also advanced a concept of *ontological security* to capture the states' identity imperative—the need to experience themselves as entities with the consistent
sense of "self."[85] In specific historical moments, ontological security might be
more important than economic or military security as a motivator of state behavior. Changing state hierarchies, caused by war outcomes, decolonization, or other
critical situations that create "radical and unpredictable disjuncture," result in a
condition of ontological insecurity—a condition that states find hard to bear. As
opposed to cognitive burdens of uncertainty that IR scholars focus on, following
Anthony Giddens's and Ronald David Laing's theorizing, social identity theory
scholars emphasize the importance of status and hierarchies. Tajfel and Turner
(1979) argued that groups are always interested in more favorable in-group evalu-
ations and more favorable comparisons with out-groups. The differentiation
between secure and insecure identities in social identity theory, therefore, calls
attention to the perceived stability of group status: the more stable and immu-
table group status is, the more secure collective identities are.[86]

Building on these approaches, in this book I zoom in on the structural pre-
conditions that elevated the potency of collective identity politics in Russia,

as well as its main elements and propagation mechanisms. Soviet collapse was undoubtedly a radical disjuncture for Russia and for the Russians who were used to thinking about the Soviet Union as "their own" territory.[87] The new Russian state's loss of international status and the condition of ontological insecurity impacted Russia's political community, producing specific points of psychological vulnerability (akin to emotional "hot buttons"). Vladimir Putin made the politicization of Russia's collective identity into the core of his legitimization strategy, which has become particularly pronounced since 2012. It was hard (but arguably not impossible) to resist such political trajectory given the political potential of collective identity-related questions. Putinism, especially in its "mature" format, could therefore be viewed as an actualization of the political potential associated with Russian society's insecure (or destabilized) collective identity.

The social identity theory also posits that, when the group perspective becomes a central anchor for individuals, leaders gain immense influence. More recently, building on Tajfel and Turner's work, Alexander Haslam, Stephen Reicher, and Michael Platow have developed a "new psychology of leadership" to explain leadership phenomena. I rely on this new approach to analyze Vladimir Putin's leadership. The allure of Putin as a leader builds on the dynamics of powerful group emotions that provide him with a larger leeway to shape public opinion by making group identity into the most salient and cognitively central element of individuals' sense of identity. Specifically, the Kremlin-constructed and heavily propagated image of Russia as a fortress besieged by foreign enemies worked well as a compensatory mechanism in the context when the Kremlin promulgated Russia's insecure, victimized collective status associated with the 1990s. Kremlin's messages worked because they fit with *social representations*—the ideas widely shared by society members in relation to Russia's recent past.[88] They encompassed 'mass common sense.'[89] Using these ideas, the Kremlin-controlled media and Russia's political and cultural elites constructed the vision of the collective trauma of the 1990s, which turned into one of the building blocks for Russian present-day national identity.

The social identity approach, along with the sociopsychological conception of collective identity, allows for bringing together societal, elite-level, and contextual factors to make sense of Putinism and the dynamics of the "post-Crimean consensus" in Russia.[90] Putin as a political phenomenon is a result of a sociocultural and political construction empowered by powerful political communication technologies that work to promulgate the image of the country's leader as a national hero and an irreplaceable politician. The importance of social and political construction, however, does not mean that it was or could be done voluntarily. Understanding the historical context and the structural conditions in which the Russian community found itself in the aftermath of the Soviet collapse is essential because the effectiveness of political communication is not predetermined by technological sophistication, but by the degree of resonance that specific messages have in the wider population. Such resonance, in turn, depends on the emotional makeup of the society, which is determined by real-life experiences.

In contrast to arguments that focus on *homo sovieticus* and on Russian societal features viewed by many to be responsible for Putinism, my focus is on the leadership process and the historical context. My normative orientation is toward *understanding* Russian society and recognizing the challenges it has encountered on its transformational path. Understanding that these challenges do not originate in innate psychological traits, differences in moral capacity, or other intrinsic features, but rather in factors that travel globally, combined with some historically unique circumstances, should work as a proof against self-righteousness and the Cold War–era sense of national superiority that might have afflicted some Western audiences vis-à-vis Russia. This orientation would have been different if I wrote this book for the Russian audience. There is a famous quote from the Soviet classic *Twelve Chairs* by Ilf and Petrov (1928) that turned into a popular proverb: "the business of saving those who are drowning is all their own" (дело помощи утопающим—есть дело рук самих утопающих).[91] This quote underscores the importance of active and constructive agency, as opposed to blaming someone or expecting help and understanding from the outside. If the aim is to transform Russia into a prosperous and free nation that values its citizens, culture, and its relations with the outside world, then reliance on the internal human and social capital, as well as economic and institutional resources, is arguably the best attitude from the perspective of Russian citizens. One important message that emerges from the following analysis that is relevant for Russia's future is that the politics and psychology of victimhood will have to be overcome if Russia wants to move forward.

On Methodology

This book benefits from a mixed-method approach to analyzing the content and the effects of social and political construction in Russia. More systematically, to study the effects of political construction, I conducted four focus-group interviews in Kazan and Samara—two large cities in Privolzhsky Federal District— in November 2016. The design and methodology underlying these focus-group interviews, as well as their main findings, are described in detail in my article "Public Opinion Formation and Group Identity: The Politics of National Identity Salience in Putin's Russia" (*Problems of Post-Communism*, 2021). I draw on this research selectively, highlighting some central findings and using most representative and colorful quotes in Chapter 2, which focuses on Putin's leadership from the social identity theory perspective; Chapter 3, which explores the core beliefs associated with the Soviet identity; and Chapter 5, which focuses on the social and political construction of the collective trauma of the 1990s.

To test the central hypotheses guiding the analysis in this book in relation to the political effects of insecure collective identity in Russia, I also conducted a nationwide survey experiment in November 2017. This survey was conducted with help from the Levada Center and became the empirical foundation for "Authoritarian Legitimation and Insecure Collective Identity in Putin's Russia"—an article manuscript that describes the technical details of this project. I refer to the design and major findings from this survey experiment in a shorter format in Chapters 2 and 7. Besides this original research into public opinion in Russia, in writing Chapters 3, 4, and 5, I also relied heavily on other opinion polls conducted by the Levada Center, the Russian Public Opinion Research Center (VCIOM), and the Public Opinion Foundation (FOM) in Russia over the past few decades.

I relied mostly on secondary research for writing Chapters 3 and 4, although some of the observations in these chapters benefit from Soviet-era materials, including poems, songs, and the 1986 "spacebridge" that connected residents of Leningrad with those of Seattle in an unprecedented uncensored exchange led by Phil Donahue (from the American side) and Vladimir Pozner (from the Soviet side). Chapters 6 and 7 are based on primary sources ranging from Vladimir Putin's speeches and press conferences to Vladimir Solovyev's political talk shows, Sergei Kurginyan's writings and presentations, Nikita Mikhalkov's documentaries, films by Alexei Balabanov, songs by Monetochka, and opinions voiced by the respondents of the focus-group interviews I conducted in Russia.

Last but not least, the book draws (more indirectly) on years of growing up in the Soviet Union, and then, later, on soaking and poking in Russia and specifically in the Republic of Tatarstan, where I spend summers traveling between various cities, towns, and villages; meeting relatives, friends, and colleagues; chatting with neighbors, former classmates, fellow travelers, and taxi drivers. It is also based on years of following political, economic, and cultural news from Russia. I follow Russia's recent literature (selectively, of course), try to watch the most recent films, and listen to the most recent music coming out of Russia. I follow Russia's popular bloggers (giving preference to Yuri Dud) and keep up with parts of the Russian intellectual diaspora abroad, especially in Washington, DC, and London. These interactions and points of discovery of things Russian are not methodologically systematic, but they create the broader foundation of my understanding of Russia.

2

The White Knight and the Red Queen

BLINDED BY LOVE?

Putin is married to Russia.

—JOSEPH KOBZON (2018)

THE RELATIONSHIP BETWEEN Vladimir Putin and Russia has been depicted in various colorful ways, verbally and nonverbally. One drawing has a bare-chested Putin, with machine gun in his hands, riding a bear with a young woman on his knees. The young woman is, presumably, his bride (Russia). The dynamism palpable in this depiction might even be telling a story of a bride "stolen" in accordance with traditional practices in some parts of Central Asia. Although the drawing is dated to the first decade of the 2000s, its prescience has only grown since Putin's third presidential term. The late Joseph Kobzon, a renowned Russian singer, noted playfully in 2015 that Putin "is married to Russia" and "thinks only about Russia."[1] This metaphor of Putin's "marriage to Russia" underscores the evolving nature of this relationship—from that of a groom to that of a husband. Building on this metaphor, one could suggest that the relationship has been fulfilling. At one moment, the wife has even become "blinded by love" and has developed faith in her husband to the point of seeing him to be irreplaceable.[2]

This relationship is by no means free and equal. The issues of control, power, and codependence in the atmosphere of controlled information flows and growing repression of alternative views and ideas play a big role in defining the nature of this relationship. But it is, on the whole, real and tangible, as evidenced by many Russian and non-Russian sociologists and as I, also, discovered in my focus-group interviews in two Russian cities, Kazan and Samara. Many Russian citizens who voted for Putin in 2018 believed in him and were willing to give up on democratic rules and principles to see him stay in power.[3] Levada-based opinion polls revealed that between 2012 and 2015 the number of Russians who associated democracy with government accountability and popular control of

The Red Mirror. Gulnaz Sharafutdinova, Oxford University Press (2020). © Oxford University Press.
DOI: 10.1093/oso/9780197502938.001.0001.

the government has dropped from 39% to 18%.[4] These changes were arguably linked to feelings of trust in Putin that spiked after the Crimea annexation. In the post-2014 political context—at least until the deeply unpopular pension reform announced in 2018—many Russians did not see Russia without Putin, and even feared any such scenario.

The idea of Putin being unique and irreplaceable is promoted in Russia in a top-down manner. The state-controlled media propagates this message coming from the Kremlin, the Orthodox Church, and the cultural elites. Russia's patriarch Kirill systematically praises Putin, pronouncing him to be Russia's savior who helped the country to avert collapse and disintegration and calling Putin's rule "a miracle of God."[5] Nikita Mikhalkov, a well-known film producer, actor, and Putin apologist, also developed these themes, which were expressed with a particularly zealous tone in his 2007 documentary celebrating Putin's fifty-fifth birthday.[6] Other influential pro-Kremlin media personalities, such as Vladimir Solovyev, propagate these ideas in a variety of media platforms, including television and radio talk shows, books, and face-to-face meetings with the public.

Vyacheslav Volodin's 2014 quote "no Putin—no Russia"[7] did not introduce a new idea to the public sphere. With an eloquent simplicity, the head of the presidential administration vocalized and channeled the sentiment shared by many Russians in the post-2014 period. The annexation of Crimea elevated Putin's leadership role and worked as a charisma-builder for the Russian president. The nature of the relationship between Putin as leader and the Russian citizens as followers shifted. Putin, the president, became Putin the state Leader (with a capital L). Russian society itself transformed in this period. Samuel Greene and Graeme Robertson referred to this new state in their book *Putin v. the People: The Perilous Politics of a Divided Russia* (2019), borrowing from Emile Durkheim, as a state of "collective effervescence."[8] Durkheim used this term to describe society coming together and "feeling together" in specific moments.[9] The new sentiments represented the psychological glue that connected Vladimir Putin to many Russian citizens.

I explore the nature of this glue and its composite materials in this chapter. This glue consists of the ideas and sentiments that many Russian citizens share in relation to their president. The main insights of the recent application of social identity theory to leadership studies relate to Putin's role as a *leader* of the Russian national community. The annexation of Crimea became the pin for Putin's leadership success. At that moment, Russia's president turned from an individual who occupied the highest position of power in the Russian state into a *charismatic national leader*, and an embodiment of the Russian nation that the people could take pride in. It was the ultimate proof of the ideas and messages long conveyed to the public. It was the moment when Putin's leadership acquired special properties because it provided the public with a more positively conceived vision of their national identity.

Vladimir Solovyev, one of the Kremlin's principal media mouthpieces channeling the state messages through television and other media platforms, has summarized his perception of Putin's role in Russia as follows:

> Returning a sense of pride to the Russians is the main thing Putin did. Putin is a living epic hero for the public consciousness. He punished the evil: Shamil Basaev is dead. He showed the Americans their place and told them in face what he thinks about them. He won the 2014 Olympics! During his rule, Putin fulfilled all the promises he made. Overall, all of his problems were resolved at once. He dealt with the oligarchs the way, neither of the previous leaders could be praised for anything like this. Yeltsin left Russia with a humiliating Khasavyurt accords, which could not be seen by Russians as anything but a brazen slap on the face. Gorbachev had lost the whole country entirely. Putin, on the other hand, won and changed the attitude towards Russia, by shifting the domestic power configuration and by making the international community view Russia as an independent and strong partner. Putin has an understanding [of] who you are and why you are. And this is important.[10]

The focus group interviews I conducted in Samara and Kazan—to study the political implications and manifestations of assuming national identity in Russia in 2016—highlighted the extent to which these views were internalized by many Russian citizens.

These interviews were held in November 2016—a moment still charged by a post-Crimea public euphoria. Samara and Kazan are both located along the Volga River and are multinational cities, each with population of over one million. Samara is the capital of Samara oblast, dominated by the Russian ethnic group, while Kazan is the capital of an ethnic Republic of Tatarstan, where Muslim Tatars comprise 53% of the population. Such location choice for these focus-group interviews—away from Moscow and in ethnically diverse regions—allowed me to explore potential differences in the popular reception of the Kremlin's identity politics in groups dominated by ethnic Russians versus non-Russian ethnic groups. I was also curious about the potential impact of age on political opinions, and I arranged for two groups to be interviewed in each city: a younger audience aged 20–35, and an audience composed of respondents above 35 years of age. The interviews lasted around 80–90 minutes and involved groups of 9–12 people.

I describe the main analytical goals, working hypotheses, the questions setup, and findings of the study based on focus group interviews elsewhere.[11] Here I highlight the selected results and most representative and interesting quotes and observations from that study.

Just as Solovyev juxtaposed Putin to previous leaders, my respondents also reasoned along very similar lines. Their attitudes toward Boris Yeltsin, as well as the last Soviet leader—Mikhail Gorbachev—in most cases could not stand in greater contrast to how they perceived Vladimir Putin. There was a clear consensus on the positive role of Putin and mostly negative memories about Yeltsin. Group members criticized Yeltsin not only for his personal vices, such as drinking and coarse manners, but also for his carelessness toward the country's strategic interests. Specifically, he was accused of allowing many former Soviet republics to go their own way, with no effort undertaken to keep them united. Russia's first president was closely associated with the rough 1990s, "when the country as such was not really there" in the aftermath of the Soviet collapse, in perceptive words of one group member.

Vladimir Solovyev's writings, once again, convey the ideas that have been propagated from the Kremlin and shared widely by the Russian public:

> In contrast to Yeltsin, Putin behaves as a real statesman. Yeltsin's rule went under the slogan "Grab anything you see." That was the time of tearing Russia apart and dispersing the lands. Putin gathers the lands. Yeltsin was losing allies; Putin finds new allies. In some sense, Putin is Yeltsin's political antagonist. [. . .] Putin has a different understanding and different life experience: he knows life better than Yeltsin. Putin is likely the most national of all the presidents we ever had. Not in a sense that he is Russian but in a sense that he is a citizen of this country and is responsible for our ancestors' graves. He cannot imagine himself apart from Russia.[12]

My focus group respondents praised Putin for (1) his personal qualities, such as competence and physical agility, as well as his policy achievements, such as (2) raising Russia's international status and (3) bringing stability (in relation to war in Chechnya, as well as a sense of economic stability, at least prior to the problems associated with Crimea and sanctions). One respondent in Samara, with evident literary skills, offered the most eloquent and nuanced evaluation of Putin's role in Russia:

> Putin is not a rocket dragging the country up; Putin is a parachute that prevented Russia from falling and crashing completely. The downward move still continues by inertia and we have not reached the bottom yet.

This metaphor was so nuanced that it took some time for the group to process its meaning. But after a moment of silence, many group members expressed a sense of amusement and admiration for the insight offered through this metaphor. In one "shot" it captured three important ideas: (1) the sense of the "free fall" Russia was in during the 1990s; (2) the perceived role of Putin in stopping this free fall and rescuing the country from a complete crash; and (3) an understanding that Russia is still in some state of stagnation (or even fall), with a potential for growth and development.

Putin's charisma was also validated in the degree of irrational faith in his foresight. One respondent expressed his faith in Putin as such:

> I believe that he [Putin] knows where he is going to; he is not doing anything without a purpose. He has a goal.

Another respondent in Kazan shared his unquestioned faith by suggesting:

> People do not need to know everything. It is sufficient that Putin knows.

The most intense approval of Putin was linked to his achievements in the realm of foreign policy and international politics. The comments in relation to Russia's new status in the world were accompanied by the words "*ne stydno*" (not shameful). These unforced comments, exerted spontaneously while someone else was talking, highlight the extent of shame many Russians had experienced in relation to how they perceived Russia's standing in the world.

A variety of public opinion polls capture similar views, revealing that many Russians view Putin through the lens described by Solovyev so well. This lens, promoting Putin as an irreplaceable leader of Russia endowed by super-qualities and worthy of special trust and faith, was propagated through national TV, radio, and other media platforms by an army of pro-Kremlin media professionals.[13]

The pro-Kremlin message is to be found everywhere in Russia. The state-controlled media is very careful about its content management. The Kremlin relies on talented and forceful interlocutors and producers of TV content. The same messages are channeled relentlessly through various media formats. The Kremlin has invested massively not only in the traditional communication channels but also in social media, attempting to dominate virtual media space. All these factors have undoubtedly played a very significant role in the successful propagation of the Kremlin's version of history and the meaning of the ongoing events in Russia and abroad. The media part of the Russian story deserves as much attention as possible. Many scholars and analysts rightfully focus on the study of the Russian media and political communication. Discounting the factor of the media as an important playmaker in the Russian political space would be foolish. In Chapters 6 and 7, I focus on the system of political communication constructed during the first decade of the 2000s and its centrality for the Kremlin's legitimation strategy.

Nonetheless, the media are only a part of the larger story. The puzzle of Putin's popularity has two keys: the state-controlled media broadcasting specific messages to the public, and the contextual variables that created the possibility for Putin's leadership phenomenon. These contextual variables—the Russian citizens' collective experience of the Soviet collapse and the ensuing transition—shaped the psychological conditions enabling such societal response when even the more educated and advanced groups in Russian society fell into the trap of irrational adulation of an individual perceived to be the collective savior.

A comparison with the Soviet system of political communication and official propaganda is instructive. The Soviet informational space and media system were more tightly controlled by the Soviet party-state, and yet the Soviet citizens developed distinct patterns of interpreting information "fed" to them and a unique capacity to read between the lines of the official propaganda.[14] Many Russian TV viewers today could still be expected to follow these Soviet-era information-processing patterns.[15] Scholars who have explored the reception of news in Russia found the Russian viewers to be highly sophisticated in interpreting the information encountered on television.[16] Therefore, looking at Putin's popularity—especially in the years following the Crimea annexation—as only the result of media propaganda is too simplistic. The Kremlin had undoubtedly harnessed the power of the media, relying on the most advanced Western media technologies. But turning the technological possibilities into real influence required a good sense of the topics and ideas that would resonate with Russian society in an emotionally intense manner. It required "emotional connection" and "emotional intelligence" on the part of the regime (and the leader), as well as the specific political choices to be made by the person who seems to share some of the main public sentiments.

Normally, the term "emotional intelligence" has a positive connotation when applied to individual interaction. Such positive connotation is not warranted here. In this book, "emotional intelligence" refers to the skillfulness with which the collectively shared emotional "hot buttons" were constructed and utilized for the specific political objective of building support for Vladimir Putin's leadership. The self-serving nature of this political objective is obvious to the outside observer. It could only be ignored in the context of the "emotionally driven" politics when such "hot buttons" were manipulated. Responsible leadership would require that such emotional weak spots are acknowledged and that political and cultural work is done in order to process and overcome them. Their use as the

tools of political manipulation in Russia has become a big stumbling block for
Russia's progression toward a state that is committed to providing public goods
as well as economic and social development.

Nevertheless, the combination of the media and "emotionally intelligent"
politics allowed Putin's leadership to become transformational for the Russian
collective identity, at least in the short to medium term, while Vladimir Putin is
himself at the top of the national power pyramid. The longevity of such transformation is questionable and the effectiveness of such politics is quickly crumbling
under the weight of the health crisis that lays open the aspects of governance that
the Kremlin tried for long to keep under the cover or claimed progress in.

What Does Social Identity Theory Teach Us about Leadership?

Popular in Russia, prominent on the world stage, and celebrated by the media
globally, Vladimir Putin is a political phenomenon and a celebrity figure all at
once.[17] Hyped by the media as well as the cognitive and emotional legacies of the
Cold War, not only lay observers, but also some high-ranking politicians view
Putin as an omnipresent, powerful dictator capable of deciding election results in
the United States, turning around the fate of the Syrian president, threatening the
Baltic countries, strategizing in energy politics—often with more success than his
Western counterparts. Many scholars, journalists, and pundits have written about
his leadership, trying to decipher his personality and find answers to the question articulated early in his presidency: "Who is Mr. Putin?"[18] His psychological
profiling has undoubtedly turned into an important challenge for the intelligence
services in many parts of the world. Many analysts have argued that Putin's personal and professional background is important for understanding his policies
and strategies as Russia's president.[19] Other commentators have countered that
paying too much attention to Putin means ignoring other important factors at
play, such as (1) Russian society and political culture, (2) Russia's political elite,
and (3) the state bureaucracy. They all are as important or even more important
than Putin. There is a "collective Putin," some pundits suggest, and Putinism as a
phenomenon would not have existed without that collective. Mikhail Zygar best
expressed the idea in his *All the Kremlin's Men* (*Vsia kremlevskaia rat': Kratkaia
istoriia sovremennoi Rossii*, 2016) suggesting that "the king is made by his court,"
and referring to hundreds of people surrounding the president and guessing what
his position might be on specific issues. Brian Taylor developed a similar idea in
his recent book, *The Code of Putinism* (2018), where he outlined a list of ideas,
habits, and emotions that characterize Russia's top brass leadership and shape
Russia's economy, politics, and institutions.

Still other observers ignore personalities and agency altogether and take a structuralist view, leveraging international or domestic structures and institutions to explain Russia's current predicament. These arguments are frequently located at the intersection of post-structural theory and the studies of post-communism.[20] Ayse Zarakol, a political scientist at the University of Cambridge, looked at the consequences of stigmatization for being non-Western in the context of dominant Western normativity. In her important book, *After Defeat: How the East Learned to Live with the West* (2010), Zarakol explored the cases of Kemalist Turkey, postwar Japan, and post-Soviet Russia to argue that the structural position the non-Western states find themselves in after major defeats might engender resentment-led, revanchist foreign policies.[21] Putin's Russia fits this story well. The foreign policy trends in Russia that emerged under Evgeny Primakov's leadership in the late 1990s also pointed to the high likelihood of Russia's reassertion on the foreign arena, one way or another. But such structural argument takes Putin out of the "explanatory equation" entirely. It suggests that the outcome we see would have occurred, a specific leader notwithstanding. The puzzle of Putin's leadership and Putinism as a political phenomenon, however, stands out, crying for an explanation. It has transformed over time, acquiring new features; it has beaten popular expectations as well as academic arguments about its staying popular appeal; it has produced an ongoing political uncertainty at home and abroad in relation to Russia's future.

The approach I found most helpful to understand the Putin phenomenon at its zenith (2014–2018) relies on social identity theory applied to the topic of leadership and known as the "new psychology of leadership." It allows for integrating societal and individual factors for explaining how and why Vladimir Putin was able to attain such unprecedented charisma and popularity in Russian society.[22] This approach rests on the understanding of leadership as a group-based phenomenon. Groups need leaders for their consolidation, and leadership makes sense only in the context of groups. Leadership is *produced* by group processes that are contingent on psychologically belonging to the group. Leadership and society are mutually constitutive—each made by, and even transformed by, the other.[23] Michael Hogg, one of the authors of the new psychology of leadership, posited that "[l]eaders and followers are interdependent roles embedded within a social system bounded by common group or category membership."[24] Therefore, the two aspects of the puzzle motivating this book—Putin's popularity and Russian societal preferences—are two sides of the same coin. They need to be explored and understood in parallel, specifically for the period of time when Putin's leadership appeared to be valued and appreciated by many Russian citizens.

Let's begin with exploring the issue of leadership. Leadership is usually understood as a capacity to influence followers, and not simply by securing compliance but by shaping beliefs, desires, and priorities.[25] In the words of Haslam et al., "good leadership is not determined by competent management, skilled decision-making, or accepted authority in and of themselves. The key reason for this is that these things do not necessarily involve winnings the hearts and minds of others or harnessing their energies and passions. Leadership always does."[26] Lay observers and many scholars, too, tend to take a personalistic approach and look into charisma and individual character traits when confronted with cases of successful leadership. The "great man" approach in history that focuses on individuals and their role in remaking history is still highly influential.[27] For observers inside the community in question, the reason for following the "great man" logic might be the fact that it is hard to resist the intuition and the energy of all those followers who recognize the magic of that "great man." Only outside observers who do not belong to that community, or those who belong but can maintain psychological "autonomy" from it, might recognize the fact that the man in question is not that "great" and that this case of successful leadership rests on a specific fit between the personal traits and messages of the individual in question and the collectively shared traits and expectations of the followers.

This view highlights that any leadership phenomenon is really a phenomenon not of one man, but of a relationship between the leader and his/her followers. This relationship rests on the significance of social identity—the shared sense of "us"—for individual well-being and the degree to which parties to the leadership process define themselves in terms of a shared group membership. As Samuel Greene and Graeme Robertson argued recently, "Putin has become dear to millions of Russians [. . .] because the music he played allowed them to feel part of something big, immanent, exciting, maybe even a little dangerous."[28]

The leader and his/her followers engage with each other as members of the same in-group, and the nature of their relationship depends on the strength and the salience of the in-group ties. Leadership potential and influence are greatest when the group members stop thinking in terms of what divides them and start thinking in terms of what unites them as group members. This also means that leadership success depends on the social context because different contexts can be characterized by varying levels of group salience, as well as by varying groups made salient in specific times. For the groups persecuted on religious grounds, for example, their religious identity might be especially salient. Therefore, the potential for the leadership phenomenon to emerge in relation to religious identity is higher than, say, any other social identity. For a group that had undergone territorial disintegration and state collapse and had not developed any intermediate collective identities to substitute for the previously dominant collective identity, people's national identity might be more prominent and salient, and the national-level leadership phenomenon might be more likely to emerge.

To make sense of the impact of the Soviet collapse on the national identity of Soviet citizens, in the following chapter I will focus in more detail on the salience and the content of the Soviet collective identity. This chapter builds on the "new psychology of leadership" to describe and explain the nature of the relationship between Vladimir Putin and his followers in Russia. This approach highlights four important principles of successful leadership, all of which are linked to the importance of social identity.

To be successful, leaders (1) must be seen as "one of us," as representing the position that best distinguishes our in-group from other out-groups. Alexander Haslam and his colleagues suggested that a successful leader must be a group prototype—someone who represents the essential features and beliefs of group members. Successful leaders (2) must be perceived to be "doing it for us." Their actions must be seen as advancing the interests of in-group. Leaders must be able to take the ideas, values, and priorities of the group and embed them in reality. Leaders need to express these priorities and make them relevant and definitive of the group. Successful leaders (3) must "craft a sense of us." They need to be actively involved in shaping the shared understanding of "who we are" and "what we are about." Without such work of defining and articulating the common sense of "we-ness," groups simply cannot exist. Good leaders are always skilled entrepreneurs of identity. They help shape, transform, negotiate, define, and perform group identity. And finally, successful leaders (4) must "make us matter." Groups always compare themselves to and compete with other similar groups, although social context always shapes such inter-group dynamics, and competitive trends are by no means universal.[29] The desire to raise group prestige and status are, on the other hand, universal. And successful leaders are those who can raise the prestige of belonging to a specific group.

Over the last two decades, Putin became a successful Russian leader on all of these four important elements of leadership. All these elements are perception-based. Leadership is a socio-cognitive phenomenon and reflects socially shared perceptions. This nuance, which appears to be simply assumed in the new psychology of leadership, opens the possibility for considering the importance of political and social construction in forging socially shared collective perceptions of the leadership. It raises the issue of the extent to which media might be crucial for promoting certain views and opinions. It also raises a question as to the lasting nature of any historically situated leadership examples. If these perceptions could be instilled from above, how long would they last? What factors influence whether the group in question continues to hold the views that are seen to be at the heart of "effective leadership?" Under what circumstance does effective leadership end? All these issues appear important in light of Russia's recent experience with Putinism. For now, though, I will illustrate perceptions about Putin's leadership at the high point of Putinism, when the Russian people saw Putin as the ultimate representative of the Russian national community: a leader who has crafted a sense of collective belonging that the Russian people desired, who has defended the priorities and interests of the Russian state and nation, and who has increased the collective prestige of the Russian community on a global scale.

What Makes Putin an Effective Leader?
Putin Is "One of Us"

Successful leaders usually have prototypical characteristics of the in-group members, which means that they share the essential features and, possibly, normative predispositions—beliefs and ideas—with the in-group. If we consider the Russian society as a group that, in its most recent past, has gone through the disruptive period of the 1990s, Vladimir Putin is indeed a good prototype. He personally experienced the collapse of the Soviet Union as a destructive event. He has lost his job in Germany; he had to give up his KGB career and look for another job as he returned to St. Petersburg. The loss of jobs and professional careers and the need to adjust to new circumstances have been experienced by millions of Russian citizens. Putin's humble background and childhood experiences of growing up in one of St. Petersburg's (then Leningrad) communal apartments, in an ordinary family, and having to fend for himself in a rugged courtyard environment, are also in some ways prototypical of the experiences of millions of his co-citizens. Putin's biographers underscore the importance of his childhood experiences for the way he relates to problem-resolution, risk-taking, and interpersonal relationships.[30]

Vladimir Solovyev, a prominent media personality in contemporary Russia, explained Putin's popularity as follows:

> Why do people love Putin so much? Because he is an absolute fairy-tale character. Everything was awful: he could not get a job, he was a so-so student, he was from a very humble background, he grew up with his peers in a rough neigborhood, he was not special and small in stature, he got his job with difficulty but then lost it without making it to the general stars; he then found something in Piter [St. Petersburg, author's note] but even at the university, he was not really appreciated. . . . A simple Russian lad, no special abilities, very calm, did his work without any zeal. And suddenly he goes through a fairy tale transformation: at his Motherland's request, he got up and made it. The fairy tales about Ivan the soldier and Ivan the fool merged. He got up and made it when he was appointed as

the FSB director. And then, later, when he became a president, that's it. All talk ended. He got to work and it suddenly became clear that the "giant" Yeltsin and the "thinker" Gorbachev are nothing in comparison to Putin because Putin is "non-nomenklatura." Putin is the first non-nomenklatura president of Russia. And suddenly we learn that a simple lad from society is better than a member of nomenklatura. This fact that he is one of us ensured such colossal support. That's why he is forgiven for everything; that's why people love him so much. Putin is archetypical like a birch tree and an embodiment of the soldier who came out of the fire.[31]

Solovyev's propagandistic effort in this passage is very effective because it is rooted in the images known to anyone who grew up reading Russian folk fairy tales and who is familiar with the magic powers of Ivan the fool. These images undoubtedly resonate among Solovyev's readers and work to mythologize Putin's image as well.

One needs to give credit to Putin himself as well for building his image as a prototypical Russian. Gleb Pavlovsky, who has worked with Putin side by side until 2008, once noted that "Putin cultivated in himself a position of an average Russian person; he always tried to understand how an average Russian looks at a particular issue."[32] Various observers—domestic and foreign alike—have long noted the special quality of Vladimir Putin to appear as an empty vessel "that could be filled with any substance, or perhaps a chameleon which adapts well to any environment."[33] Especially early in his presidency, when he met with various groups and individuals, it appeared that Putin reflected onto the viewer exactly what the viewer was looking to find in him. Stanislav Belkovsky, a Russian political analyst and director of the National Strategy Institute, referred to him as an "empty, resonating vessel."[34] Political scientist Olga Kryshtanovskaya suggested, based on her surveys, that Putin worked as a mirror that reflected onto each person his/her inner aspirations.[35] Anna Arutynyan, a Russian journalist and author of *The Putin Mystique* (2015), suggested in her book that Putin "by virtue of his character and profession (and very much through an extension of his often noted personal character trait of reflecting the tone, gestures, and mood of whoever he is listening to), he has acted as a mirror of society, a product of his times, reflecting what was desired of him on a subconsoious level."[36] Many other professionals and experts who met him in the early years of his presidency noted the openness manifested by the president. This condition—of openness and "emptiness"—has arguably ended with Putin's third term in power, which started in 2012, when the Kremlin made a drastic move toward embracing traditional and conservative values and orientations. Going along with the mirror metaphor, such transformation might mean that Putin at last learned exactly what is demanded at the wider societal level. On selected issues of national identity, he resonated with and mirrored the Russian community at large.

Putin's humble background makes him relatable and enables people to see him as "one of us" or rather even as "the best one of us." This image was procreated early on by such songs as "A Man Like Putin" that topped the Russian Music Charts in 2002 and was still very popular in 2016.[37] At the same time, the Russian cultural tradition of hierarchical authority relationships demands that national leaders be seen as "tsars." The image of Putin as a "tsar" is also actively promoted through the Russian media and noted by observers.[38] Putin is therefore able to combine the sense of "being one of us" with being at the same time exceptional and unique.

Putin Is "Doing It for Us"

Putin's early leadership is associated with the extended period of uninterrupted economic growth during 1999–2008. Scholars attribute these years of growth to a host of different factors, including (1) the very low starting conditions given the years of economic contraction in the 1990s; (2) the 1998 currency devaluation; and (3) the administrative reforms undertaken by Putin's government in the first decade of the 2000s, with the flat tax of 13% among them.[39] But most observers also agree that rapidly growing energy prices provided a key ingredient of Russia's economic success in the first decade of the 2000s.[40] Putin was very lucky to straddle the period of rising energy prices that fueled economic growth and enabled the government to not only pay off Russia's debts to international creditors, such as the International Monetary Fund (IMF) and the Paris club, but also increase salaries and pensions to Russian citizens. Given the context of wage and pension arrears in the 1990s, the Russian population undoubtedly credited Putin with this new promising development. Much of his popularity in the first decade of the 2000s was associated with favorable economic trends in Russia.[41]

Putin's "war on terror" was another important element of his legitimacy-building strategy in the early 2000s. The chain of events that transformed the course of Russian history involved an armed assault on Dagestan in August 1999, undertaken by extremist military groups from Chechnya. The same month, a series of apartment bombings occurred in Moscow and two other Russian cities. These blasts were blamed on the Chechens as well, setting the stage for public outrage directed against Chechens, who became the most disliked ethnic group in Russia around that time.[42] The reaction to these shocking events became the foundation for Putin's quick rise as the undisputed leader of Russia. Putin's reaction was quick and tough. One regional leader, Ruslan Aushev, described it laconically with the slogan, "Bei Chechniu, spasai Rossiiu" (beat Chechnya and save Russia).[43] Putin started an immediate military operation to quickly free Dagestan and re-establish federal control over Chechnya. In terms of rhetoric, one of Putin's infamous lines, "We'll follow terrorists everywhere. . . . Should we catch them in an outhouse, we'll kill them there," was coined during his press conference in Astana, Kazakhstan, in September 1999.[44] Such resolve and tough action were exactly what the Russian public craved.[45] Putin's popularity ratings surged, reflecting people's growing confidence in Russia's government and in Putin himself.[46]

The war in Chechnya is widely considered to have been key to Putin's victory in the 2000 presidential election.[47] It determined the most important item on Russia's agenda for the new millennium, which was rebuilding the state and vertically consolidating centralized power. The popular perceptions of Putin's role in saving Russia from territorial fragmentation, of bringing order and stability, are largely associated with Putin's policies to tackle terrorism and pacify the North Caucasus.

Putin Is "Crafting a Sense of Us"

Successful leadership is about relations between leader and followers, when both sides are bound together as part of a common "we." Leaders represent this "we-ness"; they help to construct it, and they are constrained by it too.[48] At the moment when Vladimir Putin came to power, the Russian national community itself did not have a sense of consolidation, solidarity, togetherness, or "we-ness" based on shared narratives and publicly expressed values and preferences. The Russian society at that moment could itself be represented as an "empty vessel," or as a fragmented community silently enduring the unexpressed trauma of shattered collective identity, painful social dislocation and economic hardship, and lost international status and prestige. The local efforts of creating the "communities of hope" out of despair did not translate onto the national level.[49] So the observations about Putin as an "empty vessel" could be paralleled by similar comparisons to the Russian society experiencing a certain type of a collective *void* and finding itself in a state of *lacking*.[50]

It is this void that Vladimir Putin attempted to fill with the help of modern political communication and public relations tools, relying on the selected visions and constructions of the past—whether Soviet or even pre-Soviet, or the more recent past linked to the painful decade of the 1990s. In Chapter 5 I explore in detail how Russia's president connected with the majority of the Russian people, building on carefully chosen moments of Russian glory and, even more importantly, articulating the "collective trauma" based on a widely shared discursive frame that resonated in Russian society. Using the power of state-controlled media, he advanced a "national story" that resonated and crafted a new, more hopeful and assertive, Russian sense of "we-ness" that linked Russian citizens across religious and ethnic boundaries and provided them with much-needed positive associations of their national belonging.

The Kremlin's efforts at advancing a new sense of national belonging were arguably successful and peaked right after 2014, when Putin himself became the embodiment of Russia's national identity. Putin's luck and perceived achievements on the economic front and his assertive foreign policy also advanced the sense of belonging to a community that is getting stronger and more consolidated. But bringing Crimea back into the fold of Russia signified this new, more positively conceived sense of "we-ness" with a particular intensity. A documentary with a revealing title, *Crimea: The Way Home* (*Krym. Put' na Rodinu*), represents this event as the epitome of Russia's resurgence, of Russia finding itself, of Russia returning to its historical, millenarian destiny. "Vladimir Putin brought us home," declared the Russians living in Crimea. "Vladimir Putin brought all Russians home," celebrated the Kremlin. This documentary was broadcast on March 15, 2015, a year after the Crimea annexation. In the capital city of Moscow, over three million viewers watched the film on Russian TV's *Rossiya* channel. On YouTube the documentary has exceeded 12 million views.

Putin did not promote an ethnicized vision of the Russian nation, viewed in exclusively Russian ethnic terms. He outlined his views on this issue in a January 2012 article, "Russia: The Ethnicity Issue," published as one of his programmatic pieces ahead of the March 2012 presidential election. This important element allows us to distinguish the current Russian political system from fascism.[51] Following Soviet political traditions, he recognized the multiethnic structure of the Russian state and the need to embrace all ethnicities and state-recognized religions in Russia. The Soviet tradition also has an important legacy of "russo-centric statism," advanced by Joseph Stalin from around the 1930s. Historians captured this ideological orientation, which replaced the early Bolshevik internationalist slogans, using the term "National Bolshevism."[52] This new ideology built the foundations of Soviet patriotism by relying on Russia-centered history, culture, and the Russian pantheon of heroes. The Soviet government was careful not to build separate political institutions to represent the Russian ethnos, similar to the representation of other national minorities in the Soviet Union; rather, it used the symbolic capital associated with the Russian people to promote the Soviet state.[53] This legacy became important in Putin's Russia, especially in the context when the language of Russian nationalism, spoken from various corners of Russian society, came to dominate the political agenda.[54] Radical nationalist opposition became especially influential in the aftermath of the 2008 financial crisis. The 2010 riots on Manezh Square were just one of the reflections of growing anti-immigrant sentiments in Russia. The makeup of the 2011–2012 protests in Russia's biggest cities was also quite politically diverse and included many protesters with illiberal and undemocratic views. Paul Chaisty and Stephen Whitefield, who interviewed protesters, found that, contrary to widespread Western assumptions, many protesters were advocating authoritarian solutions to Russia's problems, and many held ethno-nationalist views.[55]

The political challenge associated with Russian nationalism was, undoubtedly, formative for Putin's third term in the presidency. Besides its new conservative orientation, the Kremlin's national identity discourse included an accentuation of the "state-bearing" role and the foundational character of the Russian ethnic group and the Orthodox religion for the Russian state. But as in Soviet times, this discourse did not mean the rise of ethnonationalism in Russia.[56]

Putin Is "Making Us Matter"

During the Cold War the two superpowers, the United States and the Soviet Union, leading the two main global camps, viewed each other as their main nemesis. They also looked at each other as their main "external other," using negative images of the opponent to help them construct their own, positively configured identities, set in opposition to the "other."[57] After the Soviet collapse, Russia was reduced not only in its territory, but also in its international ambitions and its influence abroad. Meanwhile, the United States turned from Russia's negative "external other" into a positive "role model," as the new Russia stepped on the path of reforming its economic and political institutions, trying to become *like* the United States. Even if these radical changes were, to an extent, self-driven, they produced a radical blow to Russian society's collective self-esteem.[58] That the rest of the world perceived Russia as the losing side in the Cold War, rather than the country that willingly abandoned its system in favor of the alternative, did not help the country and its people.

Evgeny Primakov's reaction to the bombing of Belgrade in 1999 signaled the beginning of the shift in Russia's self-positioning against such geopolitical "cornering."[59] From that moment on, Russia was on the path of reasserting itself on a global scale. When Putin came to power, he started with the proactive extension of support for George Bush's war in Afghanistan, trying to frame Russia's internal war in Chechnya and the US war on terrorism as part of the common struggle that Russia and the United States were involved in. While this gesture was widely interpreted as a legitimation mechanism for Russia's own counterterrorism operation in the Caucasus, its larger, "collective identity-based" ambition went unnoticed. Early on in his presidential tenure, Putin reached out to the United

States, aiming to establish a close relationship with the US president and signaling, already then, Russia's desire for status, and Russia's vision of the country's key
"foreign partners," as opposed to "role models."

By the end of Putin's first term in 2004, this policy of the Kremlin's "extended
hand" to the United States had effectively expired. A series of electoral revolutions
in Russia's "near abroad" (the so-called color revolutions) turned into a political
threat for the Kremlin and elicited changes in its domestic and foreign tactics.
The Kremlin's September 2004 decision to abolish gubernatorial elections signaled the beginning of a new political era in the domestic realm. Putin's 2007
Munich speech, in which he accused the United States of dominating world politics and playing the role of the world police, signaled Russia's new stance in the
foreign arena.[60] Some observers compared Putin's Munich speech to the famous
1946 Fulton speech, in which Winston Churchill pronounced, "From Stettin
in the Baltic to Trieste in the Adriatic, an iron curtain has descended across the
Continent." Just as the Fulton speech had signaled the beginning of the Cold
War, Putin's Munich speech signaled the beginning of new, more adversarial
relationships between Russia and the West.[61] Russia's 2008 "five-day war" with
Georgia was an important transition point in Russia's relations with the West
and even the "reset" policy launched by President Obama in 2009 failed to bring
US-Russian relations to a better ground. Russia's international stance of opposing
the United States and asserting Russia's views and interests later manifested itself
in the 2014 annexation of Crimea, and Russia's military involvement in Syria, in
support of Bashar Assad's political regime. A systematic policy of modernizing
the Russian military forces—enabled by the economic expansion during 2000–
2007—paralleled Russia's new foreign policy.

Putin's assertive foreign policy and especially the annexation of Crimea worked
to conjure a sense of pride among Russian citizens, instilling in the Russian community a sense that "we matter," and positioning Putin as the one who "makes
us matter." As I illustrated at the beginning of this chapter, public opinion polls
and focus-group interviews highlight that foreign policy is viewed by many
Russians as Putin's strongest suit. With the state-controlled media accentuating
issues linked to Russia's international status, the foreign policy aspect of Putin's
leadership takes on a particular significance. Russian TV showers the public with
the news and entertainment, frequently merged into one, through political talk
shows that focus on foreign policy debates. The political importance of such a
tightly controlled media environment has grown in the last few years, and later in
the book I illustrate the various techniques employed by the media industry and
professionals to shape public opinion in relation to foreign policy and Russia's
role in the international arena.

That Russia is surrounded by enemies is among the key messages promoted by the Kremlin-controlled media in the past decade or so. This was not a newly invented idea. Vyacheslav Morozov in his *Russia and the Others* (2009) argued that the strategy of promoting populist antagonism between Russia and the West first resurfaced during NATO's 1999 Kosovo campaign.[62] This strategy was later replaced by Putin's attempt to build a global anti-terrorist coalition, but that did not last. The role of the narrative "Russia against the West" has acquired truly dramatic proportions after the Crimea annexation in 2014. In this specific context of Russia annexing the Crimean peninsula and the Western countries opposing Russia's actions, the Kremlin-promoted image of Vladimir Putin as a leader who secured and strengthened Russia has been consummated.

I tested this thesis about the effects of "securing" collective identity (albeit indirectly) through a survey experiment conducted in Russia in November 2017, just a few months before the March 2018 presidential elections in Russia. It also happened to be a moment of Russia finding itself in the midst of an international doping scandal, awaiting the decision of the International Olympic Committee vis-à-vis the participation of the Russian athletes accused of state-sponsored doping in the Winter Olympics in PyeongChang, South Korea.[63] The experiment was embedded in a nationally representative survey of public opinion conducted by the Levada Center. The survey involved approximately 1,600 respondents across Russia, stratified according to region, type of settlement, sex, age, and educational level. All interviews were conducted face-to-face in late November 2017. The experiment aimed at, first, activating the respondents' sense of collective (national) identity and, second, at prompting the insecurity of that identity by suggesting that it compares unfavorably to various out-groups (including such significant, from the identity perspective, out-groups as Ukraine).

The experiment involved randomly assigning respondents to the treatment group that responded to the questionnaire with two additional questions (meant to activate national identity and prompt, specifically, insecure identity), while the control group had a questionnaire without these additional questions. The additional questions went as follows:

In May 2017 Ukraine was allowed visa-free travel to the European Union. What is your opinion about this issue?

The second additional question was as follows:

On December 5–7, 2017, the International Olympics Committee will be deciding on Russian athletes' participation in the Olympic games in

PyeongChang (South Korea). Do you think our athletes will be allowed
to compete at the 2018 Olympic games?

The respondents were offered different answers to these questions that sought to
further articulate the underlying attitudes and dispositions the public might have
had in reaction to such questions.

The questions that followed these were administered to all respondents as
part of the survey. They included a question about approval for Vladimir Putin,
about the respondents' intention to vote in the upcoming 2018 presidential elections, and about the choices the respondents would make ("who would you
vote for in these elections?"). The list of presidential candidates included eight
people (Gordon, Zhirinovski, Ziuganov, Mironov, Titov, Sobchak, Putin, and
Yavlinskii), as well as the options of spoiling the ballot/don't know/won't participate (these were not offered to the respondents but were registered, when
selected autonomously).[64]

The main aim of this experiment was to measure the effects of prompting
insecure collective identity on political attitudes in relation to Putin's approval,
and voting preferences in the upcoming presidential elections. The central finding was concerned with the respondents' shifting political preferences, expressed
through their responses on "who would you vote for" in the upcoming elections.[65]
Although Putin's approval ratings were not affected by the "treatment," the two
additional questions moved the respondents in a more nationalistic direction.
Those who had to answer the questions highlighting the salience of national
identity and showing Russia in an unfavorable light in terms of international recognition tended to privilege political candidates that expressed more nationalist
positions—Vladimir Zhirinovsky and Gennady Zyuganov.

These findings corroborate expectations derived from social identity theory
and reveal the psychological mechanisms at work in constructing the Putin phenomenon. Social identity theorists have long argued that insecure collective identity tends to intensify inter-group bias and discrimination along with in-group
glorification (i.e., result in more nationalist orientations).[66] The experiment
revealed precisely such effects. Logically, securing collective identity could be
expected to produce the opposite trends. The post-Crimea public opinion trends
in Russia and particularly the growing pride in Russia as a multinational state also
confirm the change in dispositions resulting from perceived "securing" of collective identity.[67] The annexation of Crimea represented an event that *confirmed*
tangibly to many Russians what the Kremlin had been propagating for years.
Evident already from the famous 2007 Munich speech, the Kremlin sought to
construct Putin's legitimacy by increasing the salience of collective identity. This
was accomplished through promoting the double frame of Russia as a "besieged

fortress" suffering from bad intentions of the West, on one hand; and, on the other hand, Putin as a leader who can stand up to and even outplay the West through his assertive foreign policy that makes Russia matter on the global scale, thereby securing and strengthening Russia's national identity.

The experiment also revealed that Putin's authority and leadership are widely recognized because his approval ratings do not change with the manipulation of collective identity. Expectedly, support for Putin in Russia is not uniform across Russia's society. The findings from this experiment have confirmed the earlier findings that gender and age, for instance, do matter in shaping Putin's support.[68] On the voting preferences question, specifically, male and younger respondents tended to select non-Putin candidates more.[69] Putin's approval question also reveals that Russian women tend to approve Putin more than men.[70] Nonetheless, that Putin's approval levels do not change with the manipulation of collective identity (while people's voting preferences shift) reveals, arguably, the political significance of the widespread sense that there are no real political alternatives to Putin. When the question focuses on Putin's approval (and does not invoke anyone else), Russians who approve of him view him as a national symbol, and their symbolic appreciation (already earned by Putin) does not shift with the momentary suggestion about Russia's insecure identity. However, when the question does not center solely on Putin but reveals alternatives in voting choices, respondents see Putin as a political figure (even if the first among others). Insecure collective identity pushes Russian citizens toward more nationalist politicians, reflecting their sensitivity and a high degree of manipulability when collective identity is highlighted. Part of this book is concerned with digging out the contextual reasons for making collective identity such a potent force. Another part focuses on how these mechanisms are being turned on by the state-controlled media in Russia.

Vitaly Mansky captured Vladimir Putin on video on the night of his first presidential victory on March 26, 2000, at his campaign headquarters, thanking his team just after the preliminary electoral results were announced:

> everything was so accurately calculated and psychologically grounded that it really provided the results—on the streets and on the screens. Everything was built step by step and brought the results we are seeing now. I would like to thank you all and congratulate. It is your success.[71]

These words became prophetic and revealing. Putin's later success as a leader of Russia was calculated and psychologically grounded to bring the results the Kremlin desired—to maintain political power in the same hands.

PART TWO

Of History and Identity

Recent and Very Recent

Making sense of the Russian society's reaction to the Crimean annexation and the resulting rise of Putin's influence and popularity demands an excursus into the late Soviet and the early post-Soviet history of Russia.

In the following two chapters I first highlight two foundational pillars of Soviet collective identity that incorporated the taken-for-granted meanings associated with belonging to the Soviet community. Shifting from late Soviet period to the 1990s' Russia, I then discuss the identity implications of the post-communist transformation the country undertook in the 1990s.

3

Shared Mental Models of the Late Soviet Period

*Then the grinning mirror trembled with such violence that it
slipped from their hands and fell to the earth, where it shattered into hundreds of millions of billions of bits, or perhaps
even more. And now it caused more trouble than it did before
it was broken, because some of the fragments were smaller
than a grain of sand and these went flying throughout the
wide world. Once they got in people's eyes they would stay
there. These bits of glass distorted everything the people saw,
and made them see only the bad side of things, for every little
bit of glass kept the same power that the whole mirror had
possessed.*

—*THE SNOW QUEEN*, Hans Christian Anderson

IT IS NOW a truism to suggest that the Soviet collapse represented the central watershed event in the lives of the people populating the region known as the Eastern bloc, or the Second World. The global political and economic system transformed entirely as a result of the 1989 Eastern European revolutions and the 1991 Soviet collapse. And yet as time flows by and new global challenges arise, it is all too easy to lose the appreciation of the fact that we live in the aftermath of this massive historical rupture that might have contained (at least as a potential-ity) the serious ripple effects transmitted across space and time into the future. The mostly peaceful dissolution of the Soviet Union might have misled us in the direction of forgetting that history repeats itself: the first time as tragedy, and the second as farce.[1] What if we consider Putin's Russia to be one of the most power-ful ripples of the Soviet collapse? Did we underestimate the potential of these ripples? What are the main turbines generating this giant wave from the past that condition Russia's present and orient its future toward its historical past? Who is to blame? (*Kto vinovat?*) And what is to be done? (*Chto delat'?*)

The Red Mirror. Gulnaz Sharafutdinova, Oxford University Press (2020). © Oxford University Press.
DOI: 10.1093/oso/9780197502938.001.0001.

I do not aspire to answer these timeless Russian questions. My more modest intention is to develop a view that "connects the dots" of political leadership and the cognitive and affective structures shared in Russian society and situated in recent history so that the reader gets the picture of what "post-Crimea" Russia is about and how it got to the historical spot it was between 2014 and 2018, with the aftereffects likely to last longer. There are many disagreements about how long this moment will last and how strong and stable Putin's popular support is.[2] But even with the latest political developments in Russia that show the fragility of Russia's political system, especially during election times, Putin's role as a symbol of national unity and strength and Putin-style collective identity politics in Russia are bound to continue to resonate because they are inextricably associated with the Soviet collapse and the trauma of the 1990s. Such "major events" with profound resonance become inscribed in collective self-understanding and produce cognitive, emotional, and behavioral consequences, according to Ohad David and Daniel Bar-Tal, social psychologists at Tel-Aviv University, who developed a sociopsychological conception of collective identity.[3] The political potential associated with such resonance is, arguably, a major hindrance to any radical institutional and political change in Russia in the short- to medium-term horizon.[4]

Many observers who would agree with this pessimistic view of the probability of radical change in Russia may do so for reasons different from those explicated here. Let's look at the dominant views that have been recently advanced to "make sense of Putin's Russia." The evolution of theories and approaches to Russian politics is an intriguing subject by itself, and the study of the sociology of knowledge about Russia can in itself serve as the subject of many books and research projects. Such books will have to inquire into the reasons underlying the growing attention to the problem of a person in Russia (*problema cheloveka*) or, in other words, the increasingly widespread doubts about the quality of the "human material" making up Russian society. I mentioned earlier David Satter's concerns about Russians' inability to pass moral judgments and Masha Gessen's use of Levada's conception of *homo sovieticus*. The occasional commentary in the West about the alleged moral impotence of post-Soviet Russians might be simple to interpret. The returning Cold War era–related dispositions and occidental Orientalism toward a country long engaged in a catch-up development with the West at the moment of geopolitical polarization and growing tensions is not very surprising (if lamentable). Why the Russian intellectuals and, at times, ordinary folks themselves turn to self-deprecating arguments about Russia's substandard human material is more intriguing. I confronted this attitude during my focus-group interviews in Russia when a few of the respondents, confronted with the question of what they would change in their country, had an immediate reaction: "the people." The same attitude is widespread among the Russian intelligentsia as well. Some, like Liudmila Ulitskaya, turn to genetics and blame the waves of emigration, purges, and brain drain that might have affected the Russian genetic pool.[5] Others, like Masha Gessen and Vladimir Sorokin, blame the Soviet past and the specific political, social, and institutional conditions that gave rise to *homo sovieticus* and that, unpurged, have come back reflected in the return of totalitarian consciousness, a tendency to doublethink, self-lie, etc.[6] The more historically conscious intellectuals look even further back into history and highlight the experience of serfdom or *obshchiny* (peasants' communes) as an important determinant of Russia's contemporary trajectory.[7]

The term *homo sovieticus* underlies perhaps the most important variation of these cultural arguments that have sprung up with such vigor of late. The Russian sociologists working for the Levada Center developed the most important variety of such arguments. During the late Soviet period, relying on massive large-N surveys, they developed the notion of a "simple Soviet man," expecting the key features of the Soviet personality and mental habits to fade away into history as the new, post-communist institutions and the conditions of freedom would release the post-Soviet person from her/his Soviet conditioning. Two decades after the Soviet collapse, the same sociologists declared that, while epiphenomenal Soviet institutions were long gone, a "simple Soviet person" has returned. The continuing sociological surveys of the "post-Soviet man" have highlighted the continuing relevance and durability of various aspects of the presumed Soviet mentality and predispositions, more than two decades after the collapse of the Soviet Union. *Homo sovieticus*, sociologists argue, "had mutated and reproduced, acquiring along the way, new characteristics such as cynicism and aggression."[8]

I have examined the analytical foundations of the concept of the Soviet man in "Was There a 'Simple Soviet' Person? Debating Politics and Sociology of *Homo Sovieticus*."[9] This concept is based on two indisputably outdated theories from the 1950s. On the one hand, it draws on Talcott Parsons' functionalist systems theory that reduces human beings to be the "output" of the social system.[10] On the other hand, it builds on the totalitarian model developed in the 1950s, during the Cold War, to capture the similarities between Nazi Germany and Stalinist Russia. Furthermore, the concept of culturally relative personality traits that was fashionable in psychology in the 1950s has undergone a major reconsideration.[11] Theorizing in personality psychology has evolved in the direction of appreciating the context responsible for varying degrees of expression and the salience of particular personality traits and in viewing the self as reflexive and agentive.[12] These analytical developments could and should be integrated into our understanding of post-Soviet Russia and the post-Soviet person, rather than returning to concepts that reflect a strong ideological leaning and that rely on outmoded theory.

The systematic sociological work that was done by Yuri Levada and his colleagues does not need to be discarded. The empirical results of massive surveys conducted by the Levada Center can be put to a good use if we appropriate these results relying on concepts different from the personality traits and the "simple Soviet man" framework. Specifically, I argue here that we need to switch our attention from "personality traits"—understood as endurable features of an individual that are hard to change—toward "identities"—understood as collectively shared notions associated with group belonging. Levada's empirical studies can be used to understand the central pillars on which the Soviet collective identity rested.

Operating with the concept of "identity" (specifically using the concept of "collective identity" rather than "personality traits") offers several important advantages. First of all, it enables us to capture and make sense of the cognitive and affective legacy of the Soviet Union in contemporary Russia in a more nuanced way than does the concept of personality traits. The Soviet government relied on a variety of social, cultural, and political institutions to instill a sense of belonging to the Soviet nation. The Soviet collective identity incorporated specific ideas and beliefs about what it meant to be Soviet, and the Levada surveys allow for extracting some of the foundational aspects of the Soviet collective identity. Identity—understood to be socially and politically constructed, flexible, and context-dependent—is a more nuanced heuristic tool than personality traits, which are understood to be enduring, fixed, and unchanging. The influence of identity is a matter of social context and, in Russia's case, political leadership and consensus-building. The influence of personality traits is often understood in more mechanical, automatic terms. Thinking in terms of identities brings attention to the importance of social and political construction and alerts us to the important role played by the media in Russia. Personality traits, at least in the form conceptualized by Yuri Levada and his associates, are expected to be reproduced due to their congruency with the specific institutional and political environment. As the system moved in an authoritarian direction, the traits of the Soviet man had to return, according to this thinking.[13] A different version of this argument that became especially popular in the post-Crimea period views this relationship in an opposite way: the natural predilections of the Soviet man (i.e., his duplicity, respect for hierarchies, etc.) prepare the ground for growing authoritarianism and the "flight from freedom." Otherwise, how would one explain the phenomenon of Putin's sky-high popularity?

Both of these arguments view Russia's current condition as predetermined by the circumstances of the country's history and its people. They hardly leave space for political construction, agency, leadership, and other contingencies. But how can an observer ignore the outsized role played by the media in contemporary

Russia and deny the ongoing social and political "construction" process? Thinking in terms of identities rather than personality traits and, specifically, in terms of the "Soviet identity" rather than a "Soviet person" is more helpful for understanding contemporary Russian developments because it allows us to account for the ongoing social and political construction. Not only that, the concept of collective identity allows us to capture the collectively shared ideas and beliefs that have *emotional* significance and resonance in the society. It brings attention to the importance of national belonging for an individual and will be helpful in understanding the scale of loss experienced by Soviet citizens at the moment of the Soviet collapse. A more accurate understanding of the importance of collective identity to the individual psyche will also alert readers to the psychological aftermath of shattered identities and the resultant emotional vulnerabilities that could be and were exploited in Russia's case by the country's political leaders.

The Soviet Experiment with Human Nature, or Forging a Soviet Citizen?

The Soviet social experiment had a great ambition—to change human nature and create a new Soviet man. This new species—an idealized Soviet person—was supposed to love work and have a high sense of public duty, love the motherland and sacrifice her individual desires for the benefit of the collective, be fearless and intolerant toward the enemies of communism, be loyal to the state and devoted to the cause of building communism.

The 1937 song lyrics written by Vasily Lebedev-Kumach ("And Stalin Is Watching with a Smile—A Soviet Simple Person") captured that ethos of a new Soviet man and the glory of the new Soviet state:

> *The songs spread ever wider*
> *And the glory is everywhere*
> *About our only in the world*
> *Great Soviet country*
> *He proudly takes a polar walk*
> *He changes the rivers' flow*
> *He also moves the mountains*
> *The Soviet simple person.*[14]

The new Soviet man was supposed to be morally pure, truthful, and humble. These main characteristics and expectations from the new Soviet man were outlined in the Moral Code of the Builder of Communism adopted, as part of the party program, by the Communist Party in 1961. And although the code formally applied only to the political vanguard of "builders of communism"—Communist party and Komsomol members—these expectations established an ideal for the Soviet society. Ironically, the late Soviet period when this code was adopted was the time when the ideological potency of Marxism-Leninism in the Soviet system was waning. The political system did not seek ideological conversion of the type that characterized the 1930s; rather, it required an adherence to rituals, arguably, to shape the social knowledge about the (im)possibility of political change in the country. Additionally, the Communist Party leadership, especially under Leonid Brezhnev, started to recognize the importance of consumption, leisure, and other values usually associated in the Soviet Union with bourgeois societies.[15] George Breslauer, a well-known Sovietologist from the University of California at Berkeley, has dubbed this system a "welfare-system authoritarianism," emphasizing the importance of the exchange between the state and society (material satisfaction for political conformism) at the heart of the Brezhnev-era social contract.[16]

The project of building a new man evolved over the course of Soviet history. It started with the heavy, ideological, "proletarian internationalism"–infused message in the first decade and a half after the 1917 revolution, when the proletarian revolution was expected to spread and the states, as a political format for community organization, were expected to eventually die out. From the mid-1930s, for pragmatic political reasons of building the new state, this project of building a new Soviet man acquired a national tinge. David Brandenberger, a historian at the University of Virginia, explored the emergence of National Bolshevism—"a state-oriented patriotic ideology reminiscent of tsarist 'great power' (velikoderzhavnye) and russocentric traditions."[17] He mapped the formation of Russian national identity among the Russian-speaking population during the 1930s–1950s and introduced a crucial distinction between russocentrism and nationalism, with the former referring to "ethnic pride deriving from a clear sense of national identity" and the latter referring to predominantly political aspirations of sovereignty and self-rule.[18] Russocentrism, expressed through an intense reliance on iconography, myths, and imagery from the Russian national past associated with tsarist Russia, was a radical departure or an ideological about-face, in Brandenberger's terminology, from the utopian idealism of the first 15 years of Bolshevik rule that focused on promoting social identities based on class consciousness and proletarian internationalism.[19] He argued persuasively that this was a new party strategy, motivated by the pragmatic challenges of promoting mass mobilization and a popular sense of patriotism. In the end, the Soviet citizen was more Russian than Soviet.[20]

The state and political entrepreneurs played a central role in this process. A variety of social, cultural, and political institutions were put in place to realize the ambition of shaping Soviet citizens—young and old—into a new, Soviet, mold. The Soviet kindergartens and schools supported by the Soviet pedagogy[21] taught schoolchildren about the importance of a collective, instilling the values of group-oriented behavior, love for motherland, and respect for authority. The children and adolescent books espoused similar values, advancing models of heroism based on self-sacrifice and hard work.[22] The Soviet army continued education for young males, teaching obedience and loyalty to motherland.[23] The workplace reinforced the importance of group-based life in the Soviet Union by promoting the labor collectives, as well as collective-based workplace in all other spheres (white-collar, office workers, etc.), as a key social structure in the lives of Soviet adults.[24] The Soviet science, literature, cinema, art, and other forms of tightly censored mass media worked to promote the norms and values underpinning the Soviet regime.[25]

The Soviet corrective and punitive institutions targeted those who, for some reason, might have escaped the embrace of and internalization of Soviet norms and values and/or openly rejected them. Psychiatric hospitals, for example, turned into a corrective institution for Soviet dissidents.[26] Prisons and the system of labor camps and settlements were another venue for "correcting" the minds of those who did not buy into what was preached by the regime and who revealed their critical stance through activities condemned by the authorities. There was simply no social space allowed for nonconformists, even if highly talented, such as Joseph Brodsky, a Nobel Prize–winning poet, persecuted and forced to leave the country in 1972.

The Soviet project of creating a new man—a Soviet man—was, of course, a classic utopia, the communist "dream-factory."[27] The Soviet system was able to create specific *utopian enclaves*, such as the peasant communes of the 1920s, pedagogical communes organized by Anton Makarenko, and even the communes organized in the 1950s that were trying to create heroic missions for the youth of that era to make them feel worthy of their heroic parents and grandparents who had to endure war, defending their motherland.[28] But, by and large, Soviet society was not utopian, and the "dream-factory," discussed earlier, was organized as a conveyor belt that the Soviet citizens stepped on as children and never really had a chance to leave. Only a few, in the bigger cities of the late Soviet Union, could escape into "de-territorialized milieus" creating an informal social and cultural environment that was not officially approved but tolerated to an extent.[29]

The actual "Soviet civilization" resulting from the translation of utopia into the real world was a unique world with "its own heroes—real and imagined—and hero-makers, its own morals and values, its own design and fashion, science and technology, workplace and leisure, food and drink, music and cinema, humor, laughter, and other cultural items that comprise human-made reality. This unique Soviet civilization, a subject of intense research by historians and anthropologists today, in some of its achievements, was comparable to what we know as Western modernity.[30] The Soviet Union has trailed on its own socialist path to the modern world, dragging several Eastern European nations along. This "Soviet world" is frequently idealized and looked back upon with a sense of deep longing and nostalgia in current-day Russia.[31] The social and individual costs of this civilization are frequently a subject remaining in the shadow, left to the peripheral vision of the collective memory in contemporary Russia.

The majority of people in Russia today realize that the return of the Soviet Union is out of the realm of the possible. But what is not widely recognized is that the cognitive structures constructed during the Soviet era, the beliefs and ideas instilled in the Soviet population—and specifically those related to collective identity—play an important role in consolidating political support for Vladimir Putin's leadership, policies, and the political system built under his rule.

Identity as a Set of Cognitive Structures about the Collective Self

Identity is understood and conceptualized differently in various disciplines.[32] Historians study how identities are performed and practiced as individuals act out certain aspects of their collective belonging, verbally and otherwise. Sociologists and anthropologists focus on how different collective identities are constructed and negotiated. Political scientists focus on how collective identities are forged, mobilized, or contested in pursuit of specific political aims. In short, identities could be understood on behavioral, emotional, and cognitive levels. Given my interest in Soviet cognitive and affective structures and their role in contemporary Russia, I look at identities through a socio-psychological lens and view them as a set of cognitive structures—established ideas, shared mental models, or schemas—that structure collective self-understanding, expressed through individuals who see themselves as part of that group. These ideas also include the understanding of the world in terms of who the "Other" is. Just like individual identity, collective identities are always relational and hierarchical.[33]

Hazel Markus, a social psychologist and a pioneer in the field of cultural psychology at Stanford University, first incorporated cognitive structures into the conceptualization of the self, suggesting that self-schemata are "cognitive generalizations about the self, derived from past experience, that organize and guide the processing of self-related information contained in the individual's social experiences."[34] Simply put, these are the ideas we believe to be true about ourselves. One can perceive oneself to be hardworking and punctual, or lazy and easygoing; one can see oneself as an athletic, outdoor-type of person or, to the contrary, as someone who likes sitting at home and reading. These ideas are important because they help us build *mental models* about ourselves that guide our personal understanding of our past behavior. These models also facilitate information-processing so that the congruent information is quickly accepted and the information that does not fit these models is rejected.

Moving from the individual self to the collective, cognitive anthropologists refer to the concept of *cultural models* and *cultural schemas*, when exploring cognitive structures that reside outside the individual mind and that reflect a socially constructed understanding of the world that could be captured by exploring patterns of social exchanges and interactions. Cultural models are intermediary, meaning they are construction structures located between universal and smaller, more refined meanings found in communities.[35] Since national identity is one type of collective identity, we could apply the concept of self-schemata or shared mental or cultural (when culture is approached cognitively) models to understand the cognitive aspect of the Soviet identity. In other words, we could analyze national identity by exploring the shared ideas and predispositions in relation to how community members see themselves as a collective body, how they understand what their community is about and what it means to be a part of it. Studying the content of these self-schemata or mental models that are frequently taken for granted would provide us with an understanding of the broad contours or the basis of Soviet identity. Understanding these foundations and the emotional consequences of the attachment to and psychological significance of these ideas is one of the analytical levers for making sense of contemporary Russian society.

The emotional aspect of collective identities needs a special emphasis. In their seminal book, *Social Construction of Reality* (1966), Peter Berger and Thomas Luckmann have highlighted the affective basis of primary socialization resulting in the internalization of social reality. Identifications that occur in childhood are most enduring, they argue, because they are not simply a result of cognitive learning but are emotionally charged phenomena. Claudia Strauss and Naomi Quinn, who advanced a cognitive approach to the construction of cultural meaning, have also emphasized the role of emotional arousal in making these shared schemas durable.[36] Soviet collective identity inculcated from childhood also involved an emotionally laden set of meanings that motivated individual and collective behavior, and drew its force not from abstract rationality and deliberation, but from the shared conceptions of good and bad, from moral orientations and beliefs instilled in Soviet citizens throughout their lives, from rites and rituals that the Soviet government invented to construct Soviet identity.[37]

Therefore I next turn to these shared mental models as they relate to the sense of belonging forged by the Soviet state. After all, as William Faulkner famously noted, "The past is never dead. In fact it is not even past."[38]

Soviet Experience as a Cognitive and Affective Legacy: Shared Mental Models of the Self and the Other

Ronald Suny, a prominent historian of nationalism at the University of Michigan, suggested that "we have tended to underestimate the connective elements, political, cultural and affective, that made the USSR a rather cohesive state until its very last years."[39] Despite its multinational structure, the Soviet state was, for the most part, highly successful in instilling the shared awareness and recognition that Soviet citizens—whether living in the capital city of Moscow or in a peripheral town of Nazarovo—collectively share the same supranational identity of being Soviet, in addition to identifying and valuing their particular ethnicities and cultures. The strength and emotional valence of this identification varied. Soviet identity was not internalized by the non-Russian communities in the Baltic Republics of Latvia, Estonia, and Lithuania, as well as in Western Ukraine and Bessarabia—the territories annexed by the Soviet Union in 1940. These communities maintained their national sense, in opposition to the Soviet identity, as reflected in a history of resistance to Soviet rule.[40] But with these important exceptions, Soviet institutions succeeded in instilling a mostly positive affective appreciation for being a Soviet citizen. The exploration of this social-psychological heritage—the mental and affective structures developed as a result of Soviet citizens adapting to and becoming socialized into dominant ideas and institutions—is at the core of the contemporary debate about the Soviet man—*homo sovieticus*. The outstanding analytical challenge is to give credit where it is due and bring together all the necessary and sufficient conditions leading to the present political outcomes.

The Russian people themselves have recognized the impact of the Soviet experience on the post-Soviet population. In 2000, between 63% and 75% of respondents thought that the 70 years of Soviet rule had changed people.[41] How do these changes affect political and social processes in contemporary Russia? What are the conditions for and mechanisms of "reloading" the old mental "software"? Exploring these questions provides an invaluable lesson in societal experience with cognitive path-dependence and the hindered collective learning process.

In the remainder of this chapter, I focus on two cognitive structures that have been promoted by the Soviet government's intentional efforts to instill specific beliefs and ideas in the Soviet citizens. Some of these ideas might be even seen as having a longer legacy, with origins further back in Russian history. I do not claim to have discovered these ideas. A vast body of literature has explored these and other aspects of Soviet identity and political culture.[42] As explained earlier, I refer to these ideas as shared mental models and schemata. I have selected them because of their central role in structuring the Soviet identity that oriented Soviet citizens and enabled them to "locate" themselves in the world in terms of who they were, who the "other" was, and how they compared to this "other."

I show later in the book that these shared mental models carry significance for the emotional dimension of politics in the early 2000s. They have imposed a specific psychological burden on post-Soviet society, creating the emotional "soft spots" in the *body social* and preparing it for political control and manipulation later on. Their relevance during the 1990s was not evident. But the political leadership during the first decade of the 2000s relied on the preexisting identity template and used the emotionally charged images close to the hearts and minds of the average Russian, retrieved from the past to construct political legitimacy and support for new policies and institutions that took Russia away from open, pluralist political space and moved in the direction of authoritarianism.

Soviet Exceptionalism

In the Soviet system of coordinates—installed by the help of a well-designed system of Soviet education, science, and propaganda—the 1917 Bolshevik Revolution opened a new historical era. The Soviet state, at the vanguard of history, was on a special path of building socialism and, eventually, communism. This path of building a socialist system was presented to the Soviet public as being morally and institutionally superior to that of a capitalist system, which was criticized for perpetuating inequality, exploitation, and rugged individualism. Stephen Kotkin argued in his seminal book *Magnetic Mountain: Stalinism as a Civilization* (1997) that "[i]nside Stalin's USSR, the appeal of socialism had several layers, including the prospect of a quick leap, not simply into modernity, but a superior form of modernity, the corresponding attainment of high international status, a broad conception of social welfare, and a sense of social justice that was built into property relations. [. . .] It stood for a new world power, founded on laudatory ideals, and backed by tangible programs and institutions: full employment, subsidized prices, paid vacations for workers, child care, health care, retirement pensions, education, and the advancement of oneself and one's children."[43]

Even if the late Soviet public did not believe in communism anymore and was skeptical about the party's ideological rhetoric, the sense of *exceptionalism*—of living in a country that was in many ways unique and superior to the rest of the world—was deeply engrained in the psyche of Soviet individuals. The sociological study conducted by Yuri Levada and his team in the late 1980s supports this claim empirically.

The Levada project sought to highlight some commonly shared thinking patterns, dispositions, attitudes, and values of Soviet people to create a matrix of the "simple Soviet man." It was based on a massive representative survey of Soviet citizens across the USSR, with the sample of 2,700 respondents, and its findings were summarized in a book, *Sovetskii prostoi chelovek* (*A Simple Soviet Man*, 1993) that elaborated the key personality traits that could be viewed as specific to the Soviet system. The survey questions used for this project were wide-ranging. They explored, among other things, people's salient identities and identifications, captured by such questions as "Who do you feel/view yourself proudly to be?" (кем вы себя осознаете с гордостью?) They looked into people's attitudes toward the state and their sense of obligation to and expectations from the state. They analyzed people's moral predispositions, using such questions as: "Should a person be responsible for . . . ?" They tried to reconstruct popular images of the nation, people's views of important historical events and prominent historical personalities, the balance of preferences on risk and stability, levels of tolerance, views of social stratification, professional and educational aspirations, a sense of social and political efficacy, views about the Soviet collapse, and many other things. To make sense of these results, sociologists in the Levada group separated their findings along three axes: identifications (Who are we?), orientations (Where are we going?), and adaptability (How far can we adapt?).

The sense of exceptionalism and Soviet superiority was associated with the sphere of Soviet identity. Yuri Levada argued that it was supported by different narrative constructions promoted by the Soviet institutions. The postwar geopolitical discourse pitched the USSR against the United States and the capitalist West, dividing the world into two opposite camps—"ours" and "theirs." The historical narrative adopted in all school textbooks represented 1917 as the dawn of a new era, with the rest of world history reinterpreted through the Marxist framework. The normative and ethical claims postulated the existence of a communist morale, while religion was denigrated as an opiate for the masses. Even the sphere of science and knowledge production in the Soviet Union was colored by its exceptionalism. The Soviet establishment prescribed Marxist historical and dialectical materialism to be the basis for all spheres of knowledge, sciences, and even the arts.[44] The juxtaposition of "bourgeois" theories, approaches, and tendencies and the correct "socialist" ones represented the key demarcation tool used in the *Great Soviet Encyclopedia* published by the Soviet state from 1926 until 1990. Given the comprehensiveness of the Soviet effort to reframe civilizational achievements in science and technology, as well as in literature, music, and the arts, along the Marxist-Leninist doctrine, the *Soviet Encyclopedia* turned into an important ideological tool of the Soviet state.

Besides epistemological autonomy, Soviet greatness was asserted through the recognition of Russian historical greatness in modern science, literature, the arts, and music. As noted by Yuri Slezkine, the postwar official propaganda had established that "M. V. Lomonosov had laid the foundation for the modern natural sciences, I. I. Polzunov has invented the steam engine, A. S. Popov had invented the radio, A. F. Mozhaiskii had built the first airplane, and P. N. Iablochkov and A. N. Lodygin had created the first light bulbs. It turned out, in fact, that Russia had always been known in the West as 'the birthplace of light.' "[45] The pantheon of classical Russian literature—Pushkin, Tolstoy, Dostoyevsky, etc.—is also widely known. The Soviet regime relied on it to promote the sense of uniqueness and superiority of the Soviet state and community. Pre-Soviet Russian music and art also bore political significance for Soviet state-building and patriotism inculcation.[46]

The foundation of the Soviet state itself was justified based on universalist grounds. The Soviet state was not simply a state representing the self-determination of the nations comprising it, as most other states are. The Soviet state was unique because it pursued a universalist project of building a society based on social equality and justice—a beacon of a classless society in the world. As such, Soviet exceptionalism is not unique. It could be compared to American exceptionalism—a set of ideas positing the United States as unique due to its origins, values, and institutions.[47]

The Soviet state inculcated a sense of the superiority of the Soviet developmental path, ideas, and institutions from a very young age. Soviet patriotism became the state's main ideological instrument after World War II. Many school textbooks were rewritten to replace the educational focus from the class struggle to the "love for the Soviet motherland."[48] The message about Soviet uniqueness and greatness and the encouragement to rise up to the challenge of being faithful to your motherland, of defending it, of being diligent, hardworking, and of being first in everything you do was pounded onto Soviet kids from kindergarten and throughout their school years, reflecting the aspirations of the Soviet state.

This message was conveyed with enthusiasm through the cultural sphere by writers, poets, and composers, many of whom were brought up in the romantic 1930s, the period of Soviet industrial expansion, revolutionary spirit, and strong faith in the human ability to conquer nature and re-engineer human souls.[49] Those who did not fit the Socialist "mold" of inspirational and enthusiastic creativity were censored, sometimes by Joseph Stalin himself.[50] Stalin understood very acutely the critical role of the cultural intelligentsia for social construction. "The production of souls is more important than the production of tanks," he famously said during a meeting with Soviet writers in October 1932.[51] One year after that meeting, 120 Soviet writers and artists (the Writers Brigade) joined a six-day excursion to *Belomorkanal* (the White Sea—Baltic Canal) constructed by Gulag prisoners.[52] This trip resulted in a collective monograph authored by 36 writers and edited by Maxim Gorky, Leopold Averbakh, and the head of *Belbaltlag*, Semen Firin.[53] The book presented *Belomorkanal* construction to the public as an example of Soviet successes in remolding (*perekovka*) human souls from criminals into the conscientious builders of socialism. Enamored by the Soviet secret police success in *perekovka*, Bruno Jasieński wrote:

> I know: I need to learn, as a writer from *chekisty*,
> the art of being an engineer—a builder of new people[54]

Even if the Soviet romanticism of the 1930s was short-lived, the post-Stalinist cultural and intellectual life revealed important continuities.[55] Whether through the practices of self-censorship or tight censorship from above, the Soviet state ensured the continuing production and propagation of patriotic literature. Consider an example of Robert Rozhdestvensky, nicknamed "the Soviet romantic," who seems to have maintained his patriotism and faith in the Revolution and in the Soviet system throughout his life. He wrote many motivating poems, some of which were included in school curricula, and were read and recited by schoolchildren. Here is one verse from a poem by Rozhdestvensky:

> *If you are here—be first*
> *Be first, whoever you are*
> *The best song among all the songs*
> *The most real book among all the books.*[56]

This competitive orientation—"be first"—reverberated recently in Russia in the song of Timati, written as a gift to Vladimir Putin:

> *Tricolor is above my head*
> *No one is cold hearted here*
> *To be the first is our fate*
> *This is my circle, this is my home.*[57]

Soviet educational and cultural institutions made sure that citizens were exposed to exclusively patriotic literature and arts. The censorship and all kinds of controls of cultural production have grown enormously after a period of brief relaxation (the thaw period) in the 1960s to protect the public from any critical, or even different, non-socialist outlook. The 1964 trial of Joseph Brodsky turned into a historical case, but was only one of many such trials and prosecutions of *inakomyslie* (literally translated as "thinking differently") in the Soviet Union.[58]

Besides educational and cultural realms, the Soviet state tried to involve citizens in various discursive practices to further instill and propagate the sense of Soviet exceptionalism. A good example is the involvement of Soviet citizens in the "world peace agenda" (*bor'ba za mir vo vsem mire*) that provided the public with the opportunity to "practice exceptionalism" in the context of the state's larger aspirations. Russian sociologist Galina Orlova analyzed the special political and social role of the peace discourse in the Brezhnev era. She argued that the struggle for peace defined the character of Soviet ideology during the Cold War, and became the main form of Soviet citizens' legal political activity, as well the central discursive "background" (фоновый) element in the late Soviet period.[59]

The institutionalization of these practices initiated by the Soviet establishment as a central part of the Soviet discursive weapon ("toolkit") of the Cold War started in the 1950s–1960s. By the 1970s, the propagandistic efforts to promote the peace agenda in Soviet society were held in schools, workplaces, and various institutions and agencies. The Brezhnev era propaganda machine worked on translating the abstract principles advanced by the Soviet authorities into everyday personal action. The Soviet media exalted the cases demonstrating personal contributions of Soviet citizens—with money, letters, and other actions—to the world peace agenda.[60] Orlova's investigation of personal letters written by Soviet citizens to the Peace Foundation (*Fond mira*), as well as interviews about Soviet-era workplace practices related to the peace agenda, demonstrates that the peace agenda was taken for granted by Soviet citizens. It was always in the background, and Soviet individuals had choices as to how to express their involvement in this project. Whatever form their involvement took, the main purpose and, arguably, the result of it was that individuals developed a sense of engagement in something significant, bigger than their personal lives and small circles, thus enhancing Soviet citizens' sense of purpose and meaning and strengthening their shared sense of exceptionalism—being part of something unique and worthy (причастность к чему-то большему чем их личная жизнь).

The "world peace" agenda was part of the childhood experience of all those growing up as part of the late Soviet society. One of the songs taught to us in kindergarten and then reproduced and sang often in primary school was "Pust' vsegda budet solntse" ("Let there always be sunshine").[61] This children's song was also a song about the world peace agenda. Not only did children sing these songs, they were encouraged to compose their own songs about peace.[62] More generally, Soviet policies relating to children were, according to Catriona Kelly, one of the main "domains in and through which the Soviet regime rehearsed its ambitions for political, intellectual and cultural leadership before its national and international audience."[63]

The country's cultural elite, though heavily controlled through Soviet censorship, did have their "moments of truth," expressing through irony (when allowed) or Aesopian language their real views and opinions. Yuri Vizbor, a well-known Soviet bard, poet, and film actor, wrote a piece in 1964 that speaks directly and with an ironic smile about this shared sense of Soviet superiority put on display in the imagined conversation of a Soviet technologist, Petukhov, with a person from an African country:

> *But we make rockets*
> *And bridged the Yenisei*
> *And in the field of ballet*
> *We surpass the entire world,*
> *We surpass the entire world!*[64]

These words have entered the vocabulary of hundreds of thousands and more, and are remembered everytime someone wants to mock Soviet greatness.

One might wonder why such subversive verses were allowed by the system that created elaborate mechanisms for controlling cultural expression. Based on her research of the Lithuanian humor and satire journal *The Broom*, anthropologist Neringa Klumbyte provided an answer. She viewed humor and satire in the Soviet Union as an expression of political intimacy and as a sphere of shared meanings and dialogue for officials and citizens. Laughter blurred the distinctions between public and private, between the state and the citizen, and thereby allowed for subjective experiencing of the system as the people's own.[65] Humor and laughter provided an important "valve" that promoted coexistence and reduced conflict in the system.

The official ideology promoted by the Communist Party became more rigid during the late Soviet period. It was practiced mostly through adopting specific formalized linguistic constructions that were expected to accompany official meetings and political rituals, as well as creative works and scientific books.[66] Alexei Yurchak argued convincingly that Marxist ideology turned into a shell that was used to display obedience and playing by the rules, while the creative construction of meaning was going on in various official and unofficial public spaces.[67] But the Soviet collective identity that had matured after World War II was not a shell. It provided a meaningful sense of belonging to a great nation that people took considerable pride in. The Soviet Union, perceived as a superpower that had defeated fascism, that was the first to send a man into space, to explore the cosmos, to educate its people, to help other developing nations, to fight for peace, etc.—provided its citizens with a strong identification. This collective identity curiously coexisted with rising skepticism and laughter at the political regime and the leadership of the late Soviet Union. But this skepticism and the rising humor expressed through anecdotes and in various humor journals did not question the viability of the Soviet state. It was a system and a state that were perceived to stay "forever."

The Soviet dissidents repressed for their political views knew better than to believe the Soviet propaganda. They tried to disseminate information critical of the Soviet state. The *samizdat* literature, and especially "The Chronicle of Current Events" that provided regular information on human rights violations in the Soviet Union, spread in selected circles among Soviet intellectuals. But the state organs became ever more repressive in their attempts to control the public space. Some intellectuals and notable members of the Soviet cultural elite deemed threatening to the regime were forced from the country, as in the case of Alexander Solzhenitsyn, Mstislav Rostropovich and his wife, Galina Vishnevskaya, Aleksandr Galich, Sergei Dovlatov, Joseph Brodsky, and many lesser known citizens of the Soviet Union. Others, like Andrei Sakharov, were sent into internal exile and were cut off from any external communication. Thousands of Soviet citizens were prosecuted for expressing discontent with Soviet authorities, were incarcerated, or were forced into psychiatric hospitals.[68]

The outward expression of the significance of collective identity, and specifically that connecting an individual to the Soviet nation, took different shapes and forms. The culture of toasting in the Soviet Union is just one of its specific expressions in everyday life. John Steinbeck, who visited the Soviet Union in 1947, noted in his *Russian Diary*, "it is strange but here [in the USSR] people rarely toast to/for something personal. More often people drink for something grand rather than the future of a particular individual."[69]

The Soviet state's efforts to instill in the public the ideas of patriotism and a sense of pride in belonging to the Soviet political community were successful for the most part. The sense of Soviet superiority and greatness was not only widely shared, but was taken for granted in the late Soviet period. The Soviet mentality did not allow for even imagining that the Soviet Union could be compared to another country on the map.[70] This taken-for-granted belief turned into an unwillingness to accept and even shame if the country was compared to others (especially those associated with the Third World). The real sense of shock experienced by many Soviet citizens who visited a Western country for the first time in the late 1980s and early 1990s is a good reflection of deeply instilled assumptions about the Soviet superiority, shattered abruptly at the point of the encounter with the "other."[71] Even the top brass Communist nomenklatura members who did not have to deal with the supply shortages that the ordinary Soviet folks encountered in their everyday life were astounded by their first "Western supermarket" experience. Boris Yeltsin's aid, Lev Sukhanov, described Yeltsin's reaction in the aftermath of visiting an American supermarket in Houston, Texas, as part of his first unofficial trip to the United States in 1989:

> Already in the plane Boris Nikolayevich spaced out for a while. He sat holding his head with his hands clearly overwhelmed by conflicting emotions. [. . .] When he was back, he let his emotions out: "What did they do to our poor people. . . . They were told fairy tales, inventing something new. . . . But everything was already invented . . . apparently it was not for people."[72]

Arguably, the first uninhibited public glance into some of the aspects of Soviet collective identity, reflected through individual Soviet citizens, became possible at the moment when a Soviet group of citizens confronted an American group in a direct communicative action. This became possible in 1986, during an unprecedented Seattle-Leningrad spacebridge (dubbed a Citizens' Summit), anchored by Vladimir Posner and Phil Donahue.[73] This uncensored exchange between two audiences was premised on the publicly declared desire to learn about each other through direct interaction, as a counter to state propaganda. Yet the actual exchange revealed the salience of collective identities and state propaganda on both sides. The audiences presented mirror images of each other, each driven by the images of media propaganda in their own countries. The Soviet audience excelled specifically on promoting the Soviet government view and eschewing any government criticism—something that was pointed out by the American side. The Soviet participants appeared resolute and united in their appreciation for the Soviet government and Soviet policy.

Members of the American audience tried a few times to raise more personal questions and provide more reflexive and critical answers. Their attempts were thwarted somewhat by Phil Donahue, the American host, who seemed to embody the American government position, openly critical of the Soviet Union. The fact that he controlled the microphone and was not shy in offering his own commentary and interpretations did create a sense that the American side was also coming mostly from the perspective of a collective identity that was, at that moment, radically antagonistic to the Soviet one. Many questions, and Donahue's own comments, presumed that the Soviet Union was a totalitarian state that controlled its citizens and that citizens were living in fear behind the iron curtain. The Soviet participants did not appreciate the outlook, which did not include any benefit of the doubt regarding how the Soviet system operated and what Soviet citizens might have thought about their government. The Soviet side perceived a strong element of pre-judgment and openly challenged it.

Later, Phil Donahue recognized that he was under pressure of wider expectations not to present the Soviet side in a positive way.[74] But the way the Soviet participants reacted to more personal questions also did not help in developing this conversation in a more personal, amicable direction. One attempt from an American participant to bring up something more personal went as follows:

> You know this Soviet teacher, they said they asked their students what they like to know about America. I am a teacher too and I ask[ed] my students here.... We have this phrase in America—the American Dream. For some it means financial independence, for others the ability to go from, literally, the log cabin to the White House. My students want to know what is the Russian dream.

The response went as follows:

> You know, I think that each person has their very own dream . . . everyone probably has their own dreams. Because we are all individuals. So I would like to talk about my dream. I am still quite young. Perhaps I may have some idealistic notions about life: I'd like to have a lot of nice children, I'd like to have a good husband, I'd like to have a good work. I do not want to leave my beautiful city. I don't want to go anywhere. I know my city because I am an art historian by education. And my dream includes a great many parts to it. But mostly it depends on whether we really are going to be able to live in peace. Because nothing would be realized unless we make efforts to ensure that this comes about. That's why I really want to fight for peace.

From this specific response and many other comments and questions from the Soviet audience, "fighting for peace" emerges as that late Soviet dream, reflecting the official peace propaganda in the late Soviet Union.

Later, in 2012, Posner recollected the aftermath of this spacebridge that was watched by millions of Soviet citizens: "I received seventy seven thousands [*sic*] letters that contained two ideas. The first was: 'Comrade Posner, why did you invite those idiots into the studio. Why didn't you invite me?' And, the second idea was more important: 'I saw my face and I did not like it.' In short, there was a sense that people were not open."[75]

This first direct exchange between the Soviet and American audiences revealed the salience of national identity actively promoted by the Soviet state through media, educational institutions, and at the workplace. Although such salience was to be expected—given the context of communication with the most significant out-group (the Americans)—and characterized the American audience as well, its relentlessness, even in the face of self-reflexive comments on the part of the Soviet audience, is remarkable. Even when the Soviet participants noted the excessively political character of the exchange and tried to speak more personally, they reverted to collectively defined, political issues. This exchange revealed the successfulness of the Brezhnev-era propagandistic efforts centered on the issue of peace-building. This agenda was incorporated personally by the Soviet citizens, who were proud of being able to contribute to loftier goals and purposes.

I saw the lasting legacies of the Soviet "world peace" agenda in my 2016 focus-group interviews in Samara and Kazan. Two older ladies who took part in the interviews opened the group discussion immediately, without deliberating, in response to my first question on desired policy priorities, with the familiar cliché from Soviet times: they wanted world peace (*mir vo vsem mire*). In both cases, they underscored their desire for world peace, not just peace in their country, thus signaling the lasting effect of Soviet internationalist propaganda and rhetoric. In both cases, these were the very first answers to the posed question, by individuals who had their answers ready and did not need to think about their personal preferences. These answers came from group members who did not show active involvement in the subsequent conversation; the formulaic nature of their response conveyed that they either did not feel very comfortable sharing their views publicly or were detached from social issues (and probably focused on issues of a personal nature, such as assisting their children with caring for grandchildren, engaging in subsistence agriculture, etc.). The Soviet official propaganda of the 1970–1980s lives on in Russia today, showing how durable some of these cognitive structures are.

The sense of pride and faith in Soviet superiority could only be maintained among the people who stayed behind the iron curtain, in the environment with tightly controlled information and the repression of voices critical of the Soviet Union. The members of the cultural elite who had foreign travel opportunities were more aware of the living standards abroad. In his memoir, *A Life Peppered by Sclerosis* (*Склероз, рассеянный по жизни*, 2014), Alexandr Shirvindt, a famous Soviet actor, shared, with a sense of irony, the travails of the Soviet troupe, underfunded and trying to save the precious currency abroad.[76] Undoubtedly, many of them felt shame for having to bring cans of food and melted cheese on their trips from the Soviet Union, to save on coffee and meals in restaurants and to buy merchandise that was in high demand in the Soviet Union. Shirvindt described the moments when those of the group who were most ashamed, who had refused to do that (i.e., bring food with them), could easily go hungry during those trips. Of course, the Soviet camaraderie helped in the end. The sense of humor with which these stories are told only bring into sharp relief the sadness of the circumstances described and experienced by Soviet citizens who might have found themselves in tourist-like roles abroad. The humor on display in these narrations undoubtedly helped to deal with the more painful emotions of shame and humiliation.

Leonid Parfenov's *Namedni* project (*Lately: Our Era. 1961–1991*)—a multi-media digest of Soviet and the more recent Russian history—is a nice illustration and a nostalgic exploration of the key elements propping the sense of Soviet exceptionalism.[77] Through text and video format, the project summarized some of the key achievements of the late Soviet civilization: the space exploration and the first astronauts, Yuri Gagarin and Valentina Tereshkova; the achievements of the Soviet science and the Nobel Prize–winning Soviet scholars; culture (including a special focus on ballet), literature, TV programming, and Soviet cinematography.

Namedni has been compared to "an encyclopedia of Soviet life" tracing the chronology of main events on a yearly basis.[78] Composed of old Soviet footage of political, social, and cultural events, clips from films and musical videos, it includes a voice-over narration by the anchor and the author, Leonid Parfenov. Every episode starts with the promise of presenting to the viewer the "events, people, and phenomena that have defined a way of life. Without this, it is hard to imagine us, let alone—to understand." According to its authors, the project did not intend to idealize the Soviet past. Serguei Oushakine, an anthropologist from Princeton University who analyzed this project as an example of decomposing "the visual legacy of monolithic and totalizing late socialism," argued that late socialism emerges in this project as "a multilayered and multivocal visual text."[79] Oushakine recognized that this project is an attempt to "humanize" socialism, and is a response to "the dominant tendency to perceive late Soviet society as a culture in which cynical double-dealers were dominated by state control."[80] But he also notes that in their selection of autonomous and usually disconnected units of late Soviet experience, the authors of the project did not promote any coherent story. "Decomposition of the available visual stock, a persistent assault on any form of narrative linearity was its main method," noted Oushakine.[81]

Leonid Parfenov denied any linkages of his project to post-Soviet nostalgia.[82] But Roman Abramov and Anna Chistyakova, sociologists at the Higher School of Economics, suggested that this was a case of restorative nostalgia aimed at "rethinking" the past (as opposed to its idealization) and responding to a deeper societal demand of integrating the past into the present.[83] So what are these elements from the past that stand out, based on this project?

The project zooms in on people, phenomena, and events. Three types of people are featured in the project: (1) historical figures (politicians and public officials); (2) those in whom Soviet people took pride (athletes, scientists, space explorers, and ballet dancers; and (3) those whom Soviet people loved (actors, poets, writers). The variety of the late Soviet phenomena highlighted by Parfenov included mostly tangible things from Soviet everyday life—the introduction of new fashions, such as high heel shoes for women and crimplene clothing, new fads such as hula hoops, deodorants, new types of furniture, and, of course, the Soviet jeans "rush." It is these everyday things that produce feelings of coziness and warmth (at least for those who have experienced them). Even the discussion of events in this Soviet chronicle that are predominantly political in nature, such as the 1962 Cuban missile crisis, Soviet military aid in Africa, the 1962 tragedy in Novocherkassk, where the unarmed workers protesting over increases in meat and dairy prices were met with gunfire, and the war in Afghanistan, does not take away the impression of a certain degree of intimacy with which the Soviet past is brought back to the viewer's attention.[84] Although the author of the project did not want to produce any linear narrative about the Soviet past, it seems appropriate to suggest that *Namedni* became "the storage of nostalgia for the Soviet evoking 'best feelings' for the irrecoverable past."[85] The project appears now as a storage box from which post-Soviet generations can draw examples of their country's exceptionalism: people, events, and phenomena they could still be proud of today.

Conflict as the Structuring Element of the Soviet Worldview

The very intensely propagated "us versus them" mentality was another important component of Soviet identity that took on a taken-for-granted character. Yuri Levada's "simple Soviet man" project captured this very well. "Demonstrative opposition to the 'hostile surrounding,' which really meant an opposition to the rest of the world, was one of the principal particularities of the Soviet society," Levada suggested in 2001. "This was reflected in various spheres: from state policies to culture, science and human relationships. From early on an individual was formed based on a militarized and primitive opposition of all things Soviet to the rest of the world."[86] Such opposition and the outsized role of *conflict* are an essential element in Soviet citizens' view of the world and their place within it. Just like the sense of exceptionalism and Soviet superiority, this mental model—that the Soviet world lives in opposition to the rest of the world (and especially the capitalist world)—could be seen as foundational. It structured and defined the sociopolitical reality for Soviet citizens and it shaped their understanding of the society's past and present, and of domestic politics as well as the international setting.[87]

The reasons behind such an outsized role of conflict and opposition could be found at least in two different realms. The first is the ideological one. The centrality of conflict is fundamental to Marxist theory that postulated class conflict to be the "locomotive of history," i.e., the driving force of political change. Karl Marx emphasized the importance of antagonistic—unresolvable—differences that, when they accumulate, become the main source of revolutionary, radical change. In accordance with these ideological postulates, the 1917 October revolution was interpreted by mainstream Soviet historiography as the epic, watershed event. It divided the history of Russia into pre-Soviet and Soviet—the new heroic age with the new state—the USSR—presumed to represent the new era and to lead to the construction of a new world, free of private property and exploitation.

The political reasons are arguably even more important than the purely ideological. There is plenty of evidence in Soviet history confirming that Marxist ideology changed in accordance with political imperatives.[88] Conflict was essential for building the Soviet nation.[89] The Soviet Union was a multinational state and incorporated many different ethnic groups that had their own, more particularistic, ethnic and local loyalties and identifications. Juxtaposing the Soviet state and society to the rest of the world was politically convenient from the perspective of nation-building. The various ethnic groups incorporated into the Soviet state had their own linguistic, religious, and traditional affinities. Building ties based on language or traditions was not an option. Marxist ideology did turn into a sort of Soviet religion.[90] But adding to that and instilling in society a sense of a common enemy was a powerful mechanism for consolidation.

The Soviet state made conflict and opposition to the Soviet system into a crucial factor for understanding the early and mature Soviet systems. To begin with, Soviet historians highlighted the story of the new Soviet state emerging out of the struggle with international capitalist states (Britain, France, and the United States) that tried to topple the nascent Soviet government. This interpretation of the civil war of 1918–1922 pitted the new Soviet republic against the capitalist world, as opposed to the so-called White Russians who supported the Russian monarchy and fought to dislodge the Bolshevik government. Once the internationally supported struggle against the Bolsheviks was over, establishing the Stalinist system involved the "domestication" of the conflict that now involved the internal enemies of the state. World War II brought a new foreign intervention into the USSR, this time from Nazi Germany. The Great Patriotic War (1941–1945) turned into a "holy war" for the Soviet Union that enabled a true national consolidation in the country. The memory of this war plays a crucial role in current-day Russia, too. Finally, the start of the Cold War in the postwar period once again saw the Soviet Union pitting itself against the capitalist system and, more specifically, the United States, which emerged as the leading representative of the capitalist system, as well as the only rival superpower. This epochal conflict between the United States and the Soviet Union played out through numerous proxy-wars and a massive military buildup, paralleled by increasingly hostile propaganda on both sides. This conflict became the central element of Soviet citizens' worldview during the last few decades of the Soviet Union.[91]

The conflict-driven strategy of national consolidation was not a Soviet invention. Enemy-construction—whether internal or external—is a tool long tried and tested in many other locales and time periods, including the United States.[92] Scholars in various disciplines have inquired into the issue of the "need for enemies" as a psychologically, cognitively, and politically driven phenomenon.[93] Social identity theory, among other approaches, goes a long way in explaining the operation of enemy images for building in-group solidarity.[94] This does not mean, though, that enemy construction is necessary and universally used due to innate psychological processes. In words of Stephen Reicher, a prominent social identity theorist at the University of St. Andrews (Scotland), "the social identity tradition forces us to turn toward the social world. It forces us to address the ideological and structural features of that world. Only by doing so will we understand how our psychology relates to what we do."[95]

The recent scholarship concerned with Soviet public attitudes toward the United States has revealed the effectiveness of Soviet official propaganda. Ordinary Soviet people's image of America—even during the late Soviet period, when the official ideology was often derided—adhered to the representation installed by Soviet propaganda before World War II.[96] These pre-war official depictions focused on American unemployment, racial problems, lack of social benefits, and warmongering. At that time, the United States was not singled out as the main Soviet threat; it was rather perceived as part of the capitalist bloc of countries hostile to the young Soviet state.[97] After World War II, as the Cold War intensified, the official propaganda constructed new images of America as an overly militarized, evil country bent on world domination. The issue of foreign spying took the front page in the Soviet media, especially several noisy affairs of scientists accused of spying in the late 1940s.[98] The Soviet state instructed its citizens to be vigilant and watch out for American and British spies and those who might be helping them. Meanwhile, the Soviet government promoted ideas about a possible new war, this time with the United States, that undoubtedly created anxieties and fears among a population that was just emerging from the ruins of World War II.[99]

The Soviet citizens who showed interest in foreign and especially American culture were also targeted by the official anti-American and anti-foreign propaganda. The popular saying from the 1950s, "today he plays jazz but tomorrow he will betray his motherland" (сегодня он играет джаз, а завтра родину продаст), as well as its various modifications that spread in the 1970s–1980s, is revealing of the public attitudes of suspicion toward those who might have been enchanted by non-Soviet art, music, and literature (except for those exemplars that were sanctioned by the Soviet system, of course).[100]

Rósa Magnúsdóttir's recent study, *Enemy Number One* (2018), examines very carefully the high point of the Soviet postwar anti-American campaign during 1947–1951, noting the prosecution of people who voiced pro-American views or even had personal contacts with Americans.[101] The author argues that Stalin saw the impending Cold War as an opportunity to unite the Soviet people against a new enemy; Soviet propaganda now fought against the "reactionary ideology of American imperialism" as a part of "the broader anticosmopolitan campaign."[102]

In short, a Soviet citizen always had an enemy—whether domestic or foreign, Nazi Germany or American imperialism, British spies or those who helped them from the inside. The Soviet government's anti-foreign propaganda targeted all ages, starting with children who watched cartoons and read books that contrasted the happy Soviet childhood to the despair, forced labor, and exploitation experienced by children in American society, and extending to the rest of the population through television and print media.[103] The continuously reconstructed image of the enemy—however fluid and changing that enemy was—provided the means for national consolidation, worked as an instrument of political legitimacy construction, and gave an impetus for continuous mobilization of the Soviet public.[104] Given that an ordinary Soviet citizen did not have access to different views and other sources of information, this "split" vision of the world, featuring a deep divide between the moral "us" and the evil "them," developed into a core element of the Soviet collective identity, providing the basis for self-categorization and sociopolitical orientation in the world.

Why should we care about Soviet collective identity today? Soviet collective identity at the state level, along with a variety of social identities that Soviet citizens crafted for themselves as part of Soviet institutions (economic, cultural, and political), represented important pillars supporting individual-level dignity for many Soviet citizens. It was a critical source of people's self-esteem and their perceptions of in-group and out-group members. Recognizing the centrality of Soviet identity for a sense of personal self-value helps in appreciating (1) the devastating psychological impact experienced by individuals in the post-Soviet society as a result of the Soviet collapse; and (2) the crucial importance of the Kremlin's efforts to portray Putin's leadership through the frame of reclaiming the lost identity of "great Russia," to recover the sense of being unified in a nation that matters, that can stand up for its principles and interests, and that can make a difference in the world.

4

The New Russian Identity and the Burden of the Soviet Past

No man is an island,
Entire of itself,
Every man is a piece of the continent,
A part of the main.

—*John Donne (1624)*

THOSE WHO HAVE traveled to Russia regularly after the collapse of the Soviet Union have undoubtedly witnessed the dramatic change in the physical surroundings of the country over the last three decades or so. The forces of capitalism and globalization have transformed Russia's largest cities into shining and glitzy spaces, filled with cafes, restaurants, and shopping centers, entertainment and sport arenas, parks and promenades. Outside the big cities and in city outskirts, the reality is more mixed. Depending on the region and the type of settlement, one can see recent infrastructural improvements intermixed with spaces showing growing degradation, dilapidation, and abandonment. Development in Russia has been highly uneven.

The social atmosphere reflected in casual conversations between visitors from the West and the locals has changed as well. Questions common in the 1990s, arising out of curiosity about life in America, have been replaced by laments, indignation, and self-righteous accusations regarding US foreign policy, American leadership, and Western ambitions, ignorance, and arrogance. Russian citizens, long curious about and often envious of the Western lifestyle and prosperity, have recently turned into US-skeptics or America-haters, seething with anger and indignation not only about US government and foreign policy, but also about Western and American values and ideas. The tone of conversations about America in Russia has changed. The subjective, individualist "place" from which the Russian citizens think and talk about America has shifted. The nationally framed inquiry into politics and morality has replaced personal curiosity about culture and society reflected in the early fascination with anything "made

The Red Mirror. Gulnaz Sharafutdinova, Oxford University Press (2020). © Oxford University Press.
DOI: 10.1093/oso/9780197502938.001.0001.

in the USA." Today, the Russians' collective selves prevail over their personal selves whenever America comes to mind. The Russian national identity becomes personified and central in nearly every Russian citizen whenever the subject of conversation turns to the United States of America. Many Russian citizens start speaking for the nation and frequently see a nation, rather than an individual, in their interlocutors associated with the West. One cannot help but note the enormous salience of national identity in current social interactions.

The 2018 World Cup did show the boundless hospitality of the Russian people. Thousands of foreign soccer fans found Russia to be a welcoming, warm, and exciting place. The Levada Center reported that for that summer month in 2018, Russians' overall attitudes toward the United States had improved, with the number of those who thought well about the United States reaching parity with those who perceived the United States in negative terms.[1] But this "thaw" did not last. The more critical disposition returned soon after the games were over, returning the balance of attitudes toward a more stable equilibrium in which the negative predispositions dominate over positive ones by a factor of 1.5–3.[2]

What has happened to bring about such a shift in the centrality of national identity in Russia? How and why did this shift occur? To what extent was it driven by Kremlin politics and media frames? Was it historically inevitable given Russia's experience in the 1990s? In this chapter, I outline the key elements of the historical context of the 1990s that provided the crucial background for the present-day identity politics in Russia. Understanding the main features of this context—through domestic and international lenses—is essential for capturing the nature of identity politics the Kremlin has promoted under Vladimir Putin's leadership, and the public response to this identity politics.

The Russian Geopolitical Condition of Double-Negation

The new Russia that emerged as an independent state in 1991 was in a unique historical situation associated with its role as the main bearer of the legacies of the Soviet state. As opposed to all other post-communist countries, Russia did not have an external actor to blame for its communist past. All other Eastern European countries could construct their post-communist vision for change in the context of the "return to Europe" project, viewing Europe as their rightful place of belonging and interpreting their communist past as a forced derailment from their "normal" historical path.[3] The post-Soviet states in Central Asia and the Caucasus could also start building their new national identities around the discourse of national liberation.[4] Russia faced a distinct identity challenge. The end of communism brought Russian society to the psychologically complicated and, arguably, intolerable historical moment of "self-negation." As Vyacheslav Morozov argued, "In the late 1980s–early 1990s it seemed that new Russia would be built on negating Soviet authoritarianism. However, the process of reassessing the past turned so traumatic that it was thrown out as too humiliating for a country that won over Nazism and that built the first spaceship."[5]

From kindergarten to high school, college, and continually throughout their life span, people were taught that they lived in the most progressive, socially advanced, industrially developed, and peace-building country in the world. In the last years of the Soviet system, the society was confronted with the message that this was not true, and that the system was immoral, corrupt, and even criminal. The end of the Soviet Union signified the collapse of this system and the broad-based consensus about building democratic political institutions and a market economy in Russia. If given a chance, many Russians would have likely preferred a more gradual reform of the Soviet Union.[6] However, Yeltsin's political victory over Gorbachev and the implosion of the Soviet state meant that the radical vision of the need to transform the system in a wholesale fashion won over any gradual reformist approach.[7] The aims of liberal reforms in 1992 were formulated in "Westernist" terms; they claimed to return Russia back to a "normal" historical trajectory.[8] Such radical approach, criticized by some scholars as "market Bolshevism," meant that the negative agenda of purging the past had prevailed.[9]

The outright rejection of the system of values and identifications inculcated by the Soviet system represented the breakdown of the collective ideational "backbone" in Russia. The Soviet identity and values were presumably chosen by Russia herself and were not imposed from the outside, as Eastern European nations or other post-Soviet states could claim. There was no one but Russia's own self to blame for communism. Even more, others in the neighborhood also blamed Russia for that (as the main bearer of the Soviet heritage). "National victimhood" discourses became the preferred instrument used by new post-communist, nationalist elites in Eastern Europe to forge new national identities.[10] The hype over Gorbachev's perestroika and new thinking was a fleeting one. The victimhood frames that focused not merely on Stalinism and communism, but also on Russia as a historic enemy, were stickier. In a provocatively titled 1997 essay, "Is Russia Still an Enemy?," Richard Pipes, an American historian specializing on Russia and the Soviet Union, noted the lingering doubts about Russia "because so much about post-communist Russia is unfinished and unsettled."[11] Was it really about the unsettledness of Russia's transition? Or did the past weigh so heavily on perceptions of Russia as a potential threat, as became evident in many post-Soviet states?[12]

As others translated their fears of Russia, linked to the country's past, into the present, and as Russia herself turned against her own past, trying to wipe it all away and start afresh, what was there left to build on for a new national identity in Russia?

Michael Urban (1994) argued eloquently in this regard, referring to Russia of the 1990s as the "nation against itself":

> For nearly all postcommunist societies, the disassociation of communism from national identity has been facilitated by a background understanding that communism had never been "our" doing in the first place. Ultimate responsibility for the crimes inflicted and the damage done in its name belongs not to the nation itself but to those who had forcibly imposed it: another nation, Russia. . . . Russia does not enjoy this luxury. There, a discourse of identity forfeits from the outset the possibility of constructing some other nation onto which might be loaded the negative moment in the recreation of a national community. As a consequence, this negative moment has circulated through Russian politics generally, informing the code of communication with the vexed categories of identity (and culpability), and transposing onto domestic conflicts the manichaean logic of unqualified nationalism.[13]

If national identities existed only on the collective level, perhaps such rejection did not have to be personally painful. But collective identities—including national ones—are carried by and embodied in individuals. Rejecting the collective past, from the standpoint of an individual who was not simply connected to but was *made* by that past, also means rejecting the value of one's own life. With the exceptional cases of individuals who tried to live in their "castles of spirit" (as Joseph Brodsky tried, but the system did not allow him that anyway), the lives of the majority of Soviet citizens were intrinsically tied to the system, made by and through the system.[14] So the loss and rejection of the system meant (in the big picture of things) the corresponding rejection of what each (or most) Soviet citizens believed in, strived for, aspired to, accomplished, created, enjoyed, loved, and incorporated as part of themselves.

This condition of Russia's "self-negation" was shaped not only by the political choices made and outcomes procured domestically, but also by the geopolitical decisions, and political and sociocultural dynamics in the new post-Soviet nations, especially those neighboring Russia in the West. The three Baltic states, Ukraine, and Moldova—striving to consolidate their new states on nationalist grounds—proceeded in the direction of constructing their collective identities from the position of being victims to Soviet aggression and expansionism, rewriting their histories, including the moments deemed foundational for Russia's national identity, such as the meaning of the World War II.[15] Russia, which took on the role of the Soviet Union's main successor state, subsequently was turned into an "external other" for these states—never to be trusted and to be protected from with the help of Western alliances such as the European Union and NATO. The ethnic demography and, specifically, the presence of large Russian-speaking minorities in these states resulted in the politicization of ethnicity. The new nation-building projects that emphasized culture, language, and collective memory of the titular groups led to the marginalization of the Russian speakers, who found themselves alienated, struggling for inclusion and integration since the collapse of the Soviet Union.[16] These trends prevailed not only among Russia's western neighbors, but also among the nationalizing states in Central Asia and the Caucasus, although the anti-communist and anti-Soviet vectors were less pronounced in some of these new states.[17]

History does not like counterfactual analysis. But even if it did, it is hard to expect that these political cleavages could have developed differently. Ethnic identity is one of those fundamental categories that people use in their everyday life to deal with uncertainty in a complex world.[18] Furthermore, it is hard to expect that the ethnic Latvians, Estonians, and Lithuanians could have easily forgiven and forgotten that thousands of their kin and family members were deported to Siberia and other remote areas in the Soviet Union in the 1940s and 1950s. This traumatic past and the experiences of losing their loved ones, of being deported, of losing homes and losing everything, could not be "thrown out the window" for the passage of time. It is only logical to expect that this past would be integrated into the collective memory of the new political community and that the members of this community—whatever ethnic identity they may have—would have to share in that knowledge and commemoration.

But political and symbolic boundaries do not always coincide. Identities are multiple and evolving. And political entrepreneurs use strategically the emotional sensitivities, historical vulnerabilities, and symbolic differences to mobilize political support in pursuit of power. Democratic politics are based on a competition among various conflicting interests according to agreed-upon rules. The political mobilization of ethnic identities in the Baltic states is, therefore, not very surprising. It is unfortunate, nonetheless, for at least two reasons. The continuous reproduction and reinforcement of ethnic polarization limit the political space and organizational potential for the parties on the left, who could have represented people based on their economic interests.[19] Added to that trend is the nearly inevitable reverberation of these politics in Russia, fraught by the insecurities associated with the country's post-imperial historical condition, especially as Russia took on the mantle of the Soviet Union. These ethnically based political lines have meant a continuing presence of the "Russia issue" in the domestic politics in these states.

Russia's internal political transformation, initiated by Gorbachev's reforms in the late 1980s, created moral pressure within Russian society to confront the violent and sorrowful Stalinist past. It was not an easy task in a context in which the victims and their families lived side by side with their executioners. Many family members lost to terror became invisible—hidden from the family chronicles to better fit the Soviet system built on avoiding and distancing from the painful truth. This important, ethical work of memory, taking Russian society "on the road to the Temple," just began in the late Soviet period and was expected to continue in the new Russia.[20] But it was quickly overtaken by the more mundane challenges of adjustment to a painful socioeconomic transition, combined with the unprecedented "piratization" of the country's assets and enrichment of a select few.[21] The newly emerging realities of crony capitalism that played out openly in the public sphere, with rival oligarchs in control of media resources manipulating information and publishing compromising materials to defeat their opponents, did not work as a good supporting ground for sustaining the public discussion about Stalinism and the collective lessons learned from the Soviet experience. To the contrary, it became a fertile ground for profound disappointment with liberal reforms and democracy and its institutions.[22] The challenge of acutely needed moral work gave way to the imperative of survival, on the part of the masses, and enrichment, on the part of a select few.

Meanwhile, the political and geopolitical developments to the west of Russia confronted the nation with additional pressures as Russia found itself collectively "cornered"—seen to be perpetually in the "wrong" and incapable of redemption—because the nation-building processes in the Baltic states, and to a lesser degree in Ukraine and Moldova, relied on the image of Russia as a historical enemy. In the Western democracies, also, doubts about Russia's democratic choice have lingered, while fears of Russia's imperialist resurgence, led by those who might aspire to returning to the days of old glory, have grown.[23] Perhaps under the circumstances of a clear loss in war and the imposition of peace and new "politics" and "geopolitics" from above and from the outside—as in the case with Nazi Germany after World War II—such "cornering" could have produced a different outcome. But the Soviet case was fundamentally different in that the political change started from within and was driven by the Soviet political elites, supported by the enthusiastic (at least in the first five years of reforms) Soviet public, eager to adopt the Western "path."

For Russia—the main successor state to the USSR—the new transformation path was self-chosen, as was evident in the leadership role of Boris Yeltsin, the first president of the Russian Federation. As a result of the Soviet dissolution,

Russia found itself in these historically peculiar, structural conditions of a *double denial*—a geopolitical "catch 22." From the inside, it negated its own past and rejected its old collective identity, aspiring to adopt an entirely new system and move in the new direction. From the outside, it was still rejected, if symbolically, as the bearer of Soviet legacies by its closest neighbors, driven by their new, nationalist politics.

The United States, the Soviet "external other," meanwhile, rushed to claim victory in the Cold War, leaving the role of the loser to Russia. The asymmetry of power between the two countries that emerged, along with new Russia coming into existence, made this situation ever more precarious. The recently released transcripts of private conversations between Bill Clinton and Boris Yeltsin reveal Russia's position as evidently dependent on US financial support—with all the resultant vulnerability palpably felt in these conversations.[24] The American triumphalism might not have been overdrawn in such context, if shortsighted.

According to Andrey Kortunov, the director general of the Russian International Affairs Council (a Russian international relations think tank), such a triumphalist attitude, reflected in the discourse of American elites in the early 1990s, created much resentment among Russian elites.[25] Russia's one-sided dependence and vulnerability was fraught with a defensive and aggressive aftermath at some point in the near future, especially if the country did not integrate with Western political institutions and security arrangements. The absence of a newly defined and positively assertive collective identity of Russia as part of the new international order in the 1990s—understandable in the context of the far-reaching transformation the country was undergoing—presupposed the likelihood of its later resurgence under a different political flag.

The failure of economic and political reforms to transform Russia's institutions and the role of global factors in enabling that failure are another important piece of the puzzle. Russia's new economic elites seduced by the opportunities of collecting rents at home and stashing them abroad never fought to ensure the government accountability and secure property rights.[26] With the help of global financial institutions creating opportunities of institutional arbitrage for asset owners worldwide, Russia's "offshore" elites took their wealth and families abroad, investing in prime real estate in London, New York, and Los Angeles, giving birth to the phenomenon of "golden youth"—the strata of privileged sons and daughters of Russia's numerous billionaires, vacationing in Europe's most expensive resorts, on their private yachts, shopping in London, Paris, and Milan, and getting cushion job placements at the top echelons of Russia's state monopolies, investment banks, and even ministerial portfolios.[27] What positive and assertive national idea could have been promoted in these circumstances of the abominable social and economic differentiation? Could the ordinary Russians have bought into the constructively framed collective identity notions based on their present domestic conditions when the system worked in such a crooked way and the sense of injustice and social alienation only grew ever more strongly? These circumstances promoted the dynamics of scapegoating, searching for enemies and hidden conspirators.

Morozov, in his *Russia and the Others* (2009), suggests that Russia's new identity narrative, based on opposing the Soviet past, dominated until about the mid-1990s, still evident and successfully implemented in Yeltsin's 1996 electoral campaign strategy.[28] A clear displacement of this internal antagonism onto the international sphere first occurred in 1999, as a reaction to NATO actions in the former Yugoslavia. The bombing of Belgrade was seen in Russia as an assault on sovereignty and as an aggression against Europe.[29]

The Search for Collective Identity in the 1990s

Collective identities are forged by leaders, and the role of leadership is especially significant in the aftermath of social rupture, group disintegration, and the loss of existing group ties and identities that were once taken for granted. It is through the leadership process that the collection of individuals lacking a shared agreement on key normative, ideological, and cultural resources come to think of themselves as a nation (or a smaller community) and to imagine themselves, once again (in Russia's case), as a unified collective body providing each individual with an accepted and a positive sense of a collective self.[30] But the leadership process is not a matter of voluntarism. It cannot happen at any time or any place. Leadership is constrained by the social and political context. What became possible in the first decade of the 2000s in terms of forging a strong sense of national identity under the leadership of Vladimir Putin was not, arguably, attainable in the 1990s. The reasons were more than one.

A state of rupture, destabilization, and confusion is probably the best descriptor for understanding the contours of Russia's national identity after the collapse of the Soviet Union. The democratic government led by Boris Yeltsin promoted the reform agenda, motivated by the goals of de-Stalinization and breaking with the Soviet past. Yeltsin and his government rejected the Soviet past, along with all the Soviet symbols.[31] Given their political victory, the symbolic aspects of Yeltsin's reforms were mostly assumed as the government focused on economic reform priorities. But the window of opportunity for re-engaging the Soviet symbols emerged, along with the rising sea of popular opposition to economic reforms. In the absence of lustration (i.e., the removal of former communist officials from state offices) and de-communization, as well as more structural reforms in the sphere of education, the communist and nationalist forces opposed to the

Yeltsin government could use the injustice frames and appeal to patriotic symbols of the shared Soviet past to gather political support for their parties and leaders.[32] Preoccupied with economic reforms and political struggles, Yeltsin's government ignored and pre-judged the symbolic aspect of politics. It was not until the celebration of the Victory Day anniversary in 1995 when some Soviet symbols (such as the red victory banner with a five-pointed yellow star) were allowed alongside the Russian tricolor.[33]

Boris Yeltsin and his ideological allies had principled reasons not to focus their time and energy on the symbolic work and the promotion of particular ideas among the Russian population, after they had gained power and control of the state. The Soviet ideological apparatus and the state-led Soviet propaganda work were seen as a thing of the past. Therefore, any centralized and government-promoted work in the field of values was deemed to be too close a reminder of the ideological department of the Central Committee of the Communist Party. Backed by the popular support that brought them to power, the Yeltsin government logically thought it was necessary to focus on economic reforms, restructuring, and the improvement of the economic livelihoods of the population. The immediate impact of economic reforms, however, was more on the destructive side, while the political communication required for explaining the expected outcomes of reforms—in the short, medium, and long term—was not available and, frankly, was not deemed important by the liberal reformers in the early 1990s.

In an interview with Olga Romanova in 2007, Egor Gaidar, Yeltsin's first prime minister, recalled:

> Many people I highly respect, including my father, told us: "What is it that you are doing? Why don't you set-up propaganda? Why don't you create the services that would explain to the population that what you are doing is right; that it is necessary for Russia?" At one point, driven by this agitation done by people, I repeat, I highly respect, I went to Boris Nikolayevich suggesting that we indeed might have to create some type of propaganda service to explain what we are doing. Do you know how Boris Nikolayevich responded? He told me: "Egor Timurovich, you want to recreate the propaganda section of the CPSU Central Committee? While I am a president, I will not allow that to happen."[34]

Boris Yeltsin, arguably for ideological reasons, personally underestimated the need for communicating to and educating the public about the market reforms. After Gaidar's departure from his position late in 1992, there was another attempt to create the information service in support of the government-led economic reforms. The presidential decree #1647, dated December 25, 1992, created the

Federal Information Center of Russia, headed by Mikhail Poltoranin. The reaction of various liberal forces in the country was ridden with fury and sarcasm, again pointing to strong an ideologically driven, anti-Soviet rationale behind the position. "The state monopoly over the information is growing stronger, not disintegrating," protested *Nezavisimaia gazeta*. "This is a ministry of propaganda with the functions that the propaganda department of the CPSU Central Committee did not even dream about," grumbled Vladimir Logunov, the editor-in-chief of *Rossiiskaia gazeta*.[35] Various other media actors, including representatives from television channels and regional and federal newspapers, were critically predisposed to this new agency that, in the end, did not survive for more than a few months.[36] It was abolished in March 1993, thus ending the government's attempt to engage in a more purposeful political communication with the public.

In this context, it is not surprising that liberal reformers in Russia appeared as "market Bolsheviks" imposing Western-style capitalism arrogantly, from above, while disregarding any public attitudes, values, and vulnerabilities.[37] We do not know retrospectively whether resolving the problem of political communication would have changed things dramatically, given the real impact of reforms on people's livelihoods, social standing, and lost identities. In his memoir, Gaidar ruminated about "working with the public" being useless during radical reforms because "nothing would have saved us from the hyperinflation and administrative chaos."[38] Gaidar himself was sacrificed to public opinion when he was fired from his position as prime minister at the end of 1992. The enrichment of the few reform winners and the rise of Russia's infamous oligarchs, who were able to influence policymaking and, indeed, to capture the state, are also facts that could not have been dealt with through political communication only.[39] Nonetheless, the technocratic arrogance with which the Yeltsin government reformers approached the reforms precluded the government from establishing new traditions of transparency and respect for public opinion, especially when such socially painful policies were concerned. Russia's nascent political institutions would have benefited if reforms had been undertaken with greater political inclusion and with a more concerted attempt to persuade the population of their purpose and necessity.[40]

By the mid-1990s, Boris Yeltsin and his government started showing more understanding of the need for symbolic work to forge Russia's new national identity. It was emblematic that on June 12, 1996, the government launched a nationwide competition for the "Russian idea." Later that year, Yeltsin decreed that the November 7th holiday that had commemorated in the Soviet Union the October Bolshevik Revolution be renamed as a Day of Accord and Reconciliation. Alas, these symbolic actions were a lost cause at that political moment. The 1996 presidential elections brought back a highly unpopular and very ill Yeltsin, who would have very likely lost to the Communist Party candidate Gennady Zyuganov were it not for a massive media campaign discrediting the Communists, along with massive electoral fraud in selected regions of the Russian Federation, evident in the second round of the election.[41] The national contest to find a new "Russian idea," organized by the government-controlled *Rossiiskaia gazeta*, did produce public discussion, but nothing more. The contest was not even brought to a conclusion, despite the formation of a jury and a promised prize in the amount of around US$15,000. Its overall political impact was negligible, and the public reaction was cynical and dismissive.

The new commemorative days, such as the new Day of Accord and Reconciliation, the Russian Independence Day celebrated on June 12 (the day of Russia's first presidential elections in 1991), and the Constitution Day celebrated on December 12, were not adopted by the public as meaningful and significant holidays. They were accepted as days off, to be sure, but they did not carry much symbolic meaning.

The symbolic struggle of the 1990s was fought more successfully by the political opposition on the left, the Communist Party (CPRF) and the nationalist, Liberal Democratic Party of Russia (LDPR). Kathleen Smith's exploration of politics surrounding the trophy art—the cultural treasures repatriated from Germany as reparations during World War II—is a good illustration of the successful mobilization of symbolic resources by the government opposition and the political problems associated with the position of the "denial" of the Soviet past.[42] The early public sentiment in 1991–1992 was full of shame, and the artworks— mostly hidden in secret depositories in Russia's central museums—were presented by some commentators to be "the last prisoners of war" and the victims of the Soviet regime.[43] The liberal government at that moment viewed the trophy art as an embarrassment, and began the work of cataloguing the works and planning their return to the rightful owners.[44]

This early work was stalled in 1994 when the nationalist LDPR, the Communists, and the Agrarian Party deputies in the Duma, newly emboldened by their political success in the 1993 parliamentary elections, created an uproar over the government's plans to return the trophies. To prevent the transfers of these items, they adopted a new bill mandating that all these cultural treasures become Russian property.[45] The main arguments used by the opposition appealed to the Soviet losses during World War II and the unmatched Soviet efforts in bringing a victorious end to the war. Given the symbolic significance and the emotional resonance of World War II in nearly all families in Russia (where the war is better known as a Great Patriotic War that started with the Nazi invasion of the Soviet Union on June 22, 1941), these arguments, emphasizing a heroic Soviet past, had a much better chance of resonating with the public. Unsurprisingly, neither the early moral maximalism in the liberal camp, nor their later market pragmatism that sought to exchange these cultural treasures in return for some type of aid, became popular. This big symbolic clash—of patriotism based on negating one's own past, while working on a new future, and patriotism based on a heroic past— was resolved, in this case, in favor of a heroic past. As Smith argues, "Untarnished memories of victory in World War II proved to be an excellent rallying point for Communist patriots."[46] The liberal self-flagellation did not appeal to people.

Michael Urban analyzed this symbolic clash as a case of politics of reciprocal non-recognition between the liberal reformers and their opposition, in which neither side was willing to recognize the legitimate place of the other in the political spectrum. Each side instead was engaged in deploying "the language and symbols of the past [. . .] against their opponents" and in "blame-laying in the name of the nation thereby foreclose[ing] the possibility for dialogue . . ." and throwing themselves into "a pattern of irresolvable conflict."[47] Urban saw political communication strategies selected by the Russian elites to be at the root of the political instability of the 1990s. "It appears in the contemporary Russian context that the root categories of prevailing discourse have disabled those instrumental-strategic activities ostensibly aimed at negotiation, compromise, and consensus. Such forms of strategic action have been systematically subverted by a discourse of identity that binds its participants into a pattern of irresolvable conflict."[48]

One can blame the communicative codes and the discursive choices made by the elites. One can also look into the material and social outcomes of the reforms to explain why Yeltsin's liberal government lost to the opposition on symbolic issues such as the war trophy return.[49] The public disappointment with these reforms was shared by around two-thirds of the population in Russia, who were struggling to adjust to the new realities, according to opinion polls conducted by the Public Opinion Foundation (FOM) in 1996–1997.[50] The combination of these antagonistic discursive choices made by political actors and the material conditions experienced by the majority of Russians meant that the liberal establishment behind the reforms did not allow any political space for the legitimate articulation of the interests of those who lost in the transition. Those who tried to do that, such as Russia's new Communist Party, led by Gennady Zyuganov, were painted into dark colors mostly through their association with the darkest periods of Soviet communism (the Gulag, Red Terror, etc.).[51]

The media played an important role in this process. This subject—of how the media of the 1990s played into what happened in Russia in the early 2000s—still requires its own authoritative storyteller. Russian journalist Nataliya Rostova, herself a well-known reporter from the field, is among those spearheading such efforts, albeit from outside Russia at the moment. In her online project, yeltsin-media.com, focused on the Russian media of the 1990s, she reveals that the post-Soviet Russian media had no notion of objectivity and was mostly one-sided, with a strong liberal bias, reflected in silencing or ridiculing the opposing views. Unable to voice their views directly through mainstream TV channels, on June 12, 1992, the opposition parties organized a protest action, walking to Ostankino television tower in Moscow to demand access to federal media. The negotiations did not bring any clear resolution, and some protesters stayed there for the next 12 days (after which they were disbursed by the police).[52] The struggle for media control intensified in October 1993, at the height of the confrontation between the presidential and parliamentary branches of power in Russia.[53] Media control and manipulation were essential for the outcomes of the 1996 presidential elections. Rostova argues that the current media environment in Putin's Russia can be traced to the decisions and policies in this sphere taken by the Kremlin in the fateful year of 1996 in connection with the perceived need (economic elites had) to re-elect Boris Yeltsin.[54]

Masha Slonim, another journalist covering Russia in the 1990s for BBC, shared her impressions as follows:

> The Russian journalism of the 1990s is passionate journalism; journalists could not distance themselves from the events, the way BBC journalists would and are expected to by the BBC. This related to everyone. The journalists were not able to maintain objectivity and neutrality during the 1996 election as well. [...] At any moment when there are barricades on the streets, journalists here take sides.[55]

Collective Identity, Emotions, and Self-Verification

The social bonds that make groups are *affective* in nature. Emotions are fundamental to thinking about who we are, what distinguishes us from others, and what values, beliefs, and collective experiences we share, cherish, and commemorate. Among various social bonds, the national ones have proven, in the last two centuries, to be the most powerful and most emotionally charged form of group solidarity. In his *Imagined Communities*, Benedict Anderson brilliantly observed that "nations inspire love and often profoundly self-sacrificing love";[56] "conceived as a deep, horizontal comradeship [...] it is this fraternity that makes it possible, over the past two centuries, for so many millions of people, not so much to kill, as willingly to die for such limited imaginings."[57] Russian sociologist Elena Trubina also noted that "[i]f a sense of belonging is constitutive for one's formation, it is the sense of national belonging that continues to be the predominant one. [...] the nation is always there—or so it seems. Generations of politicians and intellectuals worked hard to naturalize the national frames of reference to the extent that 'the nation' becomes the only way to imagine a community! Every imagination of a community becomes overcoded as a nation."[58]

To understand the state of Russian society in the 1990s in terms of people's collective identity, we need to comprehend the emotional repercussions of the identity they have lost. Throughout its 70 years of rule, the Soviet leadership invested massive resources into consolidating the Soviet nation by constructing and reconstructing the image of the enemy of the Soviet system, as well as by providing positive markers for nurturing a sense of Soviet exceptionalism. The conflict with the outside capitalist surrounding (propagated in Stalin's era using the term "capitalist encirclement") was fundamental to the identity of the Soviet state. Who precisely the enemy was changed, depending on the nature of geopolitical challenges attended to by the Soviet leadership. But the enemy was always there.

Not surprisingly, the surveys conducted by the Levada Center in 1989 pointed to the Soviet identity as the most important collective identity for the Soviet citizens; 29% of respondents acknowledged the Soviet identity with pride; it was only second to the identity of a parent, proudly acknowledged by 43% of the respondents.[59]

The Soviet citizens' self-categorization as citizens of the Soviet state worked to promote emotions that were driven by appraisals and concerns that are nationally, rather than individually based.[60] Some of these appraisals of the national self were driven by the sense of Soviet superiority, deeply engrained through education and other social and political institutions tightly controlled by the Soviet state. The closed nature of the Soviet informational space, the censorship of the media, and the tightly controlled education process, as well as extensive propaganda in the workplace through party cells, ensured that the Soviet identity—i.e., the set of meanings attached to being a Soviet citizen—was continuously defined, regulated, and verified by Soviet media and institutions.

Soviet citizens were not driven by national concerns in their everyday life. The atomization of the Soviet society and people fending for themselves in a challenging context of the economy of shortages is a well-established fact.[61] The national identification became salient and central when people had a chance to confront the outside world, and this was very rare. But it would be a mistake not to recognize the significance of that identification (even if it might have been latent most of the time)[62] and the success with which the Soviet system instilled pride and patriotism in the Soviet public and embedded the regime's lofty goals and propaganda messages in the souls of ordinary citizens.

Of course, Soviet society was not fully homogenous. There were groups that were discriminated against by the state, such as the Jews, who were not allowed into particular higher education institutions and were restricted in employment opportunities.[63] There were political dissident groups that were repressed for being involved in the publication and dissemination of underground literature prohibited by the state.[64] The Soviet Union also had its own "orient"—the Central Asian peoples and cultures that were viewed to be culturally backward and inferior to the more advanced Russians. The same applied to the ethnic minorities in the Russian Soviet Federative Socialist Republic (RSFSR). As articulated by Ted Hopf, who advanced one of the best analyses of the post–World War II Soviet identities, "Russians were understood as the privileged carriers of the modern Soviet future to the less developed non-Russians."[65] The titular groups in the Baltic Republics—Estonia, Latvia, and Lithuania—the victims of the 1939 Molotov-Ribbentrop Act—also were different, with a much greater propensity and desire to resist the Soviet state propaganda. The members of these groups mobilized based on their non-Soviet nationalist, religious, and political identities, and developed more nonconformist attitudes toward the Soviet system.[66] Nonetheless, at large, and particularly within the RSFSR, Soviet society was a success story from the point of view of national consolidation and integration. The Soviet community was integrated along the lines of Soviet patriotism and a sense of belonging to something unique, exceptional, and everlasting: the Soviet nation. As Alexei Yurchak aptly put it in the title of his book, "everything was forever [. . .]."[67] The Soviet state was an "eternal state," or so it seemed to Soviet citizens, many of whom were stunned and shocked with the changes occurring under Gorbachev, as Yurchak illustrates in the opening to his book.[68]

Identity construction is an ongoing process. Identities are continually reproduced, negotiated, changed, or contested. Identity scholars have argued that an important part of this process could be captured using the term *self-verification*, or the tendency for people to seek confirmation of their self-views. People act "so as to bring perceived self-relevant meanings in a situation (based in part on feedback from others and in part on direct perception of the environment) into congruency with the meanings contained in their identity standards."[69] This means, more simply, that any information is selected and processed in such a way as to confirm preexisting beliefs and frames. In such a tightly controlled society as the Soviet one, the process of constant "verification" of the Soviet identity was organized by the Soviet system through education, media, and other state institutions, such as the Soviet army, state enterprises, and all other Soviet institutions. The Soviet collapse and the abandonment of Soviet ideology, along with political and social institutions propping up the Soviet identity, meant that the newly emerging Russian society lost the key symbols and meanings orienting their collective self. The entirety of the symbolic order underpinning societal consolidation and integration collapsed. What is more, it was not a natural disaster. It resulted from an intentional political action and involved active ideological criticism and opposition. As discussed earlier, Russia's new government followed an ideologically anti-communist line, making de-Stalinization and, starting in 1992, marketization into its central ideological pillars. The economic and social shock, destitution, and disorientation among large groups in the society created a strong pull toward political opposition that operated in a polarized political space.

The symbolic collapse—intangible as it is—went unnoticed, at first, as the society went through the whirlwind of economic and social change. Only with time was the phenomenon of the normative void that emerged in place of Soviet-era social values, norms, and beliefs acknowledged and decried. The sense of nostalgia for the Soviet era then came to dominate the public space, reflected in the revival of Soviet forms and aesthetics.[70] The cultural, social, and political repercussions of this void are lasting until now, reflected in the linkages between the painful transition experienced by Russian society and the societal vulnerability and openness to the political legitimation strategy based on overcoming the role of "victim" that Russia presumably experienced in the 1990s.

Russia of the 1990s through Opinion Polls and the Box Office

Public opinion polls from the 1990s speak loudly to the conditions of cultural disorientation and a widespread sense of instability and uncertainty. The Levada Center scholars reported, based on their polls, that in September 1995, for example, only 3% of the respondents in nationwide polls considered the situation in Russia as "calm and favorable;" 60% viewed it as "strained/stressful," and 29% as critical and explosive. The opinion polls also reveal that the population did not see "the light at the end of the tunnel" and believed that "the events are bringing the situation to the dead end";[71] 59% of respondents did not think that their situation would improve in the near future.[72] In 1996, 64% of FOM (Foundation for Public Opinion) poll respondents thought that they could not adapt to current realities and that their living standards were worse than they were before the reforms. Only 8% thought that their living standards were better, while 23% felt that they had adapted and lived up to the standards they had before.[73]

Public opinion polls normally try to get at public attitudes, not emotions and sentiments. But there are some polls that have tried to measure the emotional aspect of public life in Russia. Levada scholars specifically have described the prevailing social mood in the 1990s as one characterized by confusion, anxiety, depression, and fear for the future.

Confusion

The Soviet Union disappeared overnight. On December 26, 1991, the inhabitants of Russia's territory woke up in a new country. Just a few weeks later, in January 1992, Yeltsin's new government, led by liberal reformer Yegor Gaidar, took the country on a rollercoaster ride of market liberalization and privatization in the absence of preexisting knowledge about the market and market-supporting institutions, and in the context of a fiscal and monetary crisis reflected in shortages of food and other everyday necessities. The painful adjustment and the economic and social dislocation that followed have been analyzed using the term "economic involution," referring to defensive strategies of retreating to a primitive domestic economy.[74] But losing jobs and incomes was only one, material side of these losses. On the symbolic side, people faced challenges associated with their diverse social identities. The formerly respected professions—of teachers, doctors, scientists, and engineers—lost the symbolic value attributed to them, along with the compensation required to live a normal life. The financial pressures forced many professionals to leave their jobs and join the "shuttle traders" migrating back and forth between Russia and China, Turkey, Poland, or another country—to bring merchandise to sell at open-air markets—trying a new identity and a new life.

In *Secondhand Time: The Last of the Soviets* (2015), Svetlana Alexievich gathered many stories of disillusionment, struggle to adapt, poverty, and a profound shift in values in the post-Soviet society: "Libraries and theaters emptied out. They were replaced by bazaars and retail stores."[75] A story told by one of her interviewees whose mother was hospitalized first in 1991 and then, later, around 1995 was very revealing. In 1991 the hospital patients entertained themselves with stories about Stalin, Bukharin, and the death of Kirov. The second time around—in the mid-90s—the center stage was taken by the wife of a big businessman and her stories of a huge apartment, domestic servants, foreign vacations, boutique shopping, jewelry, etc.[76]

One of my interviewees in Samara in November 2016 reconstructed her sense of confusion as follows:

> In the beginning of the 1990s, when the Soviet Union collapsed and the country fragmented into small pieces, people did not know what to do. Just a moment ago they had everything: stability, a place to live, free schools and kindergartens for their kids, and so on. This all ended. A different epoch started when people divided into rich and poor. Many people lost their jobs. My parents worked in a Maslennikov factory and they simply lost their jobs. You could see that some people earned a lot through shuttle trade. It produced jealousy because not everyone could do that. Some people could not.

Professional identities were not the only ones to be compromised and sometimes lost entirely in this transition. Russian citizens had to face the challenge of losing their Soviet collective identity and to find new symbolic resources to define what it meant to be a citizen of the new Russia. But the new symbols—besides the growing significance of money—were not there. Instead, there was a void—the condition of "symbolic shortage" and "speechlessness."[77] The new Russians did not know how to define themselves in positive terms. They could only tell who they were not.[78]

Public opinion polls on foreign policy issues reveal this loss of orientation and the destabilization of the Russian citizens' national identity. Public responses on the issue of NATO expansion are especially telling. Some 35%–39% of respondents selected "hard to answer" (*zatrudniaius' otvetit'*) when confronted in 1996–1997 with the question about their preferences on Russia's policy vis-à-vis NATO. The normally residual "hard to answer" option was a preferred response for more than a third of Russian citizens not sure what to think on this issue at the moment when NATO was expanding to include the former Soviet republics in the Baltics. The remaining respondents picked one of five other alternatives, ranging between "Russia should oppose NATO expansion" to "Russia should become a part of NATO" to "Russia should not oppose NATO expansion."[79] But again, almost 40% of Russian citizens did not know what to think about NATO anymore! No, this was not about NATO. They did not know what to think about Russia.

Fear, Anxiety, and Despair

Throwing an entire civilization into a dustbin of history was painful.[80] A sense of confusion about what it meant to be a Russian in this new country coexisted alongside feelings of uncertainty, anxiety, and fear about the future. The new state did not guarantee employment or a pension anymore, the job one had did not guarantee a regular salary, the salary did not guarantee a decent life, and savings did not guarantee the stable future that one might have hoped for, given that one's life savings could be wiped out overnight as a result of government reforms. The 1992 Pavlov reforms and the 1998 financial crisis were just different moments in the state of a permanent crisis people had to learn to live with.[81] The 1998 financial crisis created a sense of profound disillusionment with liberal reforms, while the 1999 terrorist bombings and the war in Chechnya added a new sense of vulnerability. Levada polls conducted in October and December 1999 and March 2000 showed that 52%–63% of Russians felt anxiety in relation to the events in Chechnya.[82]

The sociologists associated with the Levada Center referred to the new condition that emerged in Russian society as "asthenic syndrome," characterized by mass apathy, various phobias, and a sense of vulnerability and lack of control over the ongoing events and processes.[83] The widespread interest in esoteric ideas, conspiracy theories, and the occult, evident to anyone who visited Russian bookstores or read the Russian prose of that time, could be seen as a reflection of these social anxieties and apocalyptic visions of the approaching millennium.[84] Popular writers such as Viktor Pelevin and the more serious, philosophical, and geopolitical works by Alexander Dugin, the famous far-right conservative analyst, who moved from the fringes of the Russian public space to a more visible position around 2014–2016, mashed up occultism and mysticism in their work.[85] Some commentators saw these trends as a response to the spiritual vacuum left after the end of Communism.[86]

Serguei Oushakine, a Russian-born Princeton anthropologist, studied the reaction to painful transition in Russia of the 1990s through in-depth interviews in the Siberian city of Barnaul. Based on his study, he advanced a concept of "patriotism of despair," suggesting that Russians reacted to these conditions by building new "communities of hope" united by their "vocabulary of shared pain."[87] This account of integrative trends in the society, present already in the 1990s, also works to underscore the sense of despair as a shared feeling among the Russian people.

Shame

Many Russians felt shame in the 1990s and the early 2000s. Levada opinion polls reported that a vast majority of their respondents were ashamed of their economic conditions. Responding to the question "What are you ashamed of, what makes you feel shame and regret when you think about Russian history of the 20th century?" the majority of respondents (79%) in January 1999 selected the following answer: "We're a great people, a rich country always living in poverty and misery."[88] The second most popular response in that poll showed that 48% of respondents felt shame about the collapse of the USSR. In 1996 and 2003, 80%–81% of respondents agreed (fully or partially) with the statement that "the things that are currently happening in Russia make me feel shame for it." It is telling that this number dropped to 52% in 2012, 20% in 2014, and 18% in 2015.[89]

Many people today remember the humanitarian aid received by Russia in the early 1990s from the United States and Western Europe. One can only imagine how adults who had grown up in the Soviet Union, taught from kindergarten age that they represented the greatest country on Earth, might have felt when they found themselves relying on American military food supplies left over from the Gulf War.[90] Even if they did not realize the precise sources of this aid (and after all, these were diverse sources), looking into that "collective mirror" must have been hurtful, humiliating, and shameful. How could it not be? There is little surprise in expecting such reaction on the part of people brought up on the rhetoric of helping other developing countries, and building a bright future for their children. They found themselves at the mercy of the countries that had been criticized earlier as the source of all the evil in the world.

Still, one might say that public opinion polls are not always the best barometers of sentiments in the society given that there is preference falsification and social desirability bias.[91] Cultural studies that focus on cultural production—literature, film, and visual arts—can sometimes produce a more perceptive understanding of the dominant sentiments and aspirations buried in the collective imagination of a nation. Cultural production, on the one hand, expresses and channels the emotional energy contained in a collective in relation to the shared experiences people go through; and, on the other hand, such expression (and revelation) allows the group members to collectively discuss and work through them. Film studies, in particular, can serve as a powerful tool to examine the collective psyche because films and, more specifically, the degree of public resonance with actors, characters, and depictions in specific films allow the researchers to view specific films as a mirror into collective desires and fantasies.[92] The emotional resonance with specific films could not be faked and is not affected by the social desirability bias. Such resonance could be interpreted as a good sign that specific films reflect the emotional state of the society.

Yana Hashamova analyzed a selection of Russian post-Soviet films to study Russian citizens' imagination of the West, drawing important linkages to the dynamics of Russian national identity (2007). Her analysis of Alexei Balabanov's *Brat 2* (2000), among many other Russian films, posits this film to represent, in a very crystallized fashion, Russians' main fantasies as well as their national anxieties and their wounded national pride. This film clearly divides the world into "us" versus "them," demonizing the West and promoting the image of a morally superior Russian identity. This film, a sequel to *Brat* (1997), created a cult character and a national hero, Danila, presented by Hashamova as a Russian Robin Hood.[93] This most popular and most resonant post-Soviet film has been treated as prophetic and revelational of societal hidden fears and aspirations that were brought to life in the real-life politics of Putinism and Vladimir Putin's heroic image.[94] *Brat 2* expressed loudly and clearly that by 2000 the Russian people were waiting for a group savior and a national hero.

To reiterate, the collapse of the Soviet system and the corresponding devaluation and marginalization of the basic values, ideas, identities, and institutions that comprised Soviet civilization represented an existential blow to the collective identity of the majority of Soviet citizens. The psychological shock associated with the loss of this identity and the radical social and economic changes had numerous ramifications and were expressed through fears, anxieties, shame, despair, and longing for a hero. The negation of the widely accepted and taken for granted positive self-views associated with Soviet identity was psychologically unsettling. After all, for a majority of Soviet citizens, even if they might have complained about various aspects of Soviet life, Soviet society was the only one they really knew. Many people incorporated beliefs that their Soviet state was on the "right" side of history—on the side of historical progress. Losing these beliefs hurt. The ramifications of such loss was captured by some Russian sociologists through the concept of "negative identity."

Could Identity Be Negative? Could Culture and Society Be Traumatized?

Based on public opinion polls in the 1990s, the sociologists of the Levada Center advanced a new concept of *negative identity* to capture the state of collective attitudes, identifications, and predispositions in Russia. The head of the Levada Center, Lev Gudkov, defined this concept as a particular mode of self-constitution (self-definition) that uses the opposite, the "Other," to define the self "reflected in the negation of some qualities and values of the Other as something alien, repelling, scaring, threatening and personifying everything that is unacceptable for the group or community members."[95] In short, negative identity reflected the absence of positive symbols and identifiers that Russian citizens could use to describe their sense of belonging. Gudkov and other sociologists from the Levada Center working in the tradition of Yuri Levada, the founder of this center, thought that this feature of negative identification in Russia of the 1990s represented a direct legacy of *homo sovieticus*—the model of the Soviet man constructed during the Soviet period.[96]

Yuri Levada himself recognized that the process of "differention," i.e., using the "other/s" to define the "I/we," accompanies any identification process and is universal. But he also highlighted that the demonstrative opposition of the Soviet Union—its political system, culture, science, and other aspects of Soviet life—to the outside world was very much engrained in Soviet life and was internalized by the citizens.[97] Levada shared Gudkov's argument that such tradition shaped the identification processes in post-Soviet Russia as well.

Michael Urban's conception of the "nation against itself," discussed a little earlier, points to a different source of these problems.[98] The negation of the Soviet past in Russia could not be displaced onto and blamed on the "other" due to the country's role as the main successor of the Soviet Union.[99] Instead, it was circulated through communicative codes and discursive practices that predominated

among the Russian elites in the 1990s, as different political contenders undermined each other's subject positions (and, thereby, their very right to existence).
These discursive choices, shaped by political opportunities in a country with its
given history and political culture, meant that the politics of the 1990s never produced a societal and political consensus integrating opposing political forces into
the institutional framework, legitimating all of its players. It was a political war
where the opposing party was an enemy to be destroyed and not an adversary
with whom one could compromise.[100]

Other scholars explored these negative identity aspects in Russia of the 1990s
using different theories and approaches. Sergei Oushakine introduced the concepts of *symbolic shortage* and *discursive impotence* characterizing a society that
lives in the state of emergency "near the ruins."[101] Oushakine, who interviewed
members of the first post-Soviet generation cohort (mostly students) in one of
Russia's Siberian cities, suggested that young Russians, who mostly identified
themselves as post-Soviet, were feeling "lost" between the "old Soviet" and the
"new Russian." They did not identify with either of these poles and could not
"find a proper symbol, a proper signifier to represent their post-Soviet location."
The members of this new generation did not have a clear idea as to the direction they were going. The post-Soviet *transitionality* "does not provide any cues
about the direction to follow, it does not channel one's identificatory process."[102]
Oushakine draws symbolic parallels between the wordless post-Soviet anthem
and his respondents' inability to find proper signifiers to represent their "post-
Soviet" location. Oushakine's argument resonated with the work of Russian
social psychologist Nina Naumova (whom Oushakine quotes in his text) about
speechlessness characterizing Russian society of the 1990s (*bezmolstvuyushchaya
kul'tura*). She viewed this condition as a reaction to the instability of the post-
Soviet period and lack of a sense of belonging to a social group.[103]

There were other, cultural expressions of anxiety and despair noticed by
Russia observers. Elliot Borenstein's *Overkill: Sex and Violence in Contemporary
Russian Popular Culture* (2008) looked at the explosion of public discourse about
sex, deviance, and violence (frequently referred to as *chernukha* and *bespredel*).
Borenstein argued that this was a cultural reaction to the crisis of transition that
could not be appropriated by an individual mind but could, in such cultural
form, express the intensity of the "bespredel." Russian cinematography conveyed
this reality well. The Russian director Alexei Balabanov (maker of the aforementioned *Brat 2*) was, arguably, the best in depicting the 1990s. His *Brat* (1997),
Zhmurki (*Dead Man's Bluff*, 2005), and *Kochegar* (*The Stoker*, 2010) showed most
vividly the absence of social norms and regulations and the lost value of human
life in Russia of the 1990s.

Such social and cultural context could also be understood using the term *moral void* or *anomie* as discussed by Emile Durkheim (2005), "a derangement of collective representations, a situation in which morals and standards are 'upside down,' such that the lower pole of *homo duplex* rules over the higher."[104] The psychological aspects of such moral void are sometimes analyzed using the term cultural trauma.[105] However different were the terms and approaches used by cultural theorists, sociologists, social psychologists, and anthropologists, most scholars interpreted these cultural expressions as symptoms of the traumatic process Russian society was undergoing in the 1990s.

But can we psychoanalyze a traumatized society as psychologists analyze traumatized individuals? What implications would such analysis have? After all, an individual psychoanalysis is based on a subject that, presumably, wants to solve his or her problems and deal with his or her psychological traumas. How do groups and societies deal with trauma? Even if observers might try to diagnose a group with specific syndromes, it is quite unlikely that there is a clear course of action that could be recommended from the outside (of the sort that a psychologist could recommend to his/her patients). It would be, in the least, too patronizing, even if imaginable. Such things as national pride, patriotism, and social identification processes, along with the absence of a single subject to deal with these issues, preclude any "therapy" suggestions.

The trauma paradigm I rely on in this study to address these questions is constructivist in that it views collective trauma not as an event or a happening, but a result of social construction whereby an event becomes *perceived* as a trauma. The constructivist approach to collective trauma allows for studying the dynamics of group transformation in response to perceived collective trauma by exploring the issue of *leadership*. Group identity and cohesiveness are constructed in the process of leader-follower interaction. Furthermore, the construction of the collective trauma itself—i.e., building the narrative around how a specific event has affected the group—is undertaken and supported by group leaders—political and cultural, official and unofficial—who can help the group come to terms with its past.

Vladimir Putin built his political strategy on astute and, potentially, sincere understanding of the state of symbolic loss and normative breakdown that Russian citizens experienced after the collapse of the Soviet Union. The structures of meaning making up Soviet citizens' worldview—about who they were, about the nature of the community they were part of, about the social goals and purposes of this community—were shattered in the 1990s. A sense of belonging to a community characterized by positive distinction, special meaning, purpose, and efficacy had vanished, replaced by a sense of belonging to a community that had collapsed, fragmenting along the imperial lines drawn by force and manipulation;

dragged into social and economic chaos and hardship by incompetent politicians and greedy entrepreneurs; marginalized by territorial neighbors and snubbed by former competitors.

The country was looking for a group savior, and Vladimir Putin worked to fit this role. The moment of the annexation of Crimea in 2014 and the few years that followed thereafter represented a high point of that fit, with the majority of the Russian people recognizing in Putin's persona a leader they wanted to be proud of.

PART THREE

Of Media and Opinion-Makers

Top-Down Sociopolitical Construction in

Putin's Russia

This book's journey has taken the reader, so far, through the late Soviet period and the formative era of the 1990s, highlighting the challenges that Russian society has confronted as a community and as a group. This historical excursus into the changing societal context and the degree of real and metaphysical shock that Russian society has undergone after the Soviet collapse is imperative for understanding where people come from and what their expected reactions to various political messages might be. But it is no less important to look into how these experiences have been represented—in the cultural and political realms—because the specific representations, interpretations, and explanations of events, placed in a broader context, shape public opinion and the dominant view of reality. Who exercises control over these representations and how pluralistically the cultural and communicative spheres in a country are constructed are important indicators of the balance between the state and society, a sign of who is in the driver's seat in this relationship. Understanding the cognitive embeddedness, the emotional resonance, and the shared nature of specific representations alerts us to the difficulty of changing specific frames and discursive formations and, therefore, politics that might rely on them for their legitimation.

5

Constructing the Collective Trauma
of the 1990s

In the 90s people turned up dead,
And they ran the streets buck naked.
Absolutely naked.
There was no electricity,
Only fights for jeans with coca-cola.
—MONETOCHKA (2018)

POLITICAL LEADERSHIP REQUIRES emotional intelligence. The ability to connect with followers at a deeper, emotional level helps leaders to be seen as legitimate and trusted representatives of the political community they are part of. Such ability also helps in gaining support for specific actions and policies, when policy justification is built on emotional resonance. The meaningful connections are constructed and maintained through political communication and are supported through cultural production and media. Those seeking to build such connections rely on shared ideas and beliefs deriving from shared lived experiences and underpinned by emotions generated by those experiences.[1] The paths of such emotional connection could be different. For the current Russian government and, specifically, Russia's president Vladimir Putin, an important point of emotional connection was constructed through the shared vision of the 1990s.

For the adult Russian population—or anyone who is older than 40—the most meaningful and consequential period is the experience of living through the collapse of the Soviet Union and the birth of a new Russia. This experience has been commonly captured and expressed through the umbrella term *likhie devianostye* (the wild nineties), which contains, for many people, predominantly negative memories and connotations. The widely shared belief that Russia of the 1990s was a place of disorder, criminality, impoverishment, and a very weak, collapsing state, functions today as a cognitive frame that colors political imagination and shapes Russian citizens' political judgment. This frame underpins the societal fears of liberal and any other reforms and shapes popular preferences for

The Red Mirror. Gulnaz Sharafutdinova, Oxford University Press (2020). © Oxford University Press.
DOI: 10.1093/oso/9780197502938.001.0001.

stability and non-revolutionary political change. From a cognitive perspective, this frame represents an internalized and normalized heuristic that underpins the "fast thinking" processes used for political orientation and opinion formation by millions of Russians.[2] The central and defining element of shared beliefs in Putin's Russia today, it enables the continuing legitimation of the political system, which draws on the impulse to overcome the legacy of the 1990s as if it were a bottomless well. By now, this frame represents a powerful national victimhood frame that constitutes the Russian community as a political entity. Presumably, it entitles the Russian nation to self-righteous assertions directed against those who are seen as "victimizers."[3]

The public perceptions of the 1990s in Russia could be analyzed using the concept of a "chosen trauma," a term introduced by political psychiatrist Vamik Volkan to capture "the shared mental representation of an event in a large group's history in which the group suffered a catastrophic loss, humiliation, and help-lessness at the hands of enemies."[4] Such an event becomes mythologized and deeply intertwined with a group's sense of self.[5] "Chosen trauma" is a powerful identity marker, enabling those sharing this vision to emotionally connect with each other. "Chosen trauma" is the twin sister of a "chosen glory," a shared vision about events that speak to exceptional heroism and greatness of the large group. "Chosen glory" provides the positive pillar for group consolidation, propagating emotions of pride and hope for a political community. "Chosen trauma" unites through shared pain, connecting people based on common suffering and provid-ing a sense of entitlement and claims vis-à-vis the responsible "other" (i.e., who-ever or whatever is considered to be the source of the group's problems).

Under Vladimir Putin's leadership, the Kremlin has used both of these identity-building and group-consolidating ideational devices. In the Russian political context, the place of a "chosen glory" is taken up by Russia's victory in the Great Patriotic War (the Eastern front of World War II). The mythologizing and commemoration of victory in this war has reached massive proportions in the last decade and a half, and the intensity of this commemoration has been growing as the political space narrowed down.[6] "The Great Victory," "the victori-ous people" (народ победитель), "Holy Russia," "God-bearing people" (народ богоносец)—these labels are used publicly and insistently on Russian TV and in newspapers and online media outlets—positioning Russia, God, and the "Great Victory" side by side and providing people with faith, patriotism, and a sense of self-righteousness. The opinion poll conducted by the Levada Center in January 2017 found that the victory in the Great Patriotic War is seen as the main his-torical event that elicits national pride among 83% of respondents.[7] Russians have placed this "great victory" at the top of this scale since 1999.[8] Putin's govern-ment has long realized the legitimizing potential of the war and has built on that potential. The Kremlin's attention to victory parades and the appropriation of the "Immortal Regiment" march, which started as a grassroots initiative in 2012 in Tomsk and turned into an officially organized march with millions within and outside Russia joining the procession, is an important example of this trend.[9]

The significance of World War II and Russia's victory in the Great Patriotic War to the Kremlin's symbolic politics today is widely recognized. Lev Gudkov highlighted its role as the only positive symbol that works to consolidate the Russian nation today. The growing symbolic role of the war became especially clear against the background of the erosion of other Soviet subjects of national pride, i.e., Soviet achievements in space exploration, science and technology, education, industrialization, and the status of the Soviet Union as a superpower.[10] Historian Elizabeth Wood has illustrated the great lengths to which Putin's presidential administration has gone to celebrate the victory. Wood argues that "by making the war a personal event and also a sacred one, Vladimir Putin has created a myth and a ritual that elevates him personally, uniting Russia (at least theoretically) and showing him as the natural hero-leader, the warrior who is personally associated with defending the Motherland."[11] Such symbolic politics has had intense popular appeal. It was supported by a wider "ethos of triumphalism that has swept Russian cinema and television (as well as popular history) recentering war, especially World War II as an unrivaled domain for inculcating national pride."[12] For Russians, war is a central part of who they are, argued Gregory Carleton, a professor of Russian studies at Tufts University in his recent book, *Russia: The Story of War* (2017).

Some analysts link this "chosen glory" to historical amnesia and a "strange selectivity" about the Soviet past that deter honest society-wide discussions about Soviet state violence against its own society. Dina Khapaeva, a Russian-born scholar of cultural studies, has argued that the mythologizing of the Great Patriotic War has obstructed honest reflection about the Soviet past. The war played a central role in strengthening the Soviet state and in the process of Soviet nation-building; "World War II became a 'myth of origins' that legitimized the Soviet state and the identity of the Soviet people," she argued. [13] Today, the centrality of the "sacred war" in mass consciousness as a symbol of national unity and strength indeed might work to displace other moments of Soviet history to the more shadowed spaces in collective memory.

While the glory element of Russia's national myth-making has been widely discussed by commentators within and outside Russia, the element of the "chosen trauma" and the extent to which it has been prioritized and has become the foundation for the Kremlin's policy choices and policy justifications in the elite political discourse still have not received the attention the topic deserves.[14] Most discussions of trauma in the Russian context relate to the Soviet-era trauma of

Stalinism and totalitarianism and the urgent need to integrate this painful past into public debates.[15] The trauma paradigm posits that the mass crimes of totalitarianism have traumatized Russia's collective psyche, but that Russian society has not yet developed a national consensus about the crimes of the past of the type that exists, for example, in relation to the trauma of the Holocaust. According to Alexander Etkind, the absence of closure about mass terror in Russia is reflected in the phenomenon of "warped mourning" illustrated through literary and artistic creations as well as films.[16] In "the land of the unburied," the unspeakable and unknowable past enters the present through ghosts, zombies, and other monstrous images brought to life in literary and other creative works.[17]

The debates about the selective memory of the Soviet past and the phenomenon of historical amnesia in regard to state violence are indeed essential from the point of view of Russia's future political and social development. It is hard to imagine a promising future for Russian society if the system of values in relation to state-society relationships and the sanctity of individual life are overshadowed by the centrality of the state, rather than the community and its individual members. Russia sorely needs these debates. But the intellectual and cultural elites *who live in Russia* have to be the driving force in these debates, lest one could be charged with trying to impose a value change on the society from the outside. Only if domestically inspired, such a quest might create the opening for ordinary Russian citizens to dig into their family histories and confront—in the majority of cases—the painful truth of innocent family members having faced the wrath of the Soviet system. Media attention to individual cases, such as that of Denis Karagodin, a resident of Tomsk, who investigated FSB archives in relation to his grandfather, who was imprisoned in 1937 and was shot in 1938, and published all relevant documents and findings on karagodin.org, is undoubtedly a step in this direction.[18]

The intellectual focus on the Soviet trauma misses the extent to which the "trauma" paradigm has been captured by the Kremlin and developed into the vision of the trauma of the 1990s that resonated intensely with the Russian public. The Kremlin made, at first, a strategic bet on a specific representation of the 1990s as an electoral tool. The public resonance of this narrative, however, enhanced the political expediency of turning this narrative into a lasting legitimation frame that was systematically reinforced and disseminated through the state-controlled media. Any attempts to reignite the issue of the Soviet-era Stalinist trauma in Russia—with the aim of "learning the lessons of the past"—confront and compete with this emotionally resonant narrative about the 1990s. The issue of the Soviet state terror thereby becomes overshadowed and minimized in the context of public views of the more proximate 1990s as the darkest period in their recent national history.

Some Russians are more receptive to this frame than others. Age matters, as I illustrate later in this chapter. Those who experienced a harsh period of shock therapy, struggling to adjust to the new market economy while needing to provide for a family, raise kids, change professions and jobs—especially in regions and localities other than Moscow, regions that did not experience the boom and where economic and financial resources were lacking—would arguably have the most lasting impressions of this period. How they view the personal outcomes of this adjustment process would also likely matter. If they see themselves as "winners" of the transition, if they were able to grow and develop—personally and professionally—then they are more likely to look back at the 1990s with nostalgia, as a period of limitless possibilities, openness, and growth. If they have lost from market reforms, if their struggles did not bring them to the point of being proud of their achievements, if they still find themselves in a perpetual struggle for survival, then they are likely to blame the transition and the period associated with it. At the same time, for all those who have actually experienced this decade, it is likely to be a much more complex and colorful picture, combining contradictory elements; those who grew up under Putin and the Kremlin-promoted frame of the 1990s, on the other hand, are more likely to see the period through clichéd images associated with Balabanov's *Brat 2*, depicted so brightly in Monetochka's song about the 1990s.

Today there are signs that intellectual and cultural elites in Russia recognize the importance of the 1990s, and there are attempts to reframe this era.[19] What conditions are required to bring a wider public resonance to the new, more positive, vision of the 1990s is an open and difficult question. It is not surprising that the negative framing is more resonant with the "losers" of the transition. The "winners"—however defined—could, of course, buy more easily into the argument of "no pain, no gain," especially if this argument is made under the conditions of the growing economy and improving social conditions. But even the less fortunate majority of the 1990s benefited from the years of economic growth, vibrancy, and growing prosperity in Russia of the first decade of the 2000s. But these years—associated with political stability and improved social and economic well-being, which could have been used to prop up Russia's postcommunist choice and amplify the message of painful reforms ultimately bringing the desired results—were used in Russia for a different purpose.

What became an economic miracle in postwar Germany and Japan, and was used to legitimize de-Nazification and the success of the new democratic governments, turned in Russia into a period of propagating the "90s trauma" paradigm that scapegoated the domestic liberals, along with their system of values, as well as the West with its reform agenda and liberal values. Today, the publicly supported reframing of the 1990s in the context of a stagnating economy appears close to impossible. If anything, the social and institutional deterioration could be expected to enhance the "aggressive immobility" syndrome characterizing the people who work hard to build the status quo they live in and who fear that any changes that might shift their means of getting by.[20]

The frame of the 1990s as a collective trauma is central to understanding the dynamics of the Russian politics in the twenty-first century. This frame is one of the crucial pillars of Putin's legitimation strategy. It is a very potent tool that the Russian current leadership used and continues to use to harness group emotions for the political aims of the regime. The Kremlin's decisions and policies have been defended with reference to the need of avoiding the conditions of the 1990s. If the memory of the Great Patriotic War protrudes in Russia's scarce symbolic landscape as a "stone pillar in the desert," according to Lev Gudkov, the vision of the 1990s resembles a black hole that erases the past, drawing the entire decade into the abyss.[21] Most of political achievements of the Putin regime have been evaluated with reference to the 1990s. The internalized and socially shared representation of the 1990s is therefore the foundational stone—the *boogeyman* and a *scarecrow* in the public imagination—that conditions and props up the current political system in Russia. Tracing the construction, reinforcement, and political use of this dominant frame in political communication is crucial for understanding Putin's leadership and his "emotional entrepreneurship"—the politically inspired use of group-based emotions to create the foundation for maintaining the political legitimacy and popularity of the current regime.

The 1990s as a Trauma: Reality versus Construction

Trauma scholars disagree about the nature of the events that could and should be labeled as trauma.[22] Trauma is a psychological phenomenon and is best explored within individual rather than social or cultural psychology. Cultural or social traumas that relate to groups are radically different from what is understood as trauma in individual life, and the tools of psychoanalysis commonly used to explore individual trauma are not directly relevant. One important difference is that social or cultural trauma is not something that *happens* to a collectivity, but is always something that is *socially constructed* in the public imagination and collectively mediated with the help of cultural and political entrepreneurs. The idea of the social construction of trauma is at the heart of the constructivist perspective on social trauma that was developed by American sociologist Jeffrey Alexander and his academic collaborators (2004).

This approach postulates that no event is traumatic by itself. It is the narrative surrounding it that causes the event to be experienced as traumatic. It is the claim and interpretation of societal actors that an event represents a fundamental threat to the collectivity's sense of who they are that is required for an event to "turn on" the trauma process—the process of trauma construction based on the event that, according to a collectivity, has left an enduring mark on group consciousness, fundamentally changing the social identity and imprinting the collective memory. This link to identity is underscored in Ron Eyerman's (2001, 2) definition of collective trauma as a "dramatic loss of identity and meaning, a tear in the social fabric, affecting a group of people that has achieved some degree of cohesion." What is at stake is not the existence of a group in a material sense, but its sense of identity and its stability in terms of the structures of meaning and the symbolic order underlying its identity.[23] An individual sense of self is anchored in societal norms and cultural expectations, especially when it comes to his/her collective self. These structures of meaning shared in the society provide a sense of comfort, security, and predictability in everyday life. The loss of these shared meanings therefore can be constructed as a collective trauma that has torn down the ties that tie society together.

Trauma in this constructivist view is a socially mediated process of attribution. It is driven by human agency and is influenced by political actors and social agents who compose and broadcast symbolic representations of specific events, make claims to some fundamental injury and profanation of some sacred value, and build narratives about a destructive social process, demanding emotional, institutional, and symbolic reconstitution.[24] These collective agents of the trauma process are engaged in meaning-making and the creation of a new master narrative of social suffering. The new master narrative of "victimhood" then becomes the symbolic framework that can enable social integration, ordering, and orientation, reinforcing social bonds and the sense of togetherness of the collectivity that was shocked by the disintegrative dynamics of the event that has shaken their sense of "who they are." Oushakine wrote about communities of loss based on shared pain forged in the 1990s in the Siberian city of Barnaul; in the early 2000s the nationwide shared pain in Russia has been instrumentalized and turned into an ideology of collective victimhood by linking individual experiences to the challenges confronted by the state and the nation.[25]

Not only American but also Russian sociologists, such as Lev Gudkov, recognize the importance of such collective construction in their analysis of public opinion, which

> can never keep the experience of individuals; that experience is not preserved, not transmitted, not deposited. Everything that is experienced by an individual and not reflected upon, disappears, if it is not given a special institutionalized treatment, if it is not processed through the channels of cultural reproduction, if individual opinions are not sanctioned by a higher-order institution that stands above the individual.[26]

The constructivist perspective does not imply that cultural or collective trauma could be constructed without any real phenomenon backing up such construction. It means, instead, that different meanings could be constructed around similar painful realities and, further, among various events in the history of a collectivity; the "chosen trauma" is not necessarily measurable through its tangible impact on that group.[27] Working with and through a social trauma is a challenge that is different in nature than that concerned with individual trauma. A "chosen trauma" is inherently political. It might be constructed with the purpose of promoting social cohesion and the political legitimacy of a specific group in power (and thus used as a political instrument). Furthermore, the political nature of a social trauma is evident in its generative potency of creating "victims" and "perpetrators," when the events are viewed through the "trauma" prism. Therefore, the process of choosing and constructing a trauma is intrinsically linked to the politicization of collective identity of the group.[28]

Given the importance of the social and political construction of collective trauma, it might seem that a simple act of "deconstructing" the process of trauma construction, of illustrating the instrumental use of this idea for political purposes, and revealing the alternative visions of these historical events, might be sufficient for decommissioning the specific "chosen trauma" from its place in the societal imagination. In reality, vested political and economic interests and elite politics might hinder the processes required for dealing with social trauma because of the political significance of these constructions. The powerful resonance and the emotional weight that specific representations might carry represent powerful legitimating tools for the elites that might rely on them. The chosen traumas resonate deeply because they draw on real challenges and experiences that societies go through, and they hook the public using the residue of these experiences expressed through emotions.[29]

The rise of post-Soviet nostalgia in the early 2000s—and its cultural expression in media, art, and public space could be viewed as one of the emotional reactions to the tumultuous 1990s.[30] The cultural, "nostalgia-driven" creativity in Russia was not elitist. Russian sociologist Roman Abramov writes about "popular muzeification" (or constructing a museum) of the late Soviet period, involving specifically the generation that "straddled" the era of radical change, still children or coming of age when the Soviet Union collapsed. Noting the healing power of "nostalgia," Abramov argued that "the growing nostalgic sentiments relieve stress from entire generations and specific individuals that have gone through disorienting changes in material, social and cultural environment."[31]

Originating in the middle of the 1990s, the post-Soviet nostalgia turned by the mid-2000s into a defining element of Russia's socio-cultural scene.[32] And as many commentators noted, nostalgia was not so much about the "happy" past, as it was about the unsatisfactory present.[33] In his work Abramov noted that fascination with the 1970s—long viewed as a stagnation period in the USSR—represents one of the peculiar features of the Russian experience with nostalgia. The 2012 opinion polls taken by the Levada Center on the popularity levels of the twentieth-century Soviet/Russian leaders indicated that Leonid Brezhnev, the Soviet leader in 1964–1982 (corresponding to the so-called "stagnation period"), is the most popular political leader of the twentieth century, with the favorable view of 56% of Russian respondents.[34] A popular Russian media project *Namedni*, created by Leonid Parfenov and seen by various observers to have shaped Russians' collective nostalgia, takes place in the period 1961–2003. This historical period is divided into two parts: before and after the Soviet collapse, with the pre-1991 period being the domain of nostalgia.[35]

The emergence of new Russia out of the rubble of the Soviet state was neither quick nor easy. But it did have its positive elements. For many Russian citizens, the 1990s were also a decade of political pluralism, economic opportunity, open borders, cultural creativity, and freedom of political and artistic self-expression. Many people started their own businesses, opening new schools and universities, tourist agencies, hair salons, design companies, banks, farms, and consulting agencies. Others traveled abroad and took part in exciting domestic and international projects; published new journals, read new books, and partook in activities that were unimaginable under the Soviet system. The new energy, excitement, and enthusiasm—felt especially strongly in Moscow, the epicenter of Russia's new capitalism—are still remembered fondly and are missed by those who joined the "brave new world" of post-Soviet Russia.[36]

But these positive stories have, for the most part, vanquished in the public space. This vision has been sidelined by what became the dominant view of the 1990s. Almost two decades after this period has ended, we see the society-wide internalization and sedimentation of the idea that the 1990s were dreadful. How and why did this selective and undifferentiated version of the 1990s prevail?

The 1990s as an Electoral Strategy

The initial idea to incorporate the 1990s into the political toolkit of the new president was developed by Gleb Pavlovsky, a political technologist and analyst working for the Kremlin in the 1990s and the first decade of the 2000s. In a recent interview with Ivan Krastev, Pavlovsky noted that finding the "glue" for the pro-Kremlin coalition in the upcoming electoral season of 1999–2000 was one of the important issues discussed in the presidential administration in the late 1990s. Most observers understood at that moment that the presidential power needed to be bolstered and that this task could only be accomplished if the new president were associated with a new type of politics that could indicate the end of the transition period in Russia. Pavlovsky himself articulated this moment of political change as the "Operation Losers' *Revanche*."[37] He thought that the pro-Kremlin coalition should be formed by relying on the idea that those who lost from the reforms—the teachers, doctors, scientists, pensioners, and other *biudzhetniki* (state-paid employees)—needed to be provided with a chance for a state "revanche."[38] For Pavlovsky this did not mean a complete shift and reversal in Russia's political economy. An avid political technologist, Pavlovsky was preoccupied with the issue of attaining and maintaining power. So the "losers' coalition" for him was, primarily, the "packaging" in which to "sell" to the country the new candidate chosen by the Kremlin. Pavlovsky shared as much in his recent book, where he touched upon the process of selection of the presidential candidate in the Kremlin in the late 1990s (*Eksperimental'naia rodina*):

> As a technologist [political; author's note], I was indifferent and simply waited who will be named, so that I can start promoting him. If you decide that our candidate is Nikita Mikhalkov, all right, let it be Mikhalkov. Primakov? For god's sake, yes! The emergence of a new presidential power did not depend on the personality of the candidate but on the Kremlin's influence to insist that he is elected in competition with other candidates.[39]

According to Pavlovsky, around the spring of 1999, Putin rose to the top of Yeltsin's short list of his potential successors. From August 1999, when Putin was appointed a prime minister, Pavlovsky began implementing his electoral ideas for the candidate selected by the Kremlin. At the center of his plan was the idea of creating a broad "pro-Putin majority," conceived as a coalition of social groups that have lost in the transition. In Pavlovsky's own account:

> The Kremlin's coalition was paradoxical. It included circles of disappointed and not very democratic intelligentsia that were marginalized in their impoverished industrial institutes. [...] It included medical doctors, school teachers, engineers, technicians in dying factories, in scientific towns, and workers of the military-industrial complex. There were also military officers at all levels: for them, the presidential candidate's past profession was a replacement for his [political] program. These electoral groups were not ideologically incompatible anymore, as in 1996, when the communists were juxtaposed to democrats. For them Putin was the last chance for the revanche.[40]

In short, if one trusts Pavlovsky's account, the opposition to the 1990s and signaling the start of a new political era could be seen as the birthmark of Putin's presidency.[41] The outstanding question is how this frame transformed from being an electoral tool, designed to bring a selected pro-Kremlin candidate to power, into an important ideological pillar for Putinism, into a "chosen trauma" that served the purpose of national consolidation and legitimation of the president. The answer to this question lies in the intersection of culture, politics, and media in Russia throughout the early 2000s.

The 1990s as a Legitimation Strategy

The Kremlin understood the powerful resonance of the 1990s in Russian society and chose to build further on this issue through the state-controlled channels in film industry, television and radio programming, and print newspapers. One important historical trope to capture the meaning of the 1990s was found in Russia's "times of trouble" (*epokha smuty*)—a period of interregnum in the early seventeenth century, before the establishment of the Romanov dynasty, when Russian control over the country's territory was compromised by the Polish-Lithuanian occupation and a war with Sweden. The Kremlin commissioned several films, including Vladimir Khotinenko's 2007 film *1612* and, in the same year, a documentary production, *The Times of Troubles* (*Smutnoe vremya*) by Viktor Buturlin, narrated by Mikhail Leontyev. Both films centered on the so-called time of troubles (*epokha smuty*) in the early history of the Russian state and particularly on the moment when this period ended. Khotinenko's film propagated the political ideals of strong leadership, patriotism, and victory over foreigners. The "end of the time of troubles" was one of the political messages conveyed to the audience. Its literal expression was done through the joyful declaration by one of characters at the end of the film: "People, time of troubles has ended" ("Люди, смута кончилась, кончилась смута").[42] Buturlin's film brought the message home by making direct linkages between Russia of the early seventeenth century and Russia of the 1990s.[43]

The 1990s, seen as a "time of troubles," became the big frame that the Kremlin has propagated widely and relentlessly. This was the historical equivalent selected by the Kremlin to represent the 1990s. A part of Putin's 2018 inauguration speech summarized very well this take on the 1990s, presented to the public as the one that is widely shared in Russian society:

> We all know that in the 1990s and early 2000, along with long-needed historical changes, our fatherland and the people confronted hard challenges. . . . But we also remember well that in its millennial history Russia

faced the hardships and the "times of trouble" quite a few times and she always rose up as a Phoenix, getting to unimaginable heights.[44]

The idea of the 1990s as a time of trouble was inherently linked to building the image of Vladimir Putin as a *savior* of the state and the society from these troubles; as a leader who brought the country out of the crisis; as a president who instilled hope and stability to a society torn by economic and political instability. A number of documentaries made by Putin supporters, such as the one made by Nikita Mikhalkov for Putin's fifty-fifth birthday and the Kremlin-sponsored documentary prepared by journalist Andrei Kondrashov as part of Putin's 2018 electoral campaign, have resorted to the political strategy of using the 1990s as a springboard for demonstrating Putin's achievements.

Mikhalkov's 2007 documentary is exemplary in creating the representation of the 1990s and of Putin's place in Russia's modern history that has become taken for granted in Russia just a few years later. Mikhalkov framed the film introduction by referencing Yeltsin's two radical decisions: to give up his party membership in 1990 and give up his presidency in 2000. His personal take on Yeltsin was not elaborated otherwise. What the film focused on, next, was (1) the nature of the situation and the problems that Putin inherited from the 1990s, followed by (2) Putin's achievements in the short period that has passed since. The documentary describes the state of the country using references to societal confusion, wild bandits (*likhie razboiniki*), impoverishment, foreign debt, wage delays, terrorism, army disintegration, and, finally, the pinnacle of the Kursk submarine tragedy in 2000 that became a threshold, an indicator that the Russian state was at the brink of collapse. Mikhalkov's references to *semibankirshchina*, when the country "was ripped apart, when it was divided among them" (these seven bankers), were especially fiery. "The country knelt down in front of several individuals," Mikhalkov narrated. "The country had to give up to them its riches." "We will not let you die; but you have to give up everything"—the infamous Russian oligarchs have ostensibly suggested (Mikhalkov 2007). Following the dramatism of this situation, Vladimir Putin's historical entry becomes that of a savior, not less. A savior with a Purpose (with a capital P). The results that Mikhalkov narrates are stunning. In eight years, Russia joined the 10 largest world economies. The regions forgot unemployment. The national projects in health care, education, science, and agriculture sought to revitalize the Russian infrastructure and human capital. Pacification of Chechnya meant that the danger of territorial disintegration was gone; Grozny became a city that people are jealous of. Traditional religions have united around the state. Russia has consolidated and is ready for its destiny of becoming a real leader in the world—a bridge between East and West. Mikhalkov also made a special reference to the 2007 reconciliation of the two

Russian Orthodox Churches: the Russian Orthodox Church Outside Russia and the Moscow Patriarchate. All these achievements, Mikhalkov claimed, are associated with the president's name—his personal qualities and his systematic constructive work in the interests of the country.

The most recent 2018 documentary about Putin, made in advance of the 2018 presidential elections by Andrei Kondrashov, follows the same narrative about the 1990s. The very first words about the 1990s that came from Putin referred to the alleged disparaging attitude of the West toward Russia. Putin expressed that attitude borrowing from the prisoners' jargon: "your [Russia's] place is at the latrine" ("Ваше место у параши"). Other Kremlin officials joined the chorus. Sergei Shoigu, Russia's minister of defense, referred to the 1990s as "that time when almost every federation subject had its own constitution"; it was worse than chaos. Sergei Ivanov, Putin's close associate and the chief of staff of the presidential administration during 2011–2016, complained that people tend to forget how bad it was in the 1990s. Sergei Chemezov, the CEO of Rostec, Russia's state monopoly in the military-industrial complex and arms production, and Putin's long-term associate, talked about the 1990s as the time when the army was not seen as necessary because Russia was not going to fight any wars. The country therefore was unprepared to fight international terrorism in the late 1990s. The narrator, Andrei Kondrashov, refers to the 1990s as a period when the army and the country as a whole were half-decayed/half-disintegrated. Ramzan Kadyrov, head of Chechnya, suggested that without Putin, Russia would have been no more. These were just some of the central characters whose interviews frame the central story propagated by this film: the 1990s were the time of a disintegrating, weak state and a loss of sovereignty, and Vladimir Putin emerged in that context as the national savior.

The same strategy is easily identifiable in various other pro-Kremlin mass media, including radio and TV talk shows and pro-Putin books written by pro-Kremlin commentators. Vladimir Solovyev, a pro-Kremlin journalist and a talk show host, stands out among the crowd of Putin's propagandists. He could be considered one of the chief Kremlin propaganda bullhorns in the past few years. Solovyev advanced the frame of the 1990s through his writing as well as his role as an anchor of various TV and radio talk shows. Consider Solovyev's radio show *Polnyi kontakt* (full contact) aired on January 18, 2012 (less than two months in advance of the upcoming presidential elections in March 2012), and his introductory monologue about the 1990s:

> The question is simple enough: do you want to return the 1990s? Perhaps you have a hard time remembering them. Let me remind you: the 90s is when Mavrodi was jailed for MMM and when none of the state officials

responsible for GKO [Russia government bonds] and the 1998 crisis in
Russia were held responsible. The 1990s is when the bandits felt themselves to be in absolute control, the sense shared by the Kremlin inhabitants as well, for that matter; when according to Korzhakov briefcases
of money were brought to the Kremlin administration; when state positions were bought as were oil wells. The 90s is when Russia's legitimately
elected parliament was shot down at the order of the president of the RF,
Boris Nikolayevich Yeltsin. The 90s is when the president of Russia, Boris
Nikolayevich Yeltsin, declared civil war, sent in troops and bombed the
Russian city Grozny. It is precisely the times when our army was practically
decimated. It is when Mr. Kozyrev was conducting foreign policy or, better said, did not conduct foreign policy. It was when we naively believed
that Americans are kind and honest democracy fighters and we had many
advisors coming to our country. These were the same "wonderful" advisors
who were later prosecuted in the United States for using insider knowledge and participating in privatization and personal enrichment. These
were the same "wonderful" advisors who are responsible for such privatization that resulted in the transfer of the Soviet property in some clever
ways into the hands of those who later became oligarchs. It was when it
became possible to dismantle the great Soviet economy and the military-
industrial complex. It was when population decline amounted to one million annually. It was not so long ago, really. And now, the politicians from
those times are starting to teach us. [. . .] Those were the jolly times, if
someone does not remember them. So, anyone wants to return the 90s?
The 90s, when the state practically did not exist and the word "corruption" did not make sense because there was nothing else but corruption. It
was an absolute norm for Russia's state officials/bureaucrats. [. . .] These
were the times when each oligarch owned local courts and bought off former KGB and FSB officials, who bought off the Ministry of Interior and
turned them into bandit formations, who bought off state prosecutors.
Those "boys" could do anything they wanted with the country![45]

His political talk show *An Evening with Vladimir Solovyev* regularly revisits this
topic, most recently on November 13 and November 15, 2018, using the pretext of
Sergei Ursuliak's recent film *Nenast'e* (2018), set in the 1990s.

The Ideological Crusade and the Crusaders

Sergei Kurginyan is sometimes referred to as one of Russia's Renaissance men.
He is also one of the important opinion-makers who worked on forming the

discourse about the 1990s in Russia. Born into a family of Soviet intelligentsia of Armenian origin, Kurginyan graduated with a geophysics degree from the Moscow Institute of Geological Exploration. He later attended the famous Boris Schukin's Theater School and created his own theater "On the boards" (*na dos-kakh*). Since the 1980s, Kurginyan has combined his passion for theater produc-tion with his interest in philosophy, history, and politics. His political activism started with perestroika. In 1990, he ran for a deputy position in the RSFSR elec-tions on the platform of defending the Russian economy, state, and society from disintegration. In 1993 he became an advisor to Ruslan Khasbulatov (a speaker of the Congress of People's Deputies) and played an active role in developing an alternative strategy of protest actions during the October 1993 standoff between the Supreme Soviet and the executive branch of the government (Boris Yeltsin).[46] Although he stayed politically active during the 1990s and the early 2000s, his media personality and presence became especially noticeable from around 2010, when he became a co-host (along with Nikolai Svanidze) of the program *Sud Vremeni* (The Court of History), broadcast first on Channel 5 and later trans-ferred to the *Rossiya 1* channel under the title *Istorichesky protsess* (Historical Trial). This program was developed as a series of historical debates about the turning moments in Russian history. Around the same time, in response to the 2011–2012 protests, Kurginyan created a left-wing patriotic movement, "The Essence of Times," that participated in various anti-liberal protests along with other "patriotic" forces mobilized in defense of the Kremlin. It is evident that the key programmatic ideas of this movement were worked out during the debates in which Kurginyan was involved on *Sud Vremeni*. The more conservative position outlined by him in this TV show received consistent public support (usually by a margin of 90% and more), measured through public voting at the end of each debate.[47]

Kurginyan, along with Vladislav Surkov, worked on developing the new con-ceptual, ideological, and political apparatus for Putin's Russia. This work was done in the context of the Experimental Creative Center (Kurginyan Center) that he had founded already in 1990.[48] The center's research-oriented and intellectual work focuses on several main challenges confronting Russia, including resource/ energy security, religious and cultural challenges, macro-regional and local, and a few others. One of the more notable recent publications of this center is a four-volume anthology, *The Essence of Our Times: The Philosophical Foundations of the Messianic Claims of Russia in the 21st Century*, available online.[49] It was first aired as a series of video-lectures and was later published as a book. I will summarize the central ideas from these four volumes in the next few paragraphs.

The first volume of the anthology starts with the interpretation of the most decisive event in Russia's recent history: the collapse of the USSR and the birth

of the new Russia. Dissatisfied with Putin's notion of the Soviet collapse representing a "geopolitical catastrophe," Kurginyan introduces the notion of a
"metaphysical catastrophe" and even a "metaphysical demise" that impacted
Russian society. Following what looks like the Marxist-Leninist dialectics, he
takes a binary approach to human existence as encompassing the worldly and the
spiritual and alludes to the biblical story about the conflict over primogeniture
between Jacob and Joseph. According to Kurginyan, the political debates associated with perestroika and glasnost consisted of two key messages: the liberal
forces challenged the legitimacy and value of the Soviet "primogeniture" (i.e.,
the spiritual basis of the Soviet society), and challenged the need for having any
values at all. The liberal media allegedly did not allow any space for those with
different views about the Soviet past, and the public therefore bought into these
claims, even if by 1993 the majority of Russians knew that they had been manipulated. They still believed Yeltsin's promise of bread and butter (i.e., the biblical
"lentil soup" exchanged for primogeniture).

This hegemonically propagated political message, according to Kurginyan,
caused a "cognitive shock," a wide-scale "socio-cultural trauma," and a condition
of a "broken man" unable/unfit for any social/collective action.[50] Kurginyan
explores the various aspects of this metaphysical demise, including how and why
the version of Russian capitalism was built in a particularly brutal fashion, so that
the capitalist "beast" ended up devouring all public resources.[51] He critiques the
oligarchs who have not created any new industries and rely exclusively on the productive infrastructure developed during the Soviet period. In the end, he claims
that 95% of the Russian population has lost (even materially speaking) from the
economic reforms undertaken in the 1990s.[52] He critiques the elites who traded
their country for the material riches and indulged in conspicuous consumption.
He critiques the masses who believed in the elites' promises of building capitalism quickly and solving the "bread and butter" issues in the country.

After a wide-ranging criticism of all aspects of the post-Soviet reality, Kurginyan
charts the path for personal and social salvation. The path is reigniting the spiritual, the transcendental aspect of the human being; it is based on reasserting the
primogeniture—the Soviet primogeniture—the values inculcated in the Soviet
public over the 70-year period of Soviet rule. To regain that primogeniture, one
needs to understand the central Soviet legacies, which, according to him, requires
re-establishment of the facts, re-establishment of the meanings, and exploration
of what could be returned productively into the twenty-first century.[53] Although
Kurginyan's anti-capitalist views resemble, in many ways, those of the Communist
Party of the Russian Federation (CPRF), he is a staunch Putin supporter. In fact,
the Communists claimed that Kurginyan's media activity—especially on his talk
show *Istoricheskii Protsess* (Historical Trial)—was a manipulative strategy to win

the Communist votes away from the CPRF.[54] The Russian mass audience got to know Kurginyan through his talk shows (the aforementioned *Court of History* that aired for several months in 2010 and *Historical Trial* that aired on *Rossiya 1* in 2011–2012). Both of these talk shows were attempts to recapture those lost meanings that Kurginyan wrote about in his book, through reassessing various historical events and historical figures, with the audience playing the role of an ultimate jury in this process. After the presentation of different opinions and ensuing discussion, the audience was expected to call in with their preference. The topics discussed included such politically important issues as Belovezha agreements, Gaidar's reforms, Bolsheviks' role, GKChP, Molotov-Robbentrop act, the Cold War, globalization, industrialization, collectivization, glasnost, Saddam Hussein, Nicholas II, Peter the Great, etc. The central feature of the show was the format in which these issues were discussed: through the black and white frame. The audience was expected to pick one side, and in most cases Kurginyan's more conservative and statist position was the one that was favored by the audience by margins of 88%–90%. Kurginyan always managed to stay on the side of the "good."

In addition to his own talk shows, Kurginyan is also a frequent participant in other talk shows, including those of Andrei Norkin, who works on the NTV channel, and Vladimir Solovyev, a journalist who rose to prominence in post-2014 Russia and who could be considered the single most critical media "asset" the Kremlin relies upon for constructing and delivering the "correct" political message to the audience.

In addition to the ongoing circulation of this frame about the 1990s in mass media, it is also being instilled in the younger generations in schools through their history textbooks. The Kremlin has long pushed for a more homogenous and standardized history education in Russia, aimed at inculcating patriotism in schoolchildren. The 2007 publication of a government-approved textbook *A History of Russia 1945–2006*, authored by Alexander Filippov, received much critical attention from observers, with some commentators referring to this textbook as Stalinist.[55] The Soviet past in the textbook is indeed presented through a patriotic lens, even if the Soviet state-sponsored violence is discussed in the text. The textbook presents the 1990s through a dark lens as the period when Russian society suffered an unprecedented drop in living standards and the "covert fragmentation of the state." Yeltsin is seen as "an active participant in the disintegration of the Soviet Union," as well as someone who oversaw the transition to the market (even if at the expense of his popularity).[56] Vladimir Putin and the early 2000s are presented as the period when the threat of state disintegration was averted, while political stability and governmentality (*upravliayemost'*) were restored.[57] Revealing the timing of its publication, the textbook presents the now outdated formula of a "sovereign democracy" as "a perfect political form" that allows the government to maintain a consolidated state and civil and political liberties.[58] Filippov's history textbook is not an exceptional case. Many other history textbooks aim to advance a "patriotic" frame by promoting heroic images of Stalin and Putin among Russia's youth and elaborating on Putin's role as a leader who made Russia more powerful.[59]

A similar image of the 1990s is promoted online, through a variety of "patriotic" sites for Russia's youth. In her article "Likhie 90-e: vremya kogda 'zabivali' strelku i 'rubili' kapustu," Anna Fedulova writes about homeless kids and adults, bandits (*bratva*) and killers, video salons and kiosks, drugs and prostitution, religious sects and financial pyramids, etc.[60] This grim exposition ends with: "we should remember *likhie* 90s. This is rugged/hard/bleak history of Russia plunged into chaos; of a country unable to restructure and adapt. The country was surviving as it could. Some people were destroying everything, others were trying to survive."[61] The online *YouTube* channel features numerous unofficial documentaries with similar images and representations, including one titled, "Likhie 90s. Provintsialnye istorii. Ivanteevka." The search engine "Google Trends" that allows a search of public usage of the term over time reveals that online searches using the term "likhie devianostye" and "likhie 90-e" (traced from 2004) started around October 2007 and have continued very consistently since around 2010. The usage of both terms has remained quite stable and high since.

Not only national but also regional sources of information in Russia actively rely on this frame. By using regional variation in the degree of recollection of the traumatic 1990s, Alessandro Belmonte and Michael Rochlitz demonstrated that in the regions where state-controlled media more actively recalled the painful transition, the electoral support for the regional government was higher.[62] Using statistical analysis and regional comparison, these scholars showed the linkage between collective memory–based propaganda and government support in Russia.

Vladimir Putin on the 1990s: Building Russia's Victimhood Frame

Many commentators and scholars long debated whether Vladimir Putin has an identifiable ideology.[63] Putin has shown considerable flexibility with regard to the ideas he has endorsed in the last two decades. He moved from state-rebuilding, the dictatorship of the law, and the verticality of power to the idea of "sovereign democracy"; he switched from economic liberalism to support for national economic champions; he evolved from viewing Russia as part of Europe to propagating the view of millenarian Russia that is its own civilization; he shifted from modern European values to traditional, family-oriented values, posing Russia to be the last bastion of Christianity. Observers have captured this fluidity using references to postmodern dictatorship and hybrid authoritarianism.[64] Yet there is one idea that he has stuck with since his early days in power: his rule is different from the rule of Yeltsin in the 1990s. Russia of the early 2000s is a place of rebuilding order, attaining stability and economic growth, strengthening the state, pacifying business, reigning in the oligarchs, paying the pensions and salaries, asserting the state on the international arena, etc. All these objectives and the alleged achievements have been contrasted to the situation in the 1990s. This has been one of the foundational ideas that, while not amounting to "Putin's ideology," could certainly be seen as a narrative that plays the role of Atlas (a Greek Titan) propping up the Kremlin's policies and the ruling elites' political predispositions. It is true that Putin relies on foreign policy as the driving part of his identity politics. But this does not mean that he is oblivious to domestic issues and politics; he is just secure that his foundational narrative builds on popular beliefs.

Putin learned early on that emotions matter.[65] The 1999 exchange with a reporter about what is to be done with the Chechen terrorists, which involved the infamous phrase about "wiping them out in the outhouse,"[66] indicated Putin's inclination to not be picky with words when he wanted to express specific emotions. These words helped him to be seen by the public as a strong macho man, capable of defending his country at the time of an acute weakness and insecurity.[67] Growing more confident over the years, Russia's leader has progressively moved toward an ever more skillful employment of group-based emotions for defining and defending his agenda and his policies. Through his rhetoric he has connected with and validated the powerful emotions of loss, shame, and humiliation shared by the Russian public in the aftermath of the Soviet collapse. The state-controlled media, the Kremlin advisors, and Putin himself have worked on embedding and fixing the intensely negative framing of the 1990s in the public sphere.

This frame is rather amorphous and works by painting the entire decade into dark colors, pulling together various negative economic, social, and political aspects of life in the 1990s and making any positive elements invisible and inconsequential. It does not build on any sound analysis of the reasons for the negative developments and does not have any systematic way of showing the way forward. Therefore, labeling it as an ideology would mean giving it a little too much analytical substance. Most ideologies, with an exception of fascism, perhaps, represent a relatively coherent set of ideas developed to explain the past and the present, and to provide some prescriptive guide for the future.[68] *Likhie-90e* is more of a "scaring device" in the public discourse. Its emotional appeal and its potential for building communities based on despair are more important than its rational content.[69]

Putin actively employs this specific frame about the 1990s in his own rhetoric. His annual press conferences are especially revealing of his views on this issue. His responses are not scripted at these events and therefore allow for more flexibility and spontaneity. I have analyzed *Pryamaia Liniia* conferences from 2001 until 2017 to explore Putin's take on the 1990s. There are 15 episodes, each lasting from about two and a half to four and a half hours. Putin refers to the 1990s in each of these events. All of his comments about this period are negative and derogatory; there is not a single positive reference to this period.

The overall picture that emerges in relation to the 1990s could be analyzed with regard to (1) the nature of the pain and of the victim; and (2) attribution of responsibility for what transpired in this period. Putin's representations of the main victim and the nature of pain in the 1990s include a wide range: (1) Russia overall, seen as an easy trophy by outsiders because of the weak state; facing a threat of territorial disintegration and a victim of international terrorism; (2) Russian society, which has suffered because the state did not fulfill its obligations to society (for example, by not paying the pensions) and the social sphere disintegrated; because the reforms imposed economic hardships; because institutions were not effective (such as the State Duma that made many populist decisions) or were undermined (such as the institution of family); (3) Russia's economy, suffering from stalled production and fragmented industry; from an economic policy in the 1990s that relied on faith in private property but did not take into account the importance of administration and the administrative apparatus in need of taxes from the private sector for its operation; and (4) the legal system—imperfect and full of loopholes.

According to Putin, by 1998, the Russian economy was in ruins, the social sphere and the army nonexistent; meanwhile, international terrorism and civil war put the country at the risk of collapse. It is in those conditions, Putin argues, that Evgeny Primakov started the fight for Russia's territorial integrity and he, Vladimir Putin, continued that work.

Putin attributed the responsibility for the 1990s to different actors. On the one hand, he mentioned the outsiders who want Russia to be weak, fragmented, and ultimately to disintegrate. International terrorism is another agent to blame. Finally, there are concrete individuals he mentions, such as Nemtsov, Ryzhkov, and Milov, asserting that they have been stripping the country of its assets in the 1990s, along with Berezovsky; and now that they have been dragged away from their "feeder," they want to return and fill their pockets once again (2010). "If we allow them to do that, they will not stop at counting billions, they will sell Russia off entirely."

Putin's annual addresses to the Federal Assembly are less suggestive of his own views about this epoch. Especially in the first few years of his presidency, Putin's annual speeches involve more careful references to this period and include the criticism of specific aspects of policies undertaken by the government as well as the recognition that these policies were necessary. In 2000, for example, Putin recognized the necessity of regionalization and decentralization ("это была сознательная, хотя и вынужденная политика"). In 2001, when evaluating privatization results, Putin declared that he is against property redistribution and noted that he does not doubt the aims of the privatization ("не подвергая сомнению цели и задачи которые ставились в ходе этих преобразований"). At the same time, though, he noted that the questions about the way privatization was carried out should be listened to.[70]

Putin's spontaneous responses and arguments made during his annual press conferences reveal that his personal take on the 1990s is very negative and, most likely, colored primarily by his understanding of the consequences of the fall of the Soviet Union. A few personal comments also make it clear that Putin looks with disdain at liberal politicians and liberal opposition in the early 2000s, whom he paints as thieves who have plundered Russia's riches in the 1990s and are threatening Russia with the same actions in the 2000s. It is also clear that, when making references to the 1990s, Putin understands that the frame he is using is widely shared and understood by people in ways very similar to his own. By 2015 he already made references to the 1990s framed as rhetorical questions: "Did not we have this already in the 1990s? Did not we go through this already?" These statements do not require answers. They appeal to collectively shared "truths."

Public Resonance of the 1990s Frame: The Majority View

The images of the country in the 1990s propagated by Putin and the state-controlled media and Putin's central role in reversing this situation have been widely accepted by the public in Russia. I found very similar images presented during my focus-group interviews conducted in 2016 in Samara and Kazan. My respondents reproduced most of the tropes circulating in the media (as reflected in Solovyev's opening monologue cited earlier, as reflected in Nikita Mikhalkov's 2007 documentary and in Vladimir Putin's own rhetoric).

In Samara, one respondent shared: "weekly shootings in the local market is [*sic*] one of my brightest memories of the 1990s. Then shuttle-trading. The first who got into it became rich; those who came after them, lost their apartments." Then respondent S continued: "There was outright anarchy then; consider *naperstochniki*: everyone knew they were lying but people played hoping they would win. And if someone wanted to complain, a big daddy in a leather coat would lead you to the closest corner." At the same time, he also conveyed a sense of nostalgia and nuance in his assessment of the 1990s: "About the 1990s, let me tell you: it was time of my youth. Those times seem brighter. [...] These were exciting years. [...] This was the time of experiments."

In Kazan, respondent R referred to the 1990s as the time when "the country would have all crushed if someone gave it a single kick. Banditry, gangs. ..." Respondent A referred to the non-payment of salaries, remembering the experience of her family (her dad was from the military). Respondent M shared with his feeling of progress in the early 2000s compared to the 1990s when the factories and plants stood still or might have worked at 10% of their potential.[71] Another group member noted Russia's dependence on the United States.

There were two dissenting voices in Kazan who tried to bring a bit of balance into the vision of the 1990s by mentioning freedom of speech and Yeltsin's democratic constitution, along with the idea that the "movement forward," cited by most group members in association with Putin, had begun under Yeltsin and by Yeltsin. But despite these interventions that were voiced in support of each other, it was clear that the predominant view shared by the majority took more of a "black and white" perspective on the difference between these two eras. Another dissenter from the dominant view of the 1990s in Samara argued: "I think that things are getting worse. I am 28 years old but I do not own a place to live. I do not want to pay for 25 years for the mortgage."[72]

Women tended to be more critically oriented toward the 1990s although even they recognized continuing problems such as inequality. Respondent N in Samara phrased it in this way:

> In the early 90s after the collapse of the Soviet Union, when the country was no more, it was broken up into small groups and people did not know what to do. Because just a moment ago they had everything: stability, people knew they had an apartment, their kids could go to school and pre-school for free ... and this all ended and a different era began. Society separated into rich and poor ... and people started making sense ... many were fired from their jobs; my own parents lost their jobs in the Maslennikov factory; you could see that some people went into shuttle trading and earned quite a bit. People envied them because it meant money and they could not do it. Some lacked cleverness, others opportunities. And what is going on now? Alas the gap between the rich and poor has increased. But it is a different country now.[73]

Interestingly, both in Kazan and Samara there was one group member who recognized the importance of media representations about the 1990s: respondent
A, in Samara, noted, "I have partially experienced those times that are now being
scolded at."

Public opinion polls conducted by the Levada center (see Figure 5.1) illustrate that the dominant opinion about the Yeltsin era during the early 2000s is
consistently negative. The only spike in the appreciation of his presidency—that
ultimately stands for the whole epoch of the 1990s—occurred at the moment of
his death in 2007 and is, arguably, associated with a deeply held cultural tradition
of not speaking badly about the deceased.

The Russian Public Opinion Research Center's (VCIOM) systematically
conducted surveys about Yeltsin are even more telling. They illustrate that the
Russians' assessments about Yeltsin have worsened in the last decade. In 2016,
for example, 50% of respondents blamed Yeltsin for the crisis of the 1990s, while
in 2007 that proportion was only 36%.[74] The number of respondents that could
not remember any of Yeltsin's positive achievements, on the other hand, has cor-
respondingly increased from 28% in 2007 to 52% of all respondents in 2016.[75]
Meanwhile, in the absence of centralized messages about the Yeltsin era, as the
temporal distance from the 1990s grows, one could have expected that Russians

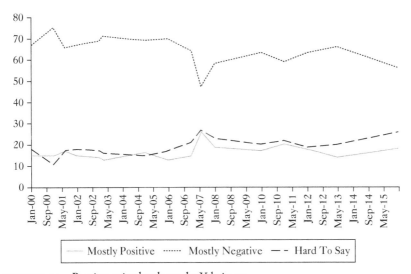

FIGURE 5.1. Russian attitudes about the Yeltsin era.

Notes: Aggregated responses to the Levada Center survey question: "Judged from a historical
perspective, did the Yeltsin era bring more positive or more negative to Russia?" (https://www.
levada.ru/2016/02/01/epoha-eltsina-i-raspad-sssr/).

would mellow somewhat toward Yeltsin. Indeed, at the beginning of the 2000s, the more neutral assessments of Yeltsin had been on the rise. In 2002 around a third of Russians expressed a neutral view about Yeltsin, when confronted with the question: "How would you define your current attitude toward Yeltsin?" (the answers ranged from "very positive" to "very negative" in a five-point scale).[76] By 2006 the number of Russians who were neutral toward Yeltsin grew to 43%. The reverse trend that is evident between 2007 and 2016 therefore must be credited to the impact of centralized media messages about *likhie 90e*—a frame that turned into a legitimation instrument right around 2007, when Mikhalkov's documentary on Putin's fifty-fifth birthday was broadcast.

Age matters in how Russians view the 1990s today. VCIOM surveys show that pensioners are more negative about the 1990s and that the youth are less negative. The experience of going through the 1990s for adults, whose identities were formed in the Soviet Union, does appear to be most painful. The youth born in the late 1990s, on the other hand, only know about it through media and family stories. Without personal recollection, the resonance and therefore political potency of this frame is apparently weaker. This idea is also supported by the fact that the VCIOM surveys conducted in 2002 show a curvilinear relationship between age and people's assessments of the Yeltsin era. The youngest respondents (18–24-year-old subgroup) in 2002 tended to be more negative in their views of the 1990s and closer in their opinions to the oldest subgroup (over 60) than to two subgroups of respondents ages 25–44.[77] The effects of the officially promoted dominant frame about the 1990s are likely to be felt more strongly in these two groups. However, these results might also indicate that the children and the pensioners—the most vulnerable groups in the society—might have borne the roughness of this era in more extreme ways that the working-age adults.

Respondents' location also matters for current perceptions of the 1990s. The residents of Moscow and St. Petersburg tend to be somewhat more positive in the assessment of Yeltsin and the decade associated with his leadership than other Russians.[78] In a 2016 VCIOM survey, the number of Moscovites (and residents of St. Petersburg) who thought that Yeltsin brought more harm to Russia was at least 10 (or more) percentage points lower than in other localities in Russia. To the contrary, the number of respondents who thought that the Yeltsin era brought more benefits was higher than in other places.[79] This is not surprising. The presence of economic and financial opportunities—most prominently in Moscow—led to social development and the rise of more cosmopolitan groups that are autonomous from the state and that value the political and civic freedoms and pluralism of the 1990s more than others in Russia.[80]

Natalya Zubarevich, a prominent economic geographer, has advanced a thesis about "four Russias," differentiating the country along the lines of socioeconomic development and related cultural and political orientations, depending on the size of settlements people live in.[81] The political developments since 2012 however seem to have split Russia into two: people in Moscow and St. Petersburg tend to exhibit different types of political and cultural attitudes, and demands.

The Dissenting Voices

Many Russian political commentators and sociologists understand the significance of the 1990s for present-day political legitimation and political stability in Russia.[82] Over the past few years, and specifically since 2015, there are also clear signs of cultural counter-mobilization against the dominant representation of the 1990s. The project *Ostrov-90kh* developed by the Yeltsin Center in Yekaterinburg and Colta.ru is arguably the most important sign of these developments. The project involves annual cultural festivals that bring together writers, artists, singers, film critics, and photographers to share their impressions about the most important creative artifacts of the 1990s. Russian political and cultural analyst Sergei Medvedev's conversation with a few Russian media professionals (mostly liberal-oriented) revealed that the 1990s could also be viewed as a time of freedom, of a shared sense of openness and opportunities, a time of creative explosion: new cinematography and the new media; new poetry and literature; new journals, magazines, and newspapers.

The Facebook flashmob—"moi 90e"—that reappears every autumn since 2015 is yet another indication of the fact that many Russians, especially those who are more educated and are more successful, disagree with the dominant view of the 1990s. The flash mob features nostalgia and sentimentality with regard to the 1990s, expressed by those who entered adulthood in the 1990s and who, from the height of their current achievements, can look at their past with a sense of nostalgia and longing. In short, those who experienced the 1990s firsthand and who find themselves in the more "well-to-do" groups in Russian society do not necessarily fall into the caricature and all-black view of this period. The question that stands out, though, and the question that is politically relevant for Russia's future, is whether those who have not experienced the 1990s firsthand will follow the dominant representation, or will they protest against it? The future is in the hands of the children of the group described in the preceding.

It is hard to expect that the counter-frame will find a wide following in Russia, at least in the short to medium term. The popularity of the Kremlin-propagated view of the 1990s could be seen through the latest cultural production that has picked up on the importance of this frame and expressed it through a slightly ironic but also very nostalgic and sentimental view of the youth, best exemplified by the young Russian pop-singer Monetochka's song about the 1990s:

> *In the 90s people turned up dead, And they ran the streets buck naked.*
> *Absolutely naked.*
> *There was no electricity,*
> *Only fights for jeans with coca-cola.*
> *It's fun to sit around and divvy up the shops,*
> *But carving up a country is where playtime stops.*
> *[...]*
> *It's only thanks to tapes and to Krovostok's song*
> *That I learned with horror what had gone wrong.*
> *That in the 90s people turned up dead,*
> *And they ran the streets buck naked.*

Maria Engström, a cultural theorist at the Uppsala University (Sweden), referred to Monetochka's songs as "the only intelligible manifesto of the aesthetics of Putin's fourth term in office."[83] Monetochka's latest album serves, according to Engström, a therapeutic function that is more "about relaxation and sleep, about the suppression of an aggressive beginning" and is more about "intentional detachment from making direct, engaged ideological statements." As such, it stands in sharp contrast to the earlier "protest art" and "actionism" reflected in the Russian protest culture of the 2010s and the creative works of *Pussy Riot* and *Voina*.[84] The explosive popularity of Monetochka, especially among the generation Z, is revealing of the current predispositions of Russian youth, especially in the provinces.

My focus-group interviews conducted in 2016 were differentiated by age groups and revealed that the young Russians often reproduce, in a rather abstract fashion, the main negative tropes about the 1990s: the country was falling apart, street crime was rampant, the government was incompetent. Compared to the young, those who had a real experience of living in the 1990s provided much more colorful images and stories from the 1990s. Among the young respondents, those who dissented from this dominant view about the 1990s (there was one in Samara and one in Kazan, referred to earlier) tended to feel marginalized. With a clear differentiation in their position, the choice made by one "dissenting" respondent was to "keep quiet" for the most of the interview. The danger of being ostracized undoubtedly played a role in such behavior.

Pro-Kremlin political analysts, and especially those more ideologically inclined among them, understand very acutely the high stakes involved in the issue as to which frame about the 1990s dominates the political and social land-scape in Russia. The official reaction to the festival *Ostrov 90kh* was derogatory and dismissive. The news anchors on *Rossiya 24* (August 22, 2016) quickly shifted attention from the festival and its ideas to what that alternative frame of the era missed: racketeers (*bratki*), impoverished pensioners, political chaos, food rationing, *chernukha*. The festival organizers were accused of urging nostalgia for the terrible 1990s, and, importantly, of hidden psychological manipulation employed by those who practice in neurolinguistic programming. The viewers of the program were thereby warned of the dangers of confusing freedom with anarchy and were advised to stay vigilant, especially when they encounter such counter-frames about the 1990s.

The denunciation of the counter-frame continued in 2017 and 2018. Sergei Kurginyan argued fiercely in a talk show *An Evening with Vladimir Solovyev* (June 2017) that the counter-frame about the 1990s associated with the Yeltsin Center in Yekaterinburg is part of the political struggle aimed at discrediting Putin's rule. In an intriguing and revealing reversal of the argument, he suggested that "this disavowal of the formula "likhie 90s" occurred in a specific moment and for a specific political purpose; it is not a matter of artistic imagery, but a clev-erly thought-out political action because all ideology was founded on present-ing the period that follows the 1990s as a moment of "saving"/escaping from the "likhie 90s." If these are not "likhie 90s" but "the sacred 90s," then they will have to be juxtaposed with the following period and we see that the Yeltsin Center is doing precisely that: their main slogan is "Yeltsin, come and take Putin away."[85] Kurginyan did his best to bring the numbers and facts in the show to demonstrate the truth behind the frame. An ideological crusader himself, he unintention-ally revealed and confirmed the crucial importance of this frame for supporting Russia's current political establishment.

The frame about the 1990s presented through stories that resonate with the public and stir emotions in the public space matters especially deeply because it creates an opportunity for emotional connection between Russia's current politi-cal leader and his followers who credit him with overcoming the 1990s. Putin's political achievements are presented to the public as a reversal of the chaos, anarchy, and disintegration of the 1990s. To the extent that the 1990s are feared ("never again"), the Kremlin looks like the country's savior.

The Kremlin did not invent this frame. In engaging, developing, and propa-gating it, the Kremlin built on the public resonance of the wider cultural produc-tion that presented the 1990s with the excess of violence and misery. The cultural entrepreneurs had their own reasons for such exaggeration and mythologizing tendencies, and there are real grounds for the societal resonance of such repre-sentations. But this resonance also provided a useful political opportunity for the Kremlin to appropriate and use this frame in favor of the political system constructed in the early 2000s.

Could the 1990s in Russia have been represented in a more balanced way? Many countries went through the dissolution of the Soviet Union and a painful transition to market economy with social and economic dislocation, confronting the challenge of constructing new collective identities. But only in Russia do the 1990s represent such a "chosen trauma," used to consolidate and unify the nation around this frame of national victimhood in the 1990s. There are undoubtedly structural reasons behind such a choice that are linked to Russia's unique geopolitical position after the collapse of the Soviet Union. Russia lost its positive identity grounding as a result of the Soviet collapse, and this "identity void" that opened up in the 1990s created the opportunities for the Kremlin to reverse the ideological backing of Yeltsin's reforms and present the 1990s as a period of state disintegration at the hands of leaders who betrayed Russia. But the presence of structural opportunities does not take away the responsibility for political choices made at the Kremlin. The implications of these choices are troublesome for Russia's future because they question the grounds for Gorbachev's and Yeltsin's reforms. They redirect attention from the need to build new institutions and new state-society relations in Russia to the symbolic issues used to promote societal consolidation that is emotionally driven and reactive in nature.

A more balanced representation of the 1990s—one that involves both the recognition of the economic and social hardships and an appreciation of the political and economic objectives pursued by reformers, as well as the reform achievements reflected in political pluralism, openness, and civil liberties enjoyed by the Russian population, along with the years of economic growth in the early 2000s that built on the reforms of the 1990s—will be necessary if and when the Russian political establishment will be ready to move beyond Putinism.

The ongoing health pandemic in Russia works to weaken the potency of this legitimation strategy that relies on the 1990s. Covid-19 forces Russian society to confront the troubled realities of the system that have been disguised by resonant symbolic and emotion-driven politics. Therefore, the power of this frame to prop the current political system and leadership in Russia will undoubtedly wane in the coming months and years.

6

MMM for VVP

BUILDING THE MODERN MEDIA MACHINE

We must occupy and at any cost
keep control of a) the telephone,
and b) the telegraph.

—LENIN, *"Sovety postoronnego"* (1920)[1]

DIFFERENT ACTORS AND institutions are involved in constructing and contesting identity narratives for a nation. Identity formation takes place within a
"relational setting of contested but patterned relations among narratives, people
and institutions."[2] Propagating any of these narratives publicly requires access to
mass media because the dominance of a specific narrative depends on its appeal
to group members. Media control therefore becomes a crucial resource if the government is bent on promoting a hegemonic, unifying identity discourse.

Putinism as identity politics relies on centralized media control, used to broadcast selected images, ideas, and messages about what it means to be a member of
the Russian national community. Media and political communication have been
central to constructing "the Putin phenomenon" and the contemporary political
landscape in Russia. Gleb Pavlovsky, one of the architects of the early Putin politics, reminiscences about the role of media in Russia in the following way:

> The Kremlin's experiments with the media politics started from the pov
> erty of the existing state toolkit—the federal center had neither money
> nor authority—rather than from the excess of cunningness. Even the
> governors followed the presidential decrees reluctantly and on occa
> sions but the central press and TV were consumed by the whole country.
> Improvising with communication, the Kremlin was trying to find new
> sources of strength.[3]

Vladimir Putin understood well the political power of the media and public communication tools. The electoral results of the 1995–1996 and 1999–2000 elections

The Red Mirror. Gulnaz Sharafutdinova, Oxford University Press (2020). © Oxford University Press.
DOI: 10.1093/oso/9780197502938.001.0001.

would have, most likely, been different if the oligarchical media resources were not deployed in support of the Kremlin.[4] The drama of media-driven politics unfolded in front of his own eyes, even before he reached the pinnacle of state power. As part of Boris Yeltsin's team, picked as Yeltsin's successor in 1999, Putin worked with self-assured political technologists such as Gleb Pavlovsky, who believed they could install anyone as Russia's president, once the Kremlin had made its choice and the media machine started working in favor of that candidate.

The founder of the Fund for Effective Politics (FEP) in 1995, Pavlovsky was involved in Russian politics as a political advisor since the early 1990s. A former Soviet dissident, he was inspired early on by the leftist theories developed in the West, reading such authors as Herbert Marcuse, whose writings were not allowed in the USSR.[5] Pavlovsky considered himself a Marxist, although the technological vision of politics that he promoted from the 1990s, focused on *managing* the voters and viewing them as an object to be controlled, brings him closer to Leninism. The technological take on politics, especially in the sphere of political agitation, political communication, and public opinion formation, was a subject highly developed by the Bolshevik political strategists.[6]

Gleb Pavlovsky was central to piloting and then propagating the use of conspiratorial ideas in the media as well as "black public relations" that relied on destroying the reputation of the political opponent as well as other instruments of political manipulation that became crucial during the 1999 parliamentary campaign.[7] He personally recalls and admits to the "imaginative" and clearly manipulative and dishonest methods he himself invented in order to discredit the Communists prior to the 1996 presidential elections. In a recent interview Pavlovsky recollected the enthusiasm with which his FEP engaged in the creation of such manipulative products as fake red-colored posters/post-its on selected buildings in Moscow, warning that this house is due to be nationalized after the June elections.[8] Pavlovsky played a central role (second only to Aleksandr Voloshin) in the 2000 presidential campaign, earning the nickname of "the Kremlin imagemaker." He also was an architect of the "Putin majority" notion that underpinned the legitimacy of the second president of the Russian Federation.[9]

Vladimir Putin's own understanding of the power of the media and communication technologies was reflected in the doctrine of Russia's informational security adopted in 2000, a few months after his election as Russia's president. This doctrine was revised and adopted anew in 2016 and reflected the Russian government's understanding of the ever-increasing political significance of information technologies and flows.[10] The 2000 doctrine was accompanied by a series of actions aimed at establishing the state control of main television channels. These actions were also associated with the Kremlin's efforts to wrestle away the political influence that Russia's so-called oligarchs wielded in the 1990s. After resolving issues with political and financial "heavyweights" from the 1990s, such as Boris Berezovsky, Vladimir Gusinsky, and Mikhail Khodorkovsky, the Kremlin focused on constructing its own "media machine."

Building the Machine: 2000–2007

Building a new media machine required (1) establishing control over the key media platforms and particularly TV channels, and (2) developing a pool of journalists, political analysts, and news anchors who would be advancing the Kremlin-defined political agenda. According to Vasily Gatov, a well-known Russian media analyst and a former chief of RIA Novosti media lab ("Novye mediatekhnologii"), Aleksei Gromov, Putin's press secretary during 2000–2008 and a deputy chief of staff of the Russian presidential administration since 2008, was the person responsible for establishing the hardware of the Kremlin's media system, along with Mikhail Lesin, the minister of the press, broadcasting, and mass communications of the Russian Federation.[11] The former chief editor of TV *Dozhd* (Rain), Roman Badanin in his new online media outlet *Proekt* (Project), also refers to Alexei Gromov as the main media operator in the Kremlin and as "the real boss of Russian TV."[12] Other journalists and researchers confirm Gromov's central role in establishing and maintaining control over the media.[13] Already from 2001, Gromov was on the board of directors of Russia's main TV channel ORT (now Channel One).[14] Mikhail Lesin, on the other hand, became the advisor to Putin on media relations during 2004–2009 and continued to work alongside Gromov on creating a system for information control and, among other things, spearheaded the creation of the global Russia Today (RT) TV channel.

Vladislav Surkov, the first deputy chief of the presidential administration during 1999–2011, became a key political figure with the responsibility for the machine's software—a new political language and the narrative articulating what new Russia was about. The main punch points of this narrative advanced from the Kremlin went through several iterations before arriving at its current, post-Crimea version. Surkov was in charge of developing and advancing the central ideological frames that guided the Kremlin's policymaking in the first decade of the 2000s. He was central to developing the main elements of the Kremlin's response to the 2004 electoral revolution in Ukraine, an event deemed deeply threatening to Russia's newfound political stability. In the aftermath of the "Orange revolution," the Kremlin increased its focus on the means and the content of political communication, producing a new "guardian discourse" (named after *okhraniteli*, the nickname used to refer to that group of pro-Kremlin analysts and journalists who propagated more conservative ideas combined with active belligerence and opposition toward the West). These analysts included Nikolai Starikov, Sergei Markov, Sergei Kurginyan, Aleksandr Dugin, Aleksandr Prokhanov, and a few others. Many of them became members of the Izborsky Club—Russia's "new conservative avant-garde"—a think-tank founded by Prokhanov in 2012.[15]

By then the Kremlin had already established full control over the main national TV channels: *Rossiya*, Channel One, and NTV, and had started to think about the online media resources as well.[16] But scholars have noted that the Kremlin controlled only the "commanding heights" of the media industry, not all the information flows, as was done during the Soviet era.[17] Even on the national TV channels, the producers made their own choices on entertainment-related programming. But the news programming was controlled from the top. Handpicked TV executives held weekly meetings in the Kremlin to receive instructions about the main agenda and the central frames to be advanced on the nightly news.[18] The rigid structure of the nightly news, with strict time allocations for covering the activities of the president and the prime minister (especially during the Medvedev's "tandem" presidency), was increasingly reminiscent of the Soviet-era *Vremya*.[19]

The so-called *temniki* (from the word "theme")—the written instructions about the thematic agenda and the main frames to be advanced by various media resources prepared by the presidential administration and distributed among the media professionals—is an interesting artifact of the Kremlin's control over media during the early 2000s.[20] As opposed to Soviet-era censorship, *temniki* took an agenda-setting, proactive approach, prescribing what events should be covered and under what light, and what events should be ignored. Marat Gelman, political analyst and a cofounder of the FEP (along with Gleb Pavlovsky), apparently invented this "managerial device" for controlling the content of political communication. He has mentioned in an interview that the *temniki* were first used in Ukraine (when Gelman and Pavlovsky got involved in Ukraine's 2004 presidential election on the side of Leonid Kuchma).[21] He suggested that *temniki* were an internal mechanism of control for creating the channel's political position:

> This is part of making sense of the daily agenda. It usually has three blocks. The first, informational, provides background to the journalist on specific topics. The second, recommendation section, includes a list of newsmakers on an issue. The third elaborates the editorial position of the channel.[22]

The weekly meetings of key television managers in the Kremlin were also apparently accompanied by written instructions about the main weekly talking points.[23] As the Kremlin's attention moved more onto other media platforms, such *temniki* presumably were distributed among other media managers as well. Curiously, these *temniki* are talked about more than they are actually seen in hard copies. Various journalists do claim to have seen at least one example of *temniki*. There are also copies of *temniki* circulating online.[24]

The prescriptive *temniki* were not the only tool for controlling the media and journalists in Russia. Journalists deemed too independent got fired or were moved to administrative positions, as happened with the talented Leonid Parfenov, Tatiana Mitkova, Savik Shuster, Stanislav Kucher, and many others.[25] The Kremlin also worked on establishing red lines on politically sensitive topics and thereby perpetuated a system of media self-censorship.[26] The "no-go zones" for journalists were referred to in the Russian media discussions using traffic rules terminology: *dvoinaia sploshnaia* (i.e., the "double yellow" line that journalists could not cross).[27] Crossing this line meant trouble with state authorities. Many Russian journalists paid with their lives for their honesty and bravery in ignoring these lines. This list, which includes Anna Politkovskaya, Ivan Safronov, Anastasia Baburova, Stanislav Markelov, Natalia Estemirova, and many other journalists across Russia, is unfortunately too long and has been growing every year.[28] In less extreme cases, the consequences of overstepping the red lines resulted in talented media managers losing their jobs and successful media outlets being closed or denied access to broadcasting (as in the case of TV *Dozhd* [Rain] station that was disconnected by Russia's TV network providers in 2014, and TV2, an independent TV channel in Tomsk oblast taken off the air in 2014 as well). Already in 2004, the Committee to Protect Journalists, a nonprofit organization that promotes press freedom worldwide, included Russia in the list of "worst countries to be a journalist."[29] These trends have not changed since.

Media observers have argued that in the first few years the Kremlin paid most attention to the television, leaving online news and the press relatively more diverse and free of direct Kremlin influence. This allowed the Russian government to defend the country's record of media freedom by referring to the large number of print outlets and radio and television companies. In Putin's own words in 2006: "we could not control them all even if we wanted to."[30] But even then, the Kremlin did care about the Internet audiences. Alexandr Morozov, an avid observer and analyst of Russian media and politics, noted that around 2003–2007 the Kremlin created a media pool financed directly from the presidential administration and tasked with fighting the political opposition not authorized or controlled by the Kremlin. The core of this media pool consisted of websites created by Konstantin Rykov and Vadim Gorshenin, such as *vzglyad.ru, pravda. ru, elektorat.ru, politonline.ru, politgeksogen.ru*, and *regnum.ru*.[31] Konstantin Kostin, then a deputy chief of the domestic policy department of the presidential

administration, Surkov's right-hand man and one of Russia's top political technologists, oversaw these online resources.

The fact that the Kremlin controlled these media platforms could be seen in
the synchronization of the messages they promoted. Their reactions to specific
events and personalities in political opposition, for example, were framed using
the same words and phrases, as if there were a centralized campaign promoted
from specific websites. Aleksandr Morozov noted, for example, that the same propaganda machine that was built by 2007 operated in reaction to the December
2011 arrests of oppositional figures (including Boris Nemtsov), because the sites
associated with the Kremlin-based media system cross-referenced each other and
used the same terminology, including references to "the fifth column," "Nemtsov's
transatlantic masters," "the State Department sponsored opposition," etc.[32]

Other instruments of the Kremlin-controlled political communication
machine were initiated in 2005 under Vladislav Surkov's guidance. *Russia Today*
(RT)—the first English-language foreign news channel funded by the Russian
government—started broadcasting in 2005. Besides expanding its communication arm, under Surkov the Kremlin also engaged closely with symbolic politics
that targeted Russia's youth through the newly created (in 2005) youth movement
Nashi.[33] At the same time, the Kremlin pushed for standardized history textbooks
and unrolled the new state program for patriotic education. The day of Unity, a
new national holiday celebrated on the 4th of November—was introduced to celebrate the events of 1612, when Moscow was liberated from the Polish-Lithuanian
occupation, ending the "time of troubles."[34] All these new, state-sponsored projects were initiated in 2005 and were driven by the Kremlin's attempt to shape the
public agenda in the direction of nurturing patriotism and, undoubtedly, a loyal-
ist stance toward the Putin-led government. Aleksandr Morozov referred to this
symbolic work during 2005–2010 as the "image factory" (*fabrika obrazov*) and as
an attempt to create a modern political public relations machine. The machine
involved several key "cultural operators," including the *Expert* magazine editor-
in-chief Valery Fadeev; the aforementioned political advisor Gleb Pavlovsky;
Vladislav Surkov's deputy in the presidential administration Aleksei Chesnakov,
and Konstantin Kostin, who replaced Chesnakov in 2008; the leader of *Nashi*
youth group Vasily Yakimenko; TV producer and the political coordinator of the
United Russia party's youth branch *Molodaya Gvardiia* Ivan Demidov; and the
aforementioned political consultant and art-manager Marat Gelman.[35] Many of
these individuals who, in essence, comprised Vladislav Surkov's operational team,
resigned from their positions in 2012. Some of them—Pavlovsky and Gelman
in particular—joined oppositional circles. Marat Gelman ended up emigrating
from Russia to Montenegro. A selected few, such as Valery Fadeev, have kept their
positions and evolved along with the system.

Stage 2: Fine-Tuning the Machine after 2011–2012 and Testing It on Ukraine

The key elements of the media control system in Putin's Russia were established during Putin's first two terms in power. But the system had to change and evolve as it confronted new political and technological challenges. The central political challenge the Kremlin faced at the start of Putin's third term in power was related to the political protests of 2011–2012. The Kremlin responded to this challenge with a major shift in political discourse. Post-2012 Russia could be represented as a country where the elites have abandoned their attempts to develop hybrid forms of ideology and identity that can combine Western values with notions and beliefs specific to Russia. The era of Vladislav Surkov and his version of postmodern creativity in the Kremlin has passed, likely deemed dangerous due to incessant ambiguities, nuances, and paradoxes evident, among other things, in the concept of "sovereign democracy" coined by Surkov. Surkov himself was replaced in his presidential administration post by a much simpler minded and more heavy-handed Vyacheslav Volodin. Surkov was later appointed a special advisor to the president on relations with Abkhazia, South Ossetia, and Ukraine. His ideas were replaced by a mix of ideas drawn from the "national-patriots" and Eurasianists such as Aleksandr Dugin, Aleksandr Prokhanov, Sergei Kurginyan, and Mikhail Leont'ev, and also relied on such Orthodox Christian thinkers as Bishop Tikhon Shevkunov, thought to be close to Vladimir Putin.[36] Vyacheslav Morozov referred to this new ideological mix as a "paleoconservatism" that drew a radical isolationist view of Russia's identity.[37]

The central elements of the media control system created by Surkov were kept largely in place. Under Volodin's and Gromov's stewardship, the Kremlin built on some of the elements that were deemed to be successful and hardened its approach in the spheres that the government deemed important to better control. The Kremlin's overall perception of the growing importance of informational tools of political control was also very clear, and was made public by Putin himself when he referred to information confrontation as one of the forms of competitive struggle, just as "the struggle for mineral resources."[38] The 2015 Freedom House report on press freedom in Russia noted that the Russian state controls, either directly or indirectly, all five of the major national television networks, national radio networks, key national newspapers, national news agencies, and more than 60% of the country's estimated 45,000 regional and local newspapers and periodicals.[39]

The Kremlin took new media initiatives in both international and domestic realms. Internationally, the Kremlin sought to build on RT's success. According to the polling firm Ipsos, within 10 years (by 2015) RT's global viewership increased to around 70 million per week (around 8 million weekly in the United States).[40] These numbers are rather small relative to other media giants such as BBC, CNN, Fox News, or MSNBC, with nightly viewership in the millions. Nonetheless, RT was among the top five foreign networks in the United States and Europe. What is even more important is that the RT network's role has been enhanced in the age of a more "democratic" media landscape driven by online communication. According to some observers, RT has formed "the hub of a new kind of state media operation: one that travels through the same diffuse online channels, chasing the same viral hits and memes, as the rest of the Twitter-and-Facebook-age media."[41]

Expanding on RT's perceived success, in 2014 the Kremlin launched another news agency, news website, and radio broadcasting service geared to non-Russian audiences. The new agency, named *Sputnik*, was created by *Rossiya Segodnya*, a new international news agency that replaced RIA Novosti in 2013. In the heat of the growing polarization between the West and Russia during 2014–2017, RT and Sputnik were referred to as the key tools of the Kremlin-waged information war against the West.[42]

The Kremlin built up its capacity to influence online communication on various social media platforms. The creation and operation of troll factories such as the Internet Research Agency (IRA)—a Russian company operating from St. Petersburg—was founded in 2013 and was first noticed in 2014–2015. The US-based investigation into the 2016 presidential election campaign has uncovered and indicted some of the employees of this company with the intent to interfere with the US political and electoral processes. The agency used fake accounts on such media platforms as Facebook and other online platforms, including newspapers, discussion boards, and video hosting services. Evgeny Prigozhin, a Russian businessman better known as "Putin's chef," is apparently in control of IRA and two other related internet trolling companies accused of trying to influence politics outside Russia. These troll factories emerged as an important tool in the informational warfare in which the Kremlin engaged especially actively in the atmosphere of polarization after the 2014 annexation of Crimea.

Domestically, the hardening in the Kremlin's approach to information control was evident in the new legislation advanced by the State Duma, the legislative branch of the Russian government, aiming to increase control over information flows and specifically in relation to online-based communication. Starting around 2012–2013, the Duma introduced and passed many conservative laws, minting the new legislation in such a rush that it was nicknamed the "mad printer."[43] The adoption of the 2012 amendments to the Law "On the Protection of Children from Information Harmful to their Health and Development" represented a turning point in state's offensive against the online media.[44] Also in 2012, the

Duma passed amendments to the law regulating the work of nongovernmental organizations (NGOs). The NGOs that receive foreign funding were required to register as "foreign agents" (the so-called foreign agents law), a term that is widely understood as "spies" in Russia. In 2013 the Duma approved amendments to the anti-extremism laws submitted by the executive branch. These changes criminalized the public advocacy of separatism and allowed the Russian Prosecutor General to block websites "promoting extremism" without court order. Later, the 2014 "Lugovoi Law" provided an additional possibility of blocking the sites "containing calls for unsanctioned acts of protest."[45]

In the same year, Putin signed into law the so-called gay propaganda bill that ostensibly protects children from "information promoting the denial of traditional family values," but in essence restricts the right to freedom of expression of LGBT community members. A related draft bill introduced in 2015 imposed fines for public displays of "non-traditional sexual relations," meaning that same-sex couples could be fined for holding hands. This bill did not pass, but it underscored the extremes to which the Russian legislators could go in their assistance to the government when it comes to controlling public space in Russia. The Kremlin's new conservative orientation empowered the "coming out" of the ultra-conservative deputies in the Duma who, suddenly, felt the public demand for their ideas and creativity. The likes of Irina Yarovaia, Elena Mizulina, Ekaterina Lakhova, Vitaly Milonov, and others came into the limelight with their sometimes scandalous ideas and bills testing the limits of the Kremlin's conservative agenda.

In 2015 the Duma passed a law that authorized the government to shut down any foreign organizations that are considered to undermine state security, national defense, or country's constitutional order. Such organizations are deemed "undesirable" by the Russian government and are banned from working within the country. As noted by various observers, the procedures for determining an organization "undesirable" are very nontransparent and uncontestable.[46]

The post-2012 recalibration of the political communication machine was not only legal in nature. It involved a "tightening of the screws" and the growing repressive orientation of the political system reflected, for example, in the enhanced use of the existing legislation, such as anti-extremism laws against individual expression, on the social media platforms.[47] In this period the Russian government began prosecuting Russian citizens based on social media use—for reposting pictures, memes, or any other content considered extremist or insulting of religious believers' feelings. The Agora legal advocacy NGO reported that around 90% of criminal cases involving social media activity in 2015 (about 200) fell under extremism law.[48] Eighteen of these cases resulted in jail terms.[49] More than half of these cases involve the most popular Russian social media platform *VKontakte*

(VK).[50] Many individuals targeted with these laws were actually active protesters against the regime, reflecting the instrumental use of this legislation against
political opposition. The return of "expert assessments," used by the authorities
in many of these cases, provides yet another flashback to Soviet times. Today, as
decades ago, the state repressive apparatus relies on conservatively oriented (or
simply compliant) historians, religious experts, linguists, and other specialists to
defend new conservative norms and laws at the courtrooms.[51]

The Kremlin initiated additional measures to bring online communication
under greater state control, requiring internet companies to retain the content
of all communications for six months and data about those communication for
three years, also making it easier for the authorities to access personal information
without any judicial oversight. In 2014, Pavel Durov, the founder of Russia's most
popular social media platform VK had to sell the shares and cede control of his
company to Putin loyalists because of his refusal to hand over the personal data of
VK users to FSB.[52] The same year, Galina Timchenko, the chief editor of the popular Russian news website *lenta.ru*, lost her job for publishing an interview with
Andrei Tarasenko, the leader of Ukraine's far-right paramilitary movement Right
Sector.[53] Three top editors of RBC, a Russian media organization that developed,
arguably, the best reporting on business and political news in Russia since 2013,
both in newspaper and website format, quit in 2016, under pressure for their
reporting on Sergei Roldugin (a lifelong Putin friend whose name emerged from
the Panama papers), Putin's daughters, and the business dealings of a businessman believed to be a husband of one of them, and Putin's palace.[54] These cases
illustrated the operation of red lines drawn by the Kremlin. Most of the talented
journalists, media managers, and entrepreneurs discussed earlier decided, in the
end, to emigrate. The brain drain from Russia has risen to extreme proportions
in the aftermath of the Crimea annexation and in the new atmosphere of "tightening the screws" in Russia.[55] Meanwhile, Russian intellectual diaspora communities have formed around the world, in cities like Kyiv, Riga, Vilnius, Prague,
London, Washington, DC, and Palo Alto.

The narrowing of the sphere of public expression in Russia was also evident
in the additional measures taken by the Kremlin to control creative expression in
art, literature, and theater. That the Kremlin's ultra-patriotic, traditional values-
driven vision became the one that was actively sponsored and endorsed by the
government structures is one important element signaling the trend. The powerful film director and long-time head of the Russia Cinematographers' Union, a
staunch Putin supporter, Nikita Mikhalkov, and the minister of culture Vladimir
Medinsky, allegedly supported by Mikhalkov, were among the leading cultural
figures promoting this vision. From 2011 Mikhalkov started disseminating his

nationalist and anti-Western views through a new program *Besogon TV* (exorcism), a video-blog broadcast on *Russia 24* (a state-owned news channel), through which the film director regularly shares his anti-liberal vision of a great Russia facing "the enemy at the gate."

The countering and purging of the remaining avant-garde, liberal voices in the cultural sphere represented the other side of this trend. Many representatives of Russia's liberal-oriented creative urban class chose to leave Russia, relocating to culturally more welcoming Western countries. Some of those who have stayed faced difficulties. The criminal persecution of Kirill Serebrennikov, the well-known, talented theater and film director, is an important example of this new trend. It has been viewed as a signal from the Kremlin about the limits of tolerance for cultural production in Russia that challenges the dominant, traditional values–oriented discourse.

The Kremlin was not always this conservative in its vision. The new discourse came to dominate the Russian public sphere only during Putin's third presidential term. The search for Russia's new political language started earlier, under Vladislav Surkov, the chief architect of the Kremlin's media machine and political strategy in the first decade of the 2000s.

Building Sovereign Political Lexicon for the Russian State
Take 1: Vladislav Surkov and the Limits of Postmodern Hybridity in Russia

Besides constructing the main elements of the Kremlin's political communication machine during 2005–2010, Vladislav Surkov was also busy with developing the content and the message to be communicated from the Kremlin. In Surkov's own terminology, Russia needed a new "political lexicon" for "communicating to ourselves and the external world images and meanings essential for a nation's historical subjectivity."[56] This was, in effect, Surkov's understanding of the need to construct Russia's national identity: "we all witnessed the Soviet Union, we all witnessed the difficult era of the 1990s, we all live today and plan to live tomorrow. But we have not worked out a consensus in our society in evaluating these recent events. It means we do not have a plan for the future."[57] The key Kremlin operator at that time, Surkov understood this to be an important political challenge:

We can speak about our experience with democracy in our own words. Because the one who does not speak, he/she listens. The one who listens, follows.[58]

Surkov's attempt at developing Russia's new political lexicon was epitomized in his hybrid notion of "sovereign democracy" that appeared in 2005. This concept responded to Putin's emphasis on Russia's sovereignty, and non-interference and autonomy from the West, articulated in a defensive response to the 2004 Orange revolution in Ukraine. It also signaled Russia's commitment—at that historical moment—to basic European norms and values of democracy and sovereignty.[59] Although widely discussed, the concept did not stand the test of time. Dmitry Medvedev, Russia's president during 2008–2012, referred to it as an oxymoron, and Putin himself did not express any particular support for this concept either. It gradually disappeared from the public space. Nonetheless, the notions of sovereignty and democracy still remain central to Russia's political elites. The currently dominant political discourse in Russia, reinforced regularly by Putin's own press conferences and interviews, asserts the Russian political system to be democratic. The polemical nature of political talk shows on TV, the invited domestic and international experts and commentators (all carefully selected to fit a specific message to be promoted at the central channels), regular elections (if tightly controlled and managed)—all these communication strategies and institutions maintain the claim that Russia has a democratic system of government and pluralist public sphere.

Surkov's vision for Russia, formulated around 2006–2007, was considerably more nuanced than the ideas that were brought forward and came to dominate Russia's discursive landscape during Putin's third and fourth terms in power. Inquiring "[S]hould the Russian state be a fortress-state?" Surkov responded in the following way:

> In terms of defending the state borders and ensuring the nuclear shield in such an unstable world, absolutely yes. But being a fortress-state in the modern economy, with financial flows and international relations is, of course, not possible. Separating from the outside world by the dikes, paling and iron curtains is a path towards stagnation and disintegration. It is an expulsion to the periphery. It is a marginalization of the state.[60]

Using his concept of "sovereign democracy," Surkov promoted a hybrid ideological construction that tried to link the idea of a globalized Russia—a legitimate part of the global economy, global financial flows, and international relations—with the idea of a sovereign Russia that is free to choose its own developmental trajectory and is free from Western interference.

Although Surkov maintained his position and continued his work in the presidential administration during Medvedev's presidency (2008–2012), the search for a new political language in this period had different accentuations.

Medvedev abandoned the more defensive, sovereignty-focused talk in favor of promoting the image of Russia developing in a progressive direction. He emphasized modernization and technological advancement, most clearly highlighted in his slogan "Rossia, vpered"—this was the title of his programmatic article published in 2009.[61] The Institute for Modern Development (INSOR)—the new think tank associated with Medvedev—had even produced some articles critical of authoritarian tendencies in Russia's political system.[62] These potentially significant ideas were largely disregarded. The political arrangement—*tandem*—that included Medvedev and Putin in power in the end worked more to maintain the key features of the system constructed in Putin's first two terms in power.

Known for his love of gadgets, Medvedev was mocked for it by his critics. The change of discourse under his leadership and the emphasis on Russia's modernization and progressive development in the end did not amount to any serious shift in strategy and was represented by observers as a "fling with the liberals" while he continued to work under Putin's shadow.[63] In the end, Medvedev's "liberalism" (if very shallow) was blamed for the 2011–2012 protests that brought the educated and well-to-do urbanites to the streets of Russia's biggest cities in demand of accountable government, honest elections, and Putin's resignation. Confronted with this political crisis, the Kremlin made a sharp turn away from the earlier hybridity of political forms and ideas and toward conservatism and a more repressive political system.

Take 2: Russia's Return to Traditional Values, National Exceptionalism, and Militarism

Elsewhere I referred to this shift as a shift from "sovereign democracy" to "sovereign morality."[64] The ideas promoted by the Kremlin since 2012 represent a major break with Western values and paradigms and a clear assertion and a defense of Russia's unique developmental trajectory and Russia's civilizational autonomy. This new paradigm of a "millennial Russia"—the last bastion of traditional Christian values (allegedly forgotten and abandoned by the decadent West)—became the guiding force for the Kremlin-controlled media and political commentary. For the Russian domestic audience, it represents a shift from a defensive stance vis-à-vis the West—"don't teach us how to build democracy in Russia"—to an offensive stance—"Russia will teach you how to stand up for your forgotten Christian values," providing the ground for turning the repressed public feelings of defeat, shame, and humiliation harbored after the fall of the Soviet Union into the revealed emotions of righteous anger, moral superiority, and even hatred. Russia was not among the followers anymore—not among those who wanted to catch up with the West and Western institutions and those who

saw the Western example as the one worthy of striving toward. This new paradigm meant that Russia was unique and exceptional; that it has its own path and
its unique mission of defending traditional (Christian) values. The space for self-
righteousness and aggression—internationally and domestically—was wide open
as the Kremlin sanctioned and promoted these collective views and emotions in
the public sphere.

This new strategic vision for Russia's place and role in the world solidified in
the euphoric atmosphere after the annexation of Crimea. The developments in
American domestic politics only fueled further the propagated sense of moral
superiority and national exceptionalism in Russia, providing a valuable fodder for
talk shows and the "infotainment" industry. In the wake of Donald's Trump's victory in the 2016 presidential elections, the issue of Russia's interference in the US
electoral process pulled "the Russia issue" into the center of American domestic
politics. The more "the Russia question" entered the epicenter of US politics, the
more geopolitically significant the Kremlin and the country as a whole became in
the eyes of the Russian population and undoubtedly the Russian elites.

The turn toward traditional and conservative social values has been the first
hallmark of Putin's third term in power. This strategic turn expressed itself in
an increasing reliance on the Orthodox Church, a mobilization of "traditional
Russian values" rhetoric, and a campaign against "nontraditional" values that are
allegedly associated with the decadent West. This shift started with the *Pussy Riot*
affair. The imprisonment of the young women associated with this punk group,
who sang in the Cathedral of Christ the Savior and uploaded the clip on *YouTube*,
became the first signal of what was to come. The Kremlin utilized this incident
to promote a new, value-based discourse that was highly moralistic and symbolic. This discursive shift was a response to the new political reality of the loss
of the acclaimed "Putin majority" of Putin's first and second terms in power that
became clear with the protests of 2011–2012.[65] It represented an attempt to construct a new majority that would exclude all the "angry urbanites" and incorporate the rest of the public on an intense emotional ground. Indeed, the moralizing
stance taken by the regime has been accompanied by the "divide and rule" political tactic whereby the establishment had juxtaposed the protesters (supposedly
rich and spoiled Muscovites) to the rest of the Russian public that the regime was
attempting to reconsolidate based on traditional, conservative values. The main
target audience of Putin's "moral" leadership was the more socially conservative,
parochial, and nationalist segments of the Russian public: those who saw themselves as the main losers of the Soviet collapse; those who made a living in struggling industrial cities and monotowns; those who held a grudge against oligarchs
and the new Russians with their lavish, cosmopolitan, glamorized lifestyles; and

finally, those who had sought a refuge in religion from the cynicism and material values of post-Soviet life.

The tenth annual Valdai Club meetings, held in September 2013, showcased a newly assertive president of Russia taking upon himself and Russia the role of a defender of Christian and moral values. In a position that reverberated abroad, Vladimir Putin criticized Euro-Atlantic countries in renouncing their spiritual roots and consequently facing a moral and demographic crisis as a result of policies that equated traditional families with same-sex marriages, and belief in God with belief in Satan. Highlighting the need for Russia's national and cultural self-determination, Putin posited Russia to be a protector of Western civilization in the face of globalization, multiculturalism, and accentuation of minority rights allegedly leading to inevitable degradation and crisis. Putin's annual address to the Federal Assembly in December 2013 reiterated the message of Russia as a global defender of traditional values, linked it with Russia's role in the successful resolution of a crisis over the use of chemical weapons in Syria, and posited Russia as the last bulwark against the West rolling down into "chaotic darkness"—the path that presumably results from forgetting about fundamental civilizational values.

Asserting Russia's national exceptionalism became the centerpiece of the symbolic turn in Russian politics. The Kremlin-based operators, with Putin at the helm, asserted Russia to be a state-civilization with over 1,000 years of history and deep cultural and spiritual roots. The opening and closing shows for the 2014 Sochi Olympics, directed by Konstantin Ernst, built on the idea of Russia's millennial history, showcasing different historical periods and the main cultural treasures deemed to be among the main Russian civilizational contributions to humanity. It is noteworthy that the historical images were associated with the reigns of Ivan the Terrible and Peter the Great, and the more recent Soviet period. The showcase of the Russian cultural treasures involved Russian avant-garde painting, classical literature (Pushkin, Tolstoy, Gogol, Lermontov, etc.), and music by Russia's classical and more modern composers (Borodin, Shnitke, Stravinsky, Khachaturyan, Artem'ev, Doga, Tukhmanov, etc.)

Besides history, culture, and values, the pro-Kremlin observers also promote a more pragmatic version of the argument about Russia's exceptionalism. This variant involves an argument about Russia's self-sufficiency due to its size and its massive natural riches. In a June 2018 political talk show, *Evening with Vladimir Solovyev*, Nikita Mikhalkov appealed very emotionally: "we have everything to live by ourselves, without them all [the West]. We should learn to produce everything that people need here at home. Goods, not the raw materials."

The same argument was voiced by one of the respondents of my focus-group interview in Kazan in November 2017:

We have everything that we need in our country. Perhaps only machine building is lacking; and we can build it up if we wanted to. So we do not have to depend on anyone. We have all our own: oil, forests, water, gas. We do not really need anyone.

This new morality and traditional values-based discourse became a solid foundation for Putin's political victory over the domestic opposition. It also provided a building ground and a moral justification for Russia's 2014 foreign policy actions with regard to Ukraine. Newly self-righteous, Russia's political leadership did not hesitate to opportunistically take over Crimea, when Ukraine was overtaken by Maidan, and to promote destabilization in East Ukraine, relying on a heated propaganda campaign.

Confronting the West—as a whole—and the United States, in particular, became another important element in the Kremlin's political communication strategy. It clearly went along with (or was another side of the coin) of the previously discussed "sovereign morality" and the assertion of Russia's own civilizational path and moral superiority. This confrontation strategy, driven by the image of Russia as a besieged fortress, involved both symbolic and real aspects. A shift from the rhetorical "global defender of traditional values" to a militarized defense of the *Russky mir* occurred almost seamlessly. The sky-high popularity of Putin's foreign policy actions testified, additionally, to the cleverness of the rhetoric advanced by the Kremlin and the degree to which the new morality-based discourse targeted the softest psychological spots in Russian society.

As noticed by other commentators, Putin's new morality discourse expressed and fed into the society-wide *ressentiment* associated with the nation's post-imperial trauma and "an extension of the inferiority complex which, in order to compensate for one's own failures, forms a system of morality that denies the values of the enemy and blames him for one's own faults."[66] Indeed, constructing the enemy was just another side of the Kremlin-initiated "morality turn." Whether embodied in the US government, a "fascist junta in Kyiv," or the "fifth column" at home—the state-controlled media pounded the message of "the enemy at the gate," fixating public attention on the economic, political, and moral problems inflicting the West, Ukraine, and the home-grown opposition, and displacing entirely any meaningful discussion of domestic problems at home. The nation's mass consciousness turned outward, with the public energy directed at degrading the symbolic "other" (whether the West, the United States, or Ukraine), while Russia herself remained in the "blind spot," unseen and imperceptible.

The theme of war became a central topic of public concern and discussion during Putin's third presidential term. Starting with "polite men" in Crimea—special service military from the GRU—who ensured the peaceful annexation of Crimea, public attention moved to Pskov paratroopers who died in Donbass in the summer of 2014,[67] then military intervention in Syria that started in September 2015, and the activities of the private military company Wagner (allegedly associated with Evgeny Prigozhin, discussed earlier in the book as a person who controls troll factories in St. Petersburg) in Syria and other countries. Meanwhile, pundits focused on the ideas of hybrid and informational war, "Gerasimov military doctrine," and cyber-warfare to describe the growing confrontation between Russia and the West. The giant statue of Mikhail Kalashnikov unveiled in Moscow in September 2017 became the perfect symbolic complement to the Kremlin's policies and rhetoric during 2014–2017.[68]

The rhetoric of war has only grown since the beginning of Putin's fourth term in power in 2018. The stage for these developments was set at Putin's annual 2018 address to the Federal Assembly, held just few weeks in advance of the March presidential elections. A big part of that speech was dedicated to boasting about Russia's new powerful weapons, including a claim for developing an unprecedented compact nuclear reactor that could power a drone. Many analysts doubted some of these statements, referring to Russia's lack of capability for such production. Others referred to Putin's nuclear "trolling."[69] Indeed, the rhetorical tactic that started in 2014 with Dmitry Kiselev's warnings of Russia's capabilities to turn the United States into "nuclear ashes" seems to have been embraced fully by Vladimir Putin in 2018.[70] In a pre-election documentary, *Miroporyadok 2018* (The Global Order 2018), produced by Vladimir Solovyev, Putin ruminates about the catastrophic consequences of nuclear war, noting, as an afterthought, "Why would we need the world if there is no Russia in it?" More recently, at an annual Valdai Club meeting, again, conjuring an image of a nuclear war, Putin suggested, "As martyrs, we will go to heaven. And they will just croak because they won't even have time to repent."[71] The image of the enemy, which had been so important to consolidating Soviet identity, has made a full comeback in Putin's Russia.

7

Le Cirque Politique à la Russe

POLITICAL TALK SHOWS AND PUBLIC OPINION LEADERS IN RUSSIA

In the middle of all open spaces there is a place
It is light and everyone is looking there
With honor and commitment all will be taught how it is
Children and elderly and all the rest.
An evening windbag!
An evening windbag!
A true labourer of our times.[1]

BORIS GREBENSHCHIKOV, "The Evening M" (2019)

RULING THROUGH PERSUASION is easier than ruling through repression. Persuasion is the main purpose of the Kremlin's media machine. Vladimir Putin is a skillful communicator and has proven it over and over again at his annual press conferences, numerous interviews, and other public performances.[2] But shaping a country's public opinion takes more than that. The Kremlin's effort at building support for the regime and for Putin involves many spokespeople, including public media personalities, influential news anchors, and talk-show hosts who promote "strategic narratives," interpretive frames, and the overall political agenda to those segments of the Russian public that could be considered to be among the more passive consumers of information.

Television remains the primary source of information for the Russian public. According to an August 2019 Public Opinion Foundation (FOM) survey, around 64% of the population get their news from watching television.[3] Levada surveys around the same time revealed that 72% of respondents used TV as their main source of information.[4] Meanwhile, 2013 Gallup polls reported that number to be at 85%.[5] The reliance on TV for getting the news in Russia has been slowly dropping, along with the level of trust. The number of those using TV as the main news source has diminished, according to FOM figures, from 87% in 2010,

The Red Mirror. Gulnaz Sharafutdinova, Oxford University Press (2020). © Oxford University Press.
DOI: 10.1093/oso/9780197502938.001.0001.

to 64% in 2019.[6] The same August 2019 FOM survey revealed that only 35% of the people trust television. The numbers on trust have been dropping, from 63% in 2015 to 50% in 2017 and 43% in 2018.[7] But the television producers and media professionals in Russia work hard on maintaining the popularity of television, copying best practices from the West in an effort to gain the most influence over the audience.[8] It is fair to say that the groups most supportive of Vladimir Putin are likely to be television viewers; however, this does not mean that those identifying themselves with political opposition do not watch TV.[9] More than half of the Russian population watch television every day as an entertainment.[10] Sarah Oates, the Russian media expert at the University of Maryland, suggested that the juxtaposition of traditional and online media systems might not be as useful as was earlier thought, when pundits hoped for "online revolutions."[11] Oates suggested that a focus on strategic narratives promoted by the state and the various informational pressures on those narratives promoted through various media platforms might prove a more fruitful path for studying informational systems in authoritarian settings.

Strategic narratives are an important part of the Kremlin-led identity politics. It is a type of nation-branding practice and rhetoric that the Kremlin relies on to advance the desired images of what Russia is about and what belonging to the Russian community means. These are the ideas used by the Kremlin to construct shared meanings about the country's past, its present, and its potential future. Strategic narratives are promoted through state-controlled news programming. The Kremlin keeps tight control over agenda setting and framing the events, including the use of *temniki* to do that. A number of prominent news anchors emerged in the last five years as the Kremlin's mouthpieces. Dmitry Kiselev, a combative host of *Vesti nedeli*; news presenter Kirill Kleimenov, who turned the traditional daily *Vremya* into something that resembles a talk-show format; the married couple Olga Skabeeva and Evgeny Popov, who cohost *60 minut*—a weeknight political talk show. These prominent media personalities are important elements in the Kremlin's media machine: they explain to the public why the Kremlin-promoted view of the world is the only correct one. Their increased visibility and political prominence reflects the changes in the Kremlin's media strategy after the 2011–2012 protests. Based on their analysis of Channel 1 and *Rossiya* broadcasts between 2010 and 2014, Vera Tolz and Yuri Teper have noted that the superficial similarity of the Russian forms of television programming that resemble the classic Western "infotainment" genre should not blur their distinct nature. They introduced the term *agitainment* to better capture the new Russian media model of "an intensive and prolonged, centrally sanctioned communication of ideologized political messages, delivered in accordance with an entertainment logic."[12]

Among various types of news programs, political talk shows provide a prime venue for studying the content of the state-promulgated strategic narratives, as well as the art of political persuasion as it is practiced in Russia today. The political talk shows supply a very convenient and cheap platform for official propaganda. A Russian media expert, Vasily Gatov, estimates that talk shows cost, on average, $15,000 per episode.[13] They serve several functions simultaneously. Framed as a platform for sharing diverse opinions, the talk shows provide an entertainment to their viewers and introduce the viewers to the main events of the day, simultaneously channeling the Kremlin's frame of analysis. The entertainment aspect of talk shows is very important. Most observers agree that Russian television has been keeping up with the global trends of privileging the popular entertainment function of television broadcasting.[14] But in the Russian case, this is not a market-driven process that reflects and promotes de-politicization and de-ideologization. To the contrary, the Russian-style *agitainment* involves coordinated ideologized campaigns on politicized topics that advance specific political messages through their constant repetition.[15]

The more the political system relies on the ongoing mass media–based ideological messaging, the more prominent the role of those who deliver these messages. The extent to which the audiences trust them determines the propagandistic impact of the media machine. Political talk shows that are very much associated with their hosts therefore carry much potential, from the Kremlin's perspective, and the hosts often turn into influential opinion leaders. Even more, the hosts sometimes turn into co-creators of the message, as long as they are trusted by the Kremlin to take a pro-Kremlin side.[16]

In this chapter I focus specifically on one important media personality whose talk shows and other creative output have acquired public prominence in Russia. Such zooming in on one case reveals specific mechanisms used in the political persuasion process and highlights—on a micro-level—the process of opinion formation and its manipulation in Russia. It also enables "reading" the main content of the ideological messages sent through the media.

Pragmatic, authoritative, and manipulative, Vladimir Solovyev is among the media personalities who have become central to forming the new political discourse and constructing the new boundaries of what is permitted, what is taken for granted, and what could still be a point of contention in political debates in Russia. Solovyev is arguably the best example of the toolkit the Kremlin relies on to propagate its messages among Russia's politically engaged (if otherwise passive) public who rely on television to form their opinions. The "us versus them" mentality, propagated using the image of external and internal enemies, and the related but mostly assumed sense of Russian exceptionalism are the two underlying ideas that are central to Solovyev's shows. Solovyev's public rhetoric and his political function from the Kremlin's perspective are the best illustration of the fact that the two ideas that used to be fundamental to the Soviet strategy of nation- and consensus-building have returned to modern-day Russia.

The Cynical King of Political Talk Shows and His Tools

Combining entertainment with news analysis, political talk shows have become the central tool of political propaganda in post-2014 Russia.[17] While many Russian talk shows aimed at de-politicizing the public, the role of political talk shows became more pronounced during the electoral seasons and at moments of active foreign-policy engagements by the Russian government. The Russian government's intervention in Syria and its policy toward Ukraine, for example, undertaken in the context of heightening polarization with the West since 2014, have been accompanied by an active reliance on propaganda tools on Russian TV.[18]

The Kremlin worked on engaging and mobilizing formerly apolitical sections of the public by targeting the primary "emotional buttons" of Russian society.[19] Specifically, it aimed at increasing the level of anger and public anxiety by reviving historically rooted national fears and hatreds associated with fascism and World War II. The political developments in Ukraine have been presented to the Russian public as a sign of fascist revival in Ukraine that is supported by the West (and the United States in particular) and that threatens Russian speakers in Ukraine.[20]

The Kremlin also tried to manipulate the national wounds associated with the loss of Russia's international stature and the perceived "greatness" of the Soviet Union, positing the return of Crimea, specifically, as a morally superior, responsible, and justified action on Russia's part. The new rule-making claimed and asserted by Russia on this international boundary issue was interpreted by the public as a "return" of the country to the category of "great powers" that are free to construct rules rather than being bound to follow existing ones.[21] The resulting ambivalence in public opinion data—showing widespread fears of a new world war, along with a newfound sense of well-being and self-confidence—is not surprising in this picture. The Russian public has been bombarded with the image of "the enemy at the gate" and the "defender" of *russky mir*—Vladimir Putin—who has taken Russia from its condition of victimhood in the 1990s into a new strength and assertiveness in the twenty-first century.

The political talk shows take up a considerable amount of daily prime time TV, and their number has increased in the last few years to over a dozen that broadcast on Russia's three major TV channels. Some of these shows get an extended time through "special editions" to cover major international breaking news. Millions of Russian viewers regularly watch the staged debates that claim to present different perspectives on key issues of the day, but in the end promote the dominant view preferred by the Kremlin. Even if sometimes these shows become very heated and relapse into fist and water fights between the opponents, they work to construct the taken-for-granted, majority worldview that is expected to be shared by the viewers of these shows.

Within the world of Russia's post-2014 TV-based propaganda, Vladimir Solovyev could rightfully be called the king of political talk shows and the central bolt of the Russian infotainment/agitainment machine. According to the sociological study of Russian citizens' attitudes toward mass media, conducted in spring 2019, Vladimir Solovyev was ranked as a number one journalist who elicits trust in his viewers; 23% of respondents picked Solovyev.[22] He was followed by Andrei Malakhov, the host of the most popular non-political talk show on Russian TV, *Let Them Talk* (*Pust' govoryat*), the Russian equivalent of the Jerry Springer show.[23] Olga Skabeeva, Andrei Norkin, and Vladimir Pozner—other well-known persons in Russia's infotainment industry—shared third place. Solovyev's popularity and high public recognition are undoubtedly due to his role as the host of political talk shows that have become central in the process of shaping public opinion in Russia.

Solovyev's television career started in 1999. He was one of the cohosts of the political talk show *The Process*, broadcast on ORT, and he had his own program on TNT. He also had a few other talk shows on TV 6 and TVS channels in the first decade of the 2000s. His show *Poedinok* (*Duel*) on TVS was followed by a very similar *K barieru!* (*To the Barrier!*) on NTV in 2003 and then returned under its original name on *Rossiya 1* channel in 2010. Solovyev's political views have evolved along with his country's ruling elites, so to say. In the 1990s and the first decade of the 2000s he positioned himself as a liberal. Around 2011 he was still defending freedom of speech and criticizing the Russian government in his talk shows. The discursive shift initiated by the Kremlin in 2012, along with the 2013 Euromaidan demonstrations in Kyiv, brought Solovyev to the "patriotic" side. Since then, Solovyev joined in earnest the state-centered agenda defending Russian foreign policy and the political establishment.

From 2012 on *Rossiya 1*, Solovyev has hosted a weekly talk show, *Sunday Evening with Vladimir Solovyev*, that has become one of the most important political programs on Russian TV. The evolution of this show and the virtuoso techniques used by Solovyev to get his message across are noteworthy given the role this show plays in shaping public opinion in Russia. From its inception, the talk show engaged with very important debates linked to Russian history and contemporary challenges such as anti-corruption policies. However, from 2014, as the crisis in Ukraine evolved, the show was offered more frequently until it turned into a daily, *An Evening with Vladimir Solovyev*. The central topics discussed in the show have also shifted in favor of foreign policy–related issues, primarily concerning Ukraine and, later, Syria and Turkey, and always the United States. The show is structured as a debate between six to eight guests led by the opinionated and browbeating host. The guest (expert) group is not very diverse. Given the continuity of this particular show, there are a number of individuals who routinely participate in the show. Among them are Vladimir Zhirinovsky, Sergei Kurginyan, Sergei Mironov, and Gennady Zyuganov. The LDPR (Liberal Democratic Party of Russia) leader Vladimir Zhirinovsky is one of the most frequent contributors, perhaps as a credit to his oratorical/stage performance skills.

The central element of the show—the expert group—is there to represent different sides of the argument. Thus, the programs that cover Ukraine would necessarily include individuals who would speak on behalf of Ukraine. And, more generally, care is taken to present diametrically different positions during the debates. The supposed diversity of the views voiced during these talk shows is there to represent the strength of Russian democracy. This view is reinforced when there are guests invited from foreign countries. Nonetheless, it is a sham democracy because, first, the experts are chosen with a very good understanding of their quality and impact on the audience. The "wrong" point of view is never represented by qualified experts, lest they credibly challenge the dominant view. At some exceptional moments such experts were actually present, but the host could simply turn off their microphones. These experts (for the opposing side) fall under the category of "useful idiots," used by the Kremlin to discredit the opposing view. Furthermore, the debate is governed by the host, whose interferences provide the necessary cues to the experts as well as the audience. The host controls whose turn it is to speak and, thereby, has an opportunity to intervene and shut the voices deemed threatening to the dominant view. Therefore, in the end, Solovyev's talk show is really about elevating Solovyev and his point of view, which is, coincidentally, also the point of view that the Kremlin wants to convey to the public.

Thus, many programs focused on Ukraine during 2014–2018 included Vyacheslav Kovtun, a political expert from Ukraine. Kovtun participated not only in many of Solovyev's shows, but also in a few other Russian political talk shows, as someone who could defend Ukraine's position. The important detail about Kovtun is that he is better known today in Russia than in Ukraine. Although he participated in Ukrainian politics and ran for *Verkhovna Rada*, Ukraine's Liberal Party's list, the party was not successful and was the last in the list of 29 parties on the electoral ballot. He is known even less in Ukraine as a political expert. After his 2014 political failure, he gained a lot of publicity in Russia, participating frequently in political talk shows and speaking on behalf of Ukraine. Indeed, he became a regular in Solovyev's program and became famous as a result.

Commentators disagree about the genuineness of his involvement, and some view him as a "fake" made by the Kremlin strategists. The nature of the public reaction to him is best described as mockery and ridicule. Many people in Russia look at him as a TV clown. The amount of negative emotions expressed and poured onto him during the shows, in the comments on the virtual media space, and, undoubtedly, on the couches and in the rooms of the show's TV viewers, is overwhelming and raises questions about the psychological factors that play into the outrage that characterizes the reception of his personality. The host is usually the leading force in articulating such outrage and anger. The audience members that largely associate themselves with the host and his position follow those signals and react accordingly. Such emotionally driven response—demonstrated by the host and adopted by the audience—ensures that the "correct" point of view becomes practically "embodied" in and by the viewers, as does the reaction to the "incorrect" viewpoint. The neural connections created in the brain as a result of emotions experienced during these talk shows—over and over—could be viewed as a sort of Russian-style, individual-based "firewall" that the Kremlin can rely upon to defend its worldview and frame of reference. Firing up emotions on specific issues on a regular basis leads to preconscious (i.e., based on sensory or perceptual experiences as opposed to cognitive efforts) formation of specific associations that influence subsequent information processing and behavioral responses.[24] The Russian talk-show viewers, who have associated themselves with the position supported by Solovyev and who ridiculed or got angry at the opponents' viewpoint, could be counted on to never make a conscious effort to consider the legitimacy of the opposite view. Through their passive participation and enjoyment of the show, they develop *tacit knowledge*, learning implicitly the key ideas and arguments that constitute the dominant, socially desirable frame of mind.[25]

Solovyev's skill in maintaining the popularity of his show therefore becomes crucial for keeping such a central propaganda mechanism in operation. His ability to gain and maintain high public recognition and wide viewership is politically significant for the Kremlin.[26]

A separate question that comes to mind is why Kovtun agrees to undergo such psychological beating and humiliation again and again. There are two plausible answers. First, he participates "because of the money." The experts who participate in these shows receive a substantial compensation for their participation. Kovtun could be considered to be a loser in Ukraine. Even if he plays the role of someone who hates Russia, that did not stop him from buying an apartment and living in Moscow. Second, it is also clear that he enjoys enormously the publicity and fame he receives through these talk shows. His Facebook account is full of pre-announcements of his shows, along with selfies made in the studio.[27]

The regular participation of Greg Veiner, presented to the audience as an American journalist, in Solovyev's shows as well as other political talk shows is another example of such "biased" choice of experts. Greg Veiner—who used to be known as Grigory Vinnikov—is a Russian émigré who left the Soviet Union in the 1980s and became a businessman in the United States. Vinnikov owned a travel company that specialized in selling airline tickets to Russia. Around 2012 the company went delinquent and, having accumulated big debt for office rent in New York, Vinnikov left the United States and returned to Russia. Many of his creditors consider him to be a fraudster, although, according to Vinnikov, he was waiting to sell his New York penthouse to pay off his debt.[28]

In Russia, Vinnikov became a regular on Solovyev's talk shows (and other shows on Channel 5), presenting the supposed American position in the debate. His role in these staged programs was very similar to that of Kovtun. Invariably, the positions he would take would be mocked and derided. A specific example from the broadcast from February 2018 with Vinnikov's participation is very revealing of the mechanisms at play in the show to produce a specific public reaction.

At *An Evening with Vladimir Solovyev* held on February 8, 2018, Solovyev expelled Vinnikov from the studio after Vinnikov's remarks about the Russian pilot who blew himself up with a grenade in order not to be caught by the Islamists in Syria.[29] While another participant was solemnly asking to honor the pilot with a minute of silence, Vinnikov disrupted him with a dismissive comment, although due to the fact that he was commenting while the other participant was talking, it was not really clear what he said. Nonetheless, this caused an outrage from all the show participants and the host, who tried to explain why such comments were unacceptable. After a few minutes of a heated exchange, Solovyev asked Vinnikov to leave.[30]

This episode underscored the theatrical and contrived nature of the entire show operation. The interesting fact, in retrospect, is that Vinnikov's remarks were not fully audible when he was interrupting the other participant. However, not only was he not allowed even a second of silence to bring his point across, but he was not even asked to clarify what he said. It appeared as if everyone knew exactly what they were supposed to think about his comment and how they were supposed to react, even if it did not make sense in that moment, given that it was not at all clear what he suggested.

As in Sergei Kurginyan's show discussed earlier, there were two opposing sides in this exchange: one side represented the "good," and the other side represented the "evil." The majority—both in the studio and, undoubtedly, in the audience, saw honoring the pilot as a sacred duty of all Russian citizens. Grigory Vinnikov, by virtue of speaking perfect Russian and being represented as an American journalist, embodied both the "unpatriotic minority" skeptical of Russia's involvement in the war in Syria and the "evil" American side, viewed as immoral and degenerate. The expulsion of Vinnikov from the studio signaled the right choice made by the host and the triumph of justice (albeit, on the scale of the small studio). But even within this limited scale, this expulsion allowed for the audience's moral outrage and anger to be vented. Further, joining on the side of the dominant view, as a result of this expulsion the audience undoubtedly felt empowered and righteous in their moral outrage against the Americans and those in Russia who might be viewed as unpatriotic.

A former State Duma deputy and a well-known associate of Sergey Kiriyenko (currently the first deputy chief of staff of the presidential administration), Boris Nadezhdin is a third case of the "whipping boys" used regularly by talk show hosts in Russia. Nadezhdin's regular participation in Solovyev's shows in the role of a Russian liberal (token liberal, to be more precise) is yet another example of such deliberate choice of experts who are not able to defend their positions and who serve the role of those "whose position is unacceptable" for the public.

Solovyev uses Nadezhdin when he needs to frame the Russian liberals and when he needs to reinforce the traumatic image of the 1990s—the idea that is foundational for Putin's legitimation. Most recently, two of Solovyev's show episodes, aired on November 13 and November 15, 2018, were dedicated to the topic of the 1990s. The opening of Sergei Ursulyak's TV series *Nenast'e*, a night before, was used as the main pretext for addressing the issue of the 1990s, a topic that could be considered one of Solovyev's favorite and well developed by now. Per usual, the cast of guests included mostly people who had the "correct" point of view about the 1990s. Vladimir Sergienko, a writer, started the first remarks, noting that the 1990s, emotionally, were all about "shame and pain." Other guests, including Aleksandr Khinshtein and Oleg Morozov (well-known State Duma deputies), Boris Slavin (MGU professor), Konstantin Kostin (political analyst with strong connections to the presidential administration) and Aleksandr Mikhailov (retired FSB general), also took a negative view about the decade, differing only in the intensity of their negativity and the types of arguments they used. When Boris Nadezhdin tried to speak a little more dispassionately and neutrally about the exaggerations present in the remarks of his peers, Solovyev practically shut him down, interrupting and shouting at him and, simultaneously, justifying his rude tactics by "I will not let you lie" (*ne dam govorit' nepravdu*). These two episodes set a new low in Solovyev's hosting style. The level of aggression in his attack on Nadezhdin was conspicuous and evidently contrived. He raised his voice and turned to accusation in an apparent attempt to close the opportunity for a more measured assessment that Nadezhdin was attempting to provide. In this episode and, apparently, in other recent episodes of his show,

Solovyev has, at times, abandoned his usual style of a well-informed arbiter who is more dispassionate and objective than his guests and has turned into an "outraged" opinion-holder who cannot keep his emotions together and resorts to aggressive, brusque, and uncivil rhetorical tactics, including name-calling, intentional diminishing of the opponent, raising his voice, pointing fingers, etc.

It would be inaccurate to pinpoint only the "whipping boys" as somehow "fake" participants used by the host to elicit specific responses from the audience.[31] All the other show participants are also fake. The nature of the talk show is a staged performance, and various experts are used by the host to delineate the diverse viewpoints and, using various rhetorical tools, show to the audience which viewpoint is the one to adopt. The choice of experts is determined by a very clear understanding of whether and how they would be viewed by the audience and, undoubtedly, preparations are made in advance for the types of strategies that would need to be used to bring the main point upfront most effectively so that there is no doubt left as to what the correct line of argumentation is, and what the audience is supposed to think about a specific issue.

Solovyev did not invent these elaborate tools and techniques himself. In the context of the US-based media, the use of deliberately inflammatory commentary aimed at provoking public emotions is referred to using the term "outrage industry."[32] Even within the Russian media, the use of "outrage" tactics is not a new phenomenon. The political journalist Aleksandr Nevzorov used a similar style and methods and became extremely influential with his *600 seconds* program from the late 1980s, which aired on Leningrad TV but was wildly popular across the Soviet Union. Sergei Dorenko is another well-known journalist and a TV anchor who used cynicism, outrage tactics, and, more generally, incivility to provoke public emotions and, thereby, influence public opinion and, ultimately, electoral results during the 1999 parliamentary elections. Vladimir Solovyev continues this tradition. The real difference today, however, is that Russian television is state-controlled and the political shows on most of the channels (with the exception of *Dozhd'*)[33] work to promote the legitimacy of the government and the elites controlling the Kremlin today, while undermining any oppositional ideas.

Vladimir Solovyev's newest political talk show, *Moscow. The Kremlin. Putin*, which aired for the first time in August 2018, is the most recent tribute to his effectiveness as the opinion leader and, indeed, opinion maker in Russia. This weekly talk show was initiated in the context of Putin's falling opinion ratings resulting from the unpopular pension reform announced by the Russian government in June 2018. The reform, in essence amounting to the government's plan to take away what people thought was rightfully theirs, planning for their retirement years ahead, caused much anger and anxiety among the public. Russia's stagnant economy, suffering from the painful consequences of the government's foreign policies, undoubtedly augmented the negative response of the public. It is in this context that Putin's popularity started to fall and the protest mood began to rise for the first time since the 2011–2012 political protests in Russia (the number of those ready to protest rising, according to Levada polls, from 37% in July to 53% in August 2018). Levada center also reported that Putin's popularity dropped to 65%–70% (from the post-Crimea "normal" of over 80%).[34]

The first edition of Solovyev's new solo program, purportedly designed to improve Putin's popularity, centered entirely on Vladimir Putin.[35] The viewers had a chance to learn about the president's extraordinarily busy schedule that took him across different cities and time zones in a matter of days. Such exposition also gave the host a chance to highlight the personal qualities revealed during the time the president engaged with his daily work or in his resting time. To do that, Solovyev interviewed a young journalist from the Kremlin pool who traveled with the president and other people making up the president's close circle (such as Peskov, his spokesperson). What emerged in the end was an image of a never-tiring superhuman who not only dedicates himself entirely to serving the public, but also is close to nature and loves children and animals, and is compassionate when it comes to such things as deceased singers (in this case the news was the passing of Joseph Kobzon, a famous Soviet and Russian singer).

The subsequent editions have, most likely, taken into account the criticisms the show received after its first week. While some commentators warned of the creation of a personality cult, others predicted that the intended message would not reach the audience as planned. According to Tatiana Stanovaya, the Russian political analyst, an image of a compassionate, children- and animal-loving superhuman propagated in the first show was just too far from the daily concerns and anxieties of Russia's population.[36] The second show changed its focus somewhat and centered on the most important political events (albeit with frequent references to Putin) but not on Putin personally. As such, the second edition of the new program continued Solovyev's hosting style and the central frames and messages he has worked on advancing in other shows.

Framing through Political Talk Shows

The main messages Solovyev promotes in his talk shows are central to the Kremlin's political legitimation strategy. They have two main goals and consist of two dominant frames. The first is to show that Russia is indeed a "besieged fortress" surrounded by the ill-wishing enemies, with the fallen West (embodied in particular countries, depending on the context) representing the main enemy. The second is to promote the taken-for-granted position of Russia's moral superiority and national exceptionalism. In the context of Solovyev's shows, these two frames are indeed two sides of the same coin. He can focus on the first frame only and his effectiveness in reaching the audience with his story would result in a simultaneous (if subtle and covert) propagation of the second frame as well. The more direct advancement of the second frame does happen at times, when the context allows, as I show in the following. But the more overwhelming and enduring focus of the show is on unmasking and denouncing the "enemies," whether they are Russian liberals representing the 1990s, fascists from Ukraine, or the Americans, the global troublemakers.

These two frames—focused on external enemies and Russia's superiority— came to dominate Solovyev's talk shows after 2014 and specifically from the moment when the Maidan movement in Ukraine unsettled the position of the Ukrainian incumbent government and President Yanukovich. Already in January 2014 the commentators on Solovyev's program openly discussed the threat of the governmental overthrow in Kyiv and the role of the West (and specifically the European Union) that is, purportedly, using the integration "bait" to levy numerous requirements on the countries aspiring to join the European Union. At the point when Yanukovich was still in power in Ukraine, the political experts in Solovyev's show suggested that Ukraine should learn from the experience of other Slavic countries (specifically Serbia) that had to compromise a lot, alleg- edly, in exchange for nothing.[37] But the lines of the conflict and Ukraine's place as the main "apple of discord" between Russia and the West were already drawn quite clearly at the beginning of 2014. From this moment on, Solovyev's shows changed dramatically in their coverage, focusing, in a campaign style, on Ukraine exclusively. This focus was being maintained even after Ukraine elected its new president, Vladimir Zelensky, in the spring of 2019.

Earlier, from its opening programs in September 2012 and until early 2014, the show has engaged with a host of issues concerned primarily with domestic affairs. Among the most topical issues discussed on the show again and again were those related to corruption, legal and illegal migrants, domestic economy, abuse of power by the police, offshores and capital flight, Russia's religious and ethnic diversity, the Russian idea, ideology, and morality, Russian history and mentality, World War II, patriotism, Stalin, Islam, and so on. Solovyev often drew attention to new laws discussed and adopted by the State Duma, such as the gay- propaganda law and the law protecting religious believers' feelings (both passed in 2013). Foreign topics also entered the debates on the show, particularly in rela- tion to the Magnitsky Act passed by the US Congress and adopted into law in December 2012. The developments in Syria also received occasional coverage, but by no means dominated the agenda.

The types of guests invited to the show is another interesting indicator of the expected tonality and ideological leanings of the show. Among the show regulars during 2012–2014 were Vladimir Zhirinovsky, Gennady Zyuganov, and Aleksandr Prokhorov—all known for their more or less radical nationalist and statist views. Nikita Mikhalkov, Maxim Shevchenko, and Sergei Shargunov are in the same ideological cohort and have occasionally participated in Solovyev's show. At rare occasions, Solovyev's guests included intellectuals well respected in Russia and abroad, such as Irina Prokhorova, Natalia Solzhenitsina, and Ekaterina Korotkova-Grossman. In general, women and liberals have always been in the minority in Solovyev's shows, and their views rarely have dominated the debate. But it is important to note that, at least, they were present (albeit rarely) between 2012 and 2014 and were represented by respectable individuals.

From early 2014, the coverage of domestic issues on the show by and large gave way to an overwhelming focus on external issues, and the show was dominated by the crisis in Ukraine, the conflict in Syria, and other external events that allowed for the constant exposition of the negative role in the world affairs played by the United States, the European Union, and Great Britain. Russia, in contrast, was presented to be both the victim of the evil West and the country that holds a high moral ground vis-à-vis countries that create problems. Such favorable exposition of Russia's intentions and foreign policy actions and the malicious view of Western democracies has been constantly privileged on Solovyev's shows, while the domestic issues have been practically ignored entirely in the past five years.

The Evening with Vladimir Solovyev that aired on September 11, 2018, is a very typical example of the central frames and messages advanced by Solovyev very consistently and rather effectively since 2014. This particular date provided an opportunity to commemorate the seventeenth-year anniversary since the tragedy of 9/11 in the United States. Remembering this tragedy at the very start of his show, Solovyev's main point was about the high moral ground that Russia demonstrated as a country, whose president (Vladimir Putin) was among the first leaders to call the American president not only with condolences, but also with the offer of and real help in finding and punishing the perpetrators of the attack:

> Because our people know what is terrorism and know what it is when the whole country is grieving over the victims of the terrorist acts. Our people who lived through the horrible 90s and the terrorist acts in the 1990s; the horrible 2000s . . . the tragic pictures that we all can list and it is hard to stop listing these cases for fear of forgetting . . . so we do understand the pain of American families who lost their loved ones. . . . Therefore, when we look today at what is happening in Ukraine, when we see how the terrorist methods are being attempted to get displaced to Russia, when we watch how the remnants of Al Qaeda in Syria continue to operate under

different labels (the same Al Qaeda that the Americans helped to nurture in the first place; the same Osama Bin Laden, named the main American enemy and who stood behind the 9/11 and Americans were so proud of getting rid of him) and now the same Al Qaeda (in different colors) sits in Idlib and the Americans do not know what to do with them.

Solovyev's long-winded introduction to the central topics of the show provides a superb demonstration of the plasticity of Solovyev's argumentation style and his ability to turn the subject upside down and inside out. Starting with the tragedy of the American people, he turned his story to underscore the "goodness" of the Russian people and the Russian president and, simultaneously, in the same long sentence, to lay the blame on the United States for (1) nurturing Al Qaeda, and (2) refusing to fight with the Islamist terrorists in Idlib. Right after his introduction, Solovyev gave the floor to Igor Markov, an outspoken deputy of the Ukrainian Verkhovna Rada (former representative of the Party of Regions), who contributed to the debate with an idea that the 9/11 tragedy might have, actually, been a conspiracy plot of the US government. Markov passionately argued that the US government cannot be trusted, historically, remembering the Kennedy assassination case as an example that supports his viewpoint. He suggested that the 9/11 tragedy might have been much worse if the planes hit two hours later, implying that those who died were seen as expendable by the US security forces who organized this terrorist act to create a pretext for war in Iraq. Solovyev's overall position appeared quite centrist in this context.

The rest of the show only developed the main frame advanced by Solovyev with the help of other participants, who included, among other people, the aforementioned Vyacheslav Kovtun, the disliked and ridiculed speaker for the "Ukrainian side."

The Social Psychology of Political Talk Shows: How Do They Impact the Public?

Talk shows focused on the personalities of their hosts, driven by moral outrage, anger, and various other techniques widely considered uncivil, are not unique to Russia. It is evident that the Russian media professionals have worked hard to learn and copy the "best" (i.e., most effective) Western practices in an effort to have the greatest impact on the audience. But if in the West the outrage-based media industry caters to specific groups who crave for safe spaces to express their political preferences (that usually do not fit with the majority opinion), in Russia these practices aim at constructing a pro-Putin majority driven by the sense of moral outrage and righteousness in relation to perceived enemies, politically mobilized and unified in defense of Russia (albeit mostly on the rhetorical level) and its leader, perceived as their main representative and defender.[38] Vladimir Solovyev, Dmitry Kiselev, Olga Skabeeva, and other such media personalities play a crucial role in constructing the dominant discourse in Russia, setting the agenda for public discussion and offering the "correct" take and interpretation of current events in the broader context. Such programs as *Vesti nedeli, 60 minut*, and *Voskresnoe Vremya*—broadcast on Russia's two main national channels—also follow the trends similar to those discussed in relation to Solovyev's show, with their exclusive focus on international news and with the intensifying promotion of the narrative "the West against Russia."[39] Some of these media personalities, such as Vladimir Solovyev, for example, not only work as a host of TV talk shows but also have their programming on radio, write books, and hold face-to-face "artistic" meetings with the public. Solovyev's public reach and influence are massive, and the most recent public ratings that place him as the "most trusted" journalist in Russia are a testament to his influence. Sergei Kurginyan, discussed earlier, is not only a recognizable TV personality, but also writes books, maintains an active online presence through his websites, and builds public organizations and movements.

But how does such intense, campaign-like media propaganda impact the Russian public? What do the viewers find in these uncivil, outrage-based media genres, and what draws viewers to the likes of Vladimir Solovyev and Olga Skabeeva?

The studies conducted in the United States produced two main types of explanations for the proliferation of outrage-based media programming. The first is social psychological in nature. It focuses on the partisan selective exposure and motivated reasoning that highlights viewers' motivation to seek out information that adheres to their preexisting beliefs in order to avoid discomforting cognitive dissonance.[40] The second explanation is sociological. It highlights the social context of political polarization in the United States and the need for constructing communities of like-minded citizens that is fulfilled through the outrage-based programs on TV and the radio. Those who feel excluded because of their views in the larger social environment, characterized by strong norms of political correctness, create powerful connections in the context of talk shows. Charismatic hosts of these talk shows create safe political spaces where the fans of these shows can feel included and connected to a larger community that shares their views and is not afraid to vocalize their opinions.[41]

The Russian case arguably follows dynamics that are different from those described in the United States. As noted earlier, the biggest difference is that the media genre development in the United States is a market-driven phenomenon. In Russia, it is directed by the state for the purposes of propping up the political system. Nonetheless, the social psychological factors—some of which are more universal and others contextually specific—are undoubtedly taken into account by the television producers in Russia. Thus, the Russian media trends toward privileging infotainment and entertainment are the same as in the West. The Russian-style political talk shows also combine the discussion of news and current events with the entertainment element. In fact, the genre of political commentary has moved into such traditional news-based programs as the daily prime time news program *Vremya*.[42]

Second, it is important to note that the audience of these shows, as well as the prime time TV news programming, tends to be older. This fact applies to TV viewership more generally in Russia.[43] But it is especially important in relation to news programming because those groups that get their main news from television tend to trust their main source of information on current events more.[44] Given that similar frames and messages are advanced through different programs and channels, the perceived homogeneity of the dominant discourse appears overwhelming and indisputable. Such homogeneity could also be expected to mobilize the mechanisms of social desirability bias so that the viewers find themselves in an inescapable "matrix" where there is a very clear differentiation between "good" and "evil" and no space in between. No gray colors are allowed, and the audience is usually expected to find themselves on the part of the "good." The ratings of Solovyev's shows, for example, very much depend on such staged juxtapositions of good and evil. The control, power, and potency exhibited by the host enable the audience to experience empowerment and hope when they observe the confrontation of the good and evil and the ultimate victory of the "good" (most of the time symbolic, but sometimes accompanied by more tangible actions such as expulsions from the studio, as in one of the episodes described earlier).

The political persuasion that results from such a mix of campaign-style focus on specific events, presented in an entertaining fashion with a big mixing in of emotions and outrage, is "peripheral" or "heuristic" in nature. It is the style of persuasion that does not require mental effort on the part of the audience. Such persuasion relies on cognitive shortcuts, simplifications, and emotions, rather than on a more systematic and deliberative exploration of values, stakes, and diverse opinions on a specific issue.[45] Such persuasion style is, albeit, common in the West as well. The difference is that in Russia it is used by the state to support the political system and is not countered by real alternative voices and alternative opinions that could clash with the Kremlin's viewpoint.

The new "morality-centered" anti-Western discourse that props up Russia's current political system is broadcast to the public in Russia using various media platforms. The political challenge of shaping public opinion brought to fame new media personalities who became true opinion leaders and opinion makers in Russia. The Kremlin relies on these individuals to transmit political messages, frames of interpretation of current events, and the boundaries of the acceptable public "deviance" allowed. They are one of the important faces of the proverbial "collective Putin" that make up Putinism as a system.[46]

This chapter has only scratched the surface of how public opinion is controlled in Russia and what specific tools and techniques these media entrepreneurs rely on. Most of their tools are borrowed from the Western models of the media and entertainment industry. The big difference is that these tools are used by the state to establish political dominance over the society.

Political persuasion *à la* Solovyev does not reach all Russian citizens. It directs the attention and shapes the attitudes of those who watch television and stay in front of their TV monitors when these programs are broadcast. But it conveys the dominant view *presented* as the one that is widely shared by the societal majority.

8

Searching for a New Mirror

ON HUMAN AND COLLECTIVE DIGNITY IN RUSSIA

"Where should I go?" —Alice.
"That depends on where you want to end up."
—The Cheshire Cat."
—LEWIS CARROLL, *Alice in Wonderland*

COLLECTIVE IDENTITY IS a crucial source of human dignity. Individuals establish their purpose and understand the meaning of their lives as members of a group—whether national, religious, professional, or ideological. Putin's success as Russia's leader stands on the shoulders of identity politics—the politics of Russia's national identity. A massive and well-coordinated media machine works to focus citizens' attention on Putin's foreign policy and on Russia's international standing, juggling the frames of "Russia against the West," Western Russophobia, and Putin's gifted leadership in securing Russia's interests in the world. Public fears and anxiety are played out against the backdrop of Soviet legacies of national exceptionalism and the politics of victimhood associated with the 1990s to conjure a sense of collective dignity, self-righteousness, and national strength to keep the political system going.

These new feelings and understandings are real. Even if they are entreated through a heavy-handed media impact, they should not be treated dismissively as something artificially created and fragile, open to dissolution in the changing circumstances. Their impact is so much stronger because they are publicly shared and broadcast and because they are also longed for, deep down, at least among those who were not able to construct new meaningful lives in the new Russia, who were not able to invent or reinvent themselves as members of new groups that share a purpose and find self-actualization in their group activities.

Nonetheless, the preceding analysis has illustrated that Putin-led identity politics in Russia depends on a centralized media control and heavy-handed and overbearing opinion leadership by chosen media personalities who promote selected ideas and narratives about Russia's past and present. If the media were

The Red Mirror. Gulnaz Sharafutdinova, Oxford University Press (2020). © Oxford University Press.
DOI: 10.1093/oso/9780197502938.001.0001.

more pluralistic, if open debate were allowed on important domestic issues, if Russia really had an active public sphere, other narratives would be disseminated, and, arguably, would have been as successful—albeit appealing more to other groups in society. These other narratives would be successful because they are also about human dignity. Only this time, they would be stories about the dignity denied to individuals and specific groups in Russian society by the Russian state.

Three short vignettes from the lives of young, old, and ordinary Russians illustrate the nature of challenges that Russian citizens face in their post-Crimean, everyday life as they confront the state and the political system in Russia. The cases discussed here reveal the cracks and fissures that exist in a system that has an increasingly hard time providing for economic development and therefore faces growing issues in providing for social stability. These are the central challenges that would have to be confronted and dealt with by Russian society and the Russian elites when the power of the Soviet "mirror" would give way to an understanding of the need for change, especially in regard to the relationship between the state and society.

"You can fool all the people some of the time, and some of the people all the time, but you cannot fool all the people all the time." The truth of Abraham Lincoln's insightful warning is sorely missed in Russia by the many who disagree with the political and sociocultural turn the country has taken in the last few years (or even two decades). But finding that "truth" in the "post-truth" era dominated by powerful media technologies used to form public opinion will be far from easy, especially when there are powerful vested interests in maintaining the status quo.

Story 1

In June 2018 the district court located in the town of Chesma (Chelyabinsk oblast, Russia) held hearings about the 5 million rubles compensation money paid to the widow of Andrei Litvinov, a contractor working for the Wagner group, the Russian paramilitary formation conducting operations in different parts of the world, including the war in Syria. In October 2017, Litvinov's burned body was returned to his family. Litvinov's wife, Svetlana Litvinova, received her husband's last unpaid salary of 160,000 rubles, an unofficial medal from the Wagner group, and a compensation package that included the 5 million rubles, as well as money for his burial.

The town of Chesma has a population of around 6,000 people, with most of them working in agriculture. The average salary in Chelyabinsk oblast in 2018 was around 35,000 rubles (over $1200).[1] In the town of Chesma the salaries are much below this average. So the 5 million ruble compensation amount (around

$180,000 at that moment) was an unheard of sum of money for the town residents.

The conflict at the center of these hearings was driven by the unwillingness of the widow to share this compensation with Andrei's parents. They wanted to receive a fifth of the sum; but Svetlana, Andrei's widow, refused that claim, allegedly telling them: "You are old; why do you need this money?"

These court hearings attracted the attention of a journalist from BBC-Russia, Ilya Barabanov, who broke a story about this case, because of the precarious status of the Wagner group in Russia. This private military organization, allegedly associated with Yevgeny Prigozhin, a friend of Vladimir Putin, is not recognized as an existing organization by the official state registry. The Wagner group is more of an illegal militarized formation that exists, arguably, only due to being sanctioned by the Russian president. Its operations might be driven by a combination of private interests and, at times, Russian state interests, especially at moments when the Kremlin can benefit from hiding its involvement in specific actions.[2] As such, the Wagner group could be viewed as one of the mechanisms in the new type of war Russia had waged during recent years—the hybrid war. The actions undertaken during the hybrid war are of such a nature that the Russian government could claim not to have participated in them. This tactic of ensuring and maintaining "plausible deniability" has been central to the Kremlin's covert actions in various parts of the world including Ukraine, and Syria, for example.[3]

The court hearing in Chesma represented a case of the state court dealing with the money given by an officially "nonexistent" organization to real individuals, survivors of those who were killed in action. Therefore, this was an important test case for how the state institutions deal with lower-level conflicts that involve such organizations.

What unfolded in the Chesma courtroom can be rightfully added to the "hall of fame" of dialogues one could have seen when reading Lewis Caroll's *Alice's Adventures in Wonderland*, or George Orwell's *Animal Farm*, or listening to the beloved Soviet stand-up comedian Arkady Raikin. I reproduce here part of the dialogue between the judge and the plaintiff (Andrei's mother), as transcribed by Ilya Barabanov, who witnessed them himself in the courtroom in Chesma:

THE JUDGE (SHUL'GIN): So what is this money?

ANDREI'S MOTHER: We received a document from voenkomat that he is not part of the military. But we know that along with the Ministry of Defense there are private military companies working in Russia.

JUDGE: Why do you think so? What kind of private military company is that? It is better if you watch and listen to mass media less. What kind of organization is that? Is it some type of group formation?

MOTHER: It is an organization that helps our military forces in Syria. Our son is
  not the only one who died there.

JUDGE: I do not understand why your son went there? To earn money? The representative for the defendant told us during the preliminary meeting that he
  went there to grow strawberries.

MOTHER: Can you imagine someone who goes to grow strawberry into the country that is going through several years of war?

JUDGE: Have you been there yourself?

MOTHER: I see it on television.

JUDGE: Why watch anything on television? It is harmful to watch and listen to
  the news, too. I have a very specific question: where is this money from and
  why do you think that you can claim it?

MOTHER: We cannot prove that he was a military. But we can assume that he was
  supposed to get this money for his military service. This is a compensation
  for his death.

JUDGE: You rely only on speculations, Plaintiff. You might have assumptions, but
  we are interested in proof and facts.

MOTHER: My son's death is a proof.[4]

This short dialogue gives a good impression of the potential outcome of these
court hearings. The claim (petition) by Nadezhda Litvinova to part of the compensation package received by his son's widow was rejected by the regional court
in Chesma.

"There will be a time when our government will recognize that our children were there and they were true patriots"—these were Nadezhda Litvinova's
words as she left the courtroom. This undoubtedly will remain one of her main
wishes—that the state recognizes those who fight for it—as she goes on with her
life in Chesma. The dignity associated with the recognition of her son's service
to his country was denied to her, as it was to many others in a similar situation.[5]
Meanwhile, this case also raises an issue of the legitimacy of the actions by the
Russian leadership, which relies on non-state military formations such as the
Wagner group to promote state interests.

Story 2

June 14, 2018, was the opening day of the FIFA world championship. The Russian
soccer team played with Saudi Arabia, winning 5:0. On the same day, and no
doubt intentionally so—Russia's prime minister, Dmitry Medvedev, announced
the government's plans to raise the retirement age for men from 60 to 65 and for
women from 55 to 63. This decision came with no public discussions on the topic.

Furthermore, a few years ago, in 2005, Vladimir Putin stated his opinion on the matter in the following way:

> I am opposed to raising the retirement age [in Russia]. As long as I am president, no such decision will be made. Altogether, I believe that there is no need in our country to raise the retirement age. We can and need to boost the economy and the interest of people to continue working but without infringing on their rights to retirement. I will say this again: I am against raising the retirement age.

So this decision does seem like a measure of the government desperate to expropriate money from its population. In the context of foreign sanctions and economic stagnation in Russia (only showing signs of little growth in the past one to two years), this indicates a mechanism the government wants to rely on to plug the holes in the budget.

Anyone who lives in the West—with better health care, longer lives, and retirement accounts normally planned years and even decades ahead—would be surprised that the decision of the Russian government might be found to be problematic. The fifties are the new forties, and the sixties are the new fifties—we are all primed in this new attitude. Sending a woman to retirement at age 55 appears like an incredible luxury and a waste of years of potentially productive time in life. After all, longevity in Russia has improved dramatically during the early 2000s.[6] In the 1990s the average life span for a man in Russia had bottomed at 57 years (in 1995); it has now increased to 66.5 (2016). For women, the life span has grown from 71 (in 1995) to 76.3 (2016).[7]

But even with these improvements in the expected life span, the new pension reform represents a type of a highway robbery committed by the government that ignores the massive human costs associated with this change. Using the Human Mortality Database and Rosstat's predicted mortality rates, the scholars of the Higher School of Economics have predicted that 17.4% of men and 6.5% of women won't live to collect retirement payments once the government raises Russia's retirement age. Furthermore, for any person who has to delay his or her retirement year by eight years, even if that individual's pension is at the lowest bound of 10,000 rubles, the savings for the government (i.e., the amount taken from a single citizen's pocket) amounts to 1.8 million rubles (compounded at 8% real interest rate). This is, once again, an amount taken away from one person who was expecting to receive the lowest pension amount.

It is hard to believe that this reform is a reaction to the changing realities and attitudes concerning aging in the modern society. If that was the case, one could expect (1) a society-wide discussion of the issue with the aim of finding a common ground in various societal groups; (2) the reform would have concerned those who have just entered the workforce, not those who have worked for many decades under the assumption of going into the retirement at a certain age.

The pension reforms—perhaps not of such a magnitude—are not unique to Russia. The Universities Superannuation Scheme (USS) pension reform was at the root of public strikes in the UK higher education sector over the spring of 2018. The public reaction to the pension reform in Russia was also fierce. For the first time after the annexation of Crimea, major opinion pollsters in Russia—VCIOM, FOM, and the Levada Center—registered a drop in presidential popularity levels to pre-Crimea popularity levels. From the moment of announcing the pension reform in June 2018, the proportion of FOM respondents who "would vote for Putin" if the elections were held next Sunday dropped by 20 points, down from 65%–68%.[8] The Levada Center reported that trust in Putin has dropped by 17 percentage points.[9]

Most observers agree that the pension reform was driven by Russia's economic troubles and the financial squeeze the Russian government has been feeling in the context of economic stagnation, Western, Ukranian, and Russia's own economic sanctions, and dropping investment in the Russian economy. These economic difficulties also reflected the irony of the Crimea annexation that initially boosted the Putin presidency to unprecedented highs but ended up placing the Kremlin into a catch-22 situation, dragging the presidential popularity down. The short-term gain associated with the territorial acquisition and identity politics had undercut Russia's potential for longer-term economic growth and development. Putin undoubtedly understands the significance of economic growth for his country. But the power imperative and the economic interests of the elites vested in Russian crony capitalism, which operates based on personalized access to the state, represent an insurmountable obstacle for significant policy changes and institutional reforms that would be necessary to change Russia's economic trajectory. In such a context, foreign policy issues, along with the resonant frame of the dreadful 1990s, remain the Kremlin's only playing cards. At least that was the case until the 2020 pandemic crisis has revealed the problems that have accumulated in this system in all their gravity, disabling "business as usual" and weakening Vladimir Putin's leadership strategy dramatically.

Story 3

On November 22, 2018, Husky (Dmitry Kuznetsov), a popular rapper with a wide following among young Russians, was arrested and sentenced to two weeks in jail in Krasnodar for ignoring police orders and performing on the street, after his concert was canceled. Husky is one of Russia's new wave of rap musicians (along with NoizeMC, Oxxymiron, and others) who seem to channel young Russians' social, economic, and political frustrations. Over the following weeks, several other rap musicians' concerts were canceled in Russia's regions, with law enforcement agencies citing concern with extremism and drug possession.[10] This chain of events signaled yet again the big chasm between the morality turn that the Russian authorities have undertaken after 2012 and that urges more prohibitive dispositions on the part of authorities, and the new generation of Russians who grew up in the early 2000s in the new environment of digital media, quick and easy communication, and market economy (even after Putin nationalized its most strategic sectors). Even when apolitical, this generation is used to maintaining boundaries in their personal lives and having choices over what music to listen to, what type of clothing to wear, and how to self-express. A moralizing state and a state that takes repressive measures in relation to specific forms of cultural expression are not what they are used to.

These three stories bring up the current problems in Russia's state-society relations, as they have unfolded during 2018. They also speak to issues related to human dignity. Only in this case, it is dignity that is not allowed by Russia's unaccountable government that has usurped the power of the broadcast media in its own interests.

The publicly expressed demand for dignity in Russia has started with the 2011–2012 protests. Furthermore, despite the post-Crimea euphoria in Russia, the societal demand for horizontal linkages and collective identities other than national is high and arguably growing.[11] New technologies help in this process of creating these much needed horizontal linkages and social capital that is independent of the state. But these links are also frequently perceived as a challenge to the state's control over Russian society. Many of Russia's activists who tried to mobilize people on issues of the day—whether to save a park, protest against rubbish landfills, or protest government corruption—learned this the hard way. The role of the state's repressive apparatus has clearly increased in Russia since 2012.[12] Still, the technologically motivated societal modernization is not likely to stop any time soon. How the state adapts to such modernization and how the authorities react to the pressures of resorting to more repressive measures, on one hand, and how Russian society will make its choices of mobilizing or learning to circumvent the state, on the other, is likely to determine Russia's future developmental trajectories.[13]

We do know that the Kremlin does not want to marginalize the youth. Husky (discussed earlier) was released before finishing his two-week sentence, evidently at a prompt from the presidential administration.[14] But the structural conflict between the traditional values–oriented Kremlin presiding over an authoritarian state deeply infiltrated by corruption and the modernized and technologically apt society that is used to certain freedoms in their cultural preferences and everyday practices (or at least growing parts of it) is only likely to grow. The recent cases of quick societal mobilization in response to specific events, such as the November 2018 crowdfunding campaign to save an independent news magazine *The New Times*, which could have otherwise gone bankrupt under a heavy fine, could be seen as a snub to the state.[15] A growing societal mobilization over police brutality is another important case that matters for youth and their parents.[16] Liudmila Alexeeva, the late Russian human rights activist, argued that Russia needs two "unbeaten generations" for freedom to take hold.[17] The public discussion today of the police beatings in Russia is reflective of the moment when the first "unbeaten generation" has come of age and has entered the public arena.

It is only natural to place one's hopes in the younger generations. Neither the surveys done by the Levada Center nor the results of the World Values Survey, however, bring much optimism in regard to political change in Russia originating in youth activism. Russia's younger generation is very similar to their Western peers in their apolitical attitudes.[18] While their social attitudes seem to evolve in a more liberal direction (at least when it comes to levels of tolerance in relation to homosexuality), their political preferences are not that different from those of their parents and grandparents.[19]

Nonetheless, the sources of social change are always present in any society. An array of external and internal factors can move the present equilibrium in Russia to a different point. The question is only in timing and in the confluence of different factors responsible for the direction of change because there are no guarantees that the change will be progressive for the society and for the individual. Therefore, Russia's future is deeply uncertain. The deterioration of the economy and the social situation in the country raise demands for order and discipline, creating opportunities for populists and Stalin-esque leaders to come to the fore. Economic growth and the rise of the middle class are, on the other hand, often associated with demands for political participation and accountability. The present Russian government's structural inability (for reasons discussed earlier) to spur economic growth represents therefore its biggest liability to Russian society. One way or another, even those enamored by Russia's leader for reasons of national identity will have to face this inconvenient and disconcerting truth.

Epilogue

A LEISURELY WALK at the Novodevich'e cemetery (Moscow, July 2016)—a place where history is peaceful and dreamlike—brings Soviet civilization into sharp relief and imparts meaning in Vladimir Putin's oft-quoted words: "whoever does not miss the Soviet Union, has no heart."[1] Famous Soviet writers (Vladimir Mayakovsky, Bella Akhmadullina, Agnia Barto, Vasily Shukshin) and world-renowned composers (Sergei Prokof'ev, Dmitry Shostakovich, Alfred Shnitke); beloved actors (Sergei Bondarchuk, Leonid Bronevoi, Rolan Bykov, Tatiana Samoilova) and cherished singers (Klavdia Shul'zhenko, Galina Vishnevskaya); talented playwriters, cartoonists, and film directors, treasured physicists, mathematicians, chemists, biologists, surgeons, cardiologists, philosophers, sculptors, historians, musicians, dancers, engineers, etc.—it is hard to stop. The most significant creators of this parallel universe that the Soviet Union was, those who made the alternative modernity possible and real—are all in there. Soviet politicians—Khrushchev and Yeltsin—are there, too. And many military generals, admirals, and marshals, the upper echelons of the repressive apparatus of the Soviet Union lie there as well, highlighting the militarized nature of the state and the permanent conflict by which the Soviet Union was defined.

A walk through the Novodevich'e makes it easy to understand the roots of Soviet nostalgia and the power of the cognitive and emotional residue associated with the Soviet Union. Of course, one has to be familiar with the names and the creations of the individuals buried there. One has to have lived through that world in order to have an attachment to it. One has to have shared the faith in that world once, to be able to experience nostalgia for it, ignited by the disillusionment in the present developments. And, importantly, one has to have forgotten, if for that moment, "the land of the unburied" victims of the system.

This parallel universe does not exist anymore. The speed of the dissemination of global fads,[2] usually coming from the West, of best practices and modern lifestyles shows that Russia is not the center of invention of new forms, styles, and technologies that the Soviet Union could claim to be. Today Russia is learning from Western and other models, while looking nostalgically back and experiencing the phantom pains of the lost "limb of Soviet greatness."

This quick reality check means that the political agenda proposed by Putin to Russian society—that of juxtaposing Russian values and aspirations to those of the West—cannot stand for long. It is not supported by any substantive idea; it is not supported by any credible organization of the society and institutions that could support the creation of new ideas and practices, except for those practices associated with support for the existing regime. Vladimir Putin will be known in history as the person associated with *"new authoritarianism"*—a political system based on a cynical exploitation of the emotional sore spots—societal vulnerabilities, domestic and global—to defend the political system he constructed. In that—i.e., in using the vulnerabilities of the opponent to his own advantage—Putin has stayed true to his training, also confirming the old adage of "you never have a *former* security officer."[3]

How long such exploitation can last is not an easy question to answer. Given the role of personality politics in contemporary Russia, this system, which takes its vitality from the Soviet past and a focus on Russia's national identity, could last *at least* as long as Putin lives and stays in power and, potentially (if Putin finds a dynamic and competent replacement) even longer. It is hard to imagine this political system reforming dramatically. The Soviet past and the revitalized collective identity associated with the Soviet past serve as a national glue of contemporary Russia. But this is not the glue that could enable Russia's economic, social, and cultural revival. The revanchist, victimization-driven consolidation can only drag Russia down the path of dangerous political confrontation and economic stagnation. The true greatness of the country and its people would be tested through its ability to abandon the defensively oriented ideas of "Russia as a fortress" in favor of more constructively conceived ideals around which the Russian nation could consolidate.

Russia would also need to rethink its "chosen traumas." Both the moral void of the 1990s and the state-sponsored terror of the Soviet period need to be brought together as important historical lessons for Russia's political community.

One only needs to learn about skeletons hidden in the closets of many families in Russia. You cannot find them in the Novodevich'e cemetery in Moscow—the showcase of Soviet civilization. But they are the reverse side of that civilization. My family experienced the state terror of Soviet times and the lawlessness of the 1990s. My great-grandfather died of hunger, jailed as a *kulak* in Chistopol, Russia, in the early 1930s. My grandfather was jailed in 1943, as part of the group accused of mishandling grain in the village of Tukmakovo (Chistopol'ski district, TASSR). He was freed after the lost documents connected to the case resurfaced, but my grandmother also has a story of her trip to Kazan to meet the judge, asking for help in that case. Such stories—unfit for the official Soviet narratives—have often been hidden in family histories by the older generations. I also learned about them relatively recently, as an adult.[4]

The 1990s have scarred my family, too. My aunt—one of the most generous and kind people I know—was unfortunate to be involved in the shuttle trade of the 1990s. She was made responsible for lost cargo and, hence, the money borrowed to buy the goods, and was sent to jail in 1997–1998. Freed one year after, she did not live long afterward. The official family story has it that her heart stopped beating and she was found dead in the bathtub. She was 46 (my age as I was writing this book).

Alas, there is nothing unique about such stories in Russia. They are, in some sense, typical. The main prototype of these stories is a victimized individual—in Soviet times and in the 1990s alike; the politics of victimhood therefore works well as a political tool in Russia. Still, the human capacity for reflexiveness and creative agency is unbounded. Shifting the public focus from victimhood to a proactive political position and from the Russian state to the Russian citizen and to the sanctity of individual life (as opposed to the sanctity of the state) remains a crucial imperative for Russia's political and societal future.

Notes

PREFACE

1. A Russian political analyst, Kirill Rogov, first referred to "Crimean syndrome" (2016).
2. Coplan and Goldie (2011), 17.
3. Batson et al. (2011).
4. https://twitter.com/tedtalks/status/989894465585340416?lang=en
5. Fukuyama (2018).

CHAPTER 1

1. *Многое из того, что происходит сейчас, — это неизжитые комплексы советского прошлого [. . .]: советское прошлое не было похоронено в должное время, то есть в 1990-е годы. Его не похоронили, и вот оно восстало в таком мутированном и одновременно полуразложившемся виде. И мы теперь должны с этим чудовищем жить. Его очень умело разбудили те, кто хорошо знал его физиологию, нервные центры. Воткнули в них нужные иголки. Такое вот отечественное вуду. Боюсь, последствия этого эксперимента будут катастрофичны.* Vladimir Sorokin, "Postsovetskii chelovek razocharoval bol'she chem sovetskii" (2015).
2. http://www.ponarseurasia.org/memo/american-lessons-path-toward-russian-progressivism (Sharafutdinova 2012).
3. On the legacy of these protests, see Zavadskaya (2018a).
4. http://www.rbc.ru/society/05/04/2017/58e4e4939a79470e66621255.
5. https://www.levada.ru/2019/04/16/dinamika-otnosheniya-k-stalinu/; Trudoliubov(2019)(http://www.kennan-russiafile.org/2019/04/19/stalin-as-super-man-and-the-dangers-of-polling-in-an-autocracy/
6. http://www.rbc.ru/politics/15/02/2017/58a33b919a79472a55281e2a?from=main
7. Ibid.
8. Gordeev (2018), https://www.rbc.ru/society/19/12/2018/5c197ede9a79475481d5e3ef?utm_source=fb_rbc&fbclid=IwAR0C8Wj-je701Nh43vzGcRrsyaStJjceAhW4uV5dLvMER6RdZCKxTxtnEWM

9. https://www.levada.ru/2018/12/19/nostalgiya-po-sssr-2/
10. Khapaeva (2009).
11. Irisova (2018).
12. Satter (2011), 301.
13. Khapaeva (2009), 359.
14. Ibid.
15. Kalashnikov (2018).
16. Arseny Roginsky, "The Memory of Stalinism," cited by Maria Tumarkin in "The Long Life of Stalinism: Reflections on the Aftermath of Totalitarianism," *Journal of Social History* 44, no. 4 (2011): 1052.
17. Kalashnikov (2018), 625–626.
18. Aron (2012).
19. Galperovich's FB account, Dec. 10, 2018.
20. Gatov (2018).
21. Herbst and Erofeev (2019) (https://publications.atlanticcouncil.org/putin-exodus/The-Putin-Exodus.pdf)
22. Clément (2019); Gabowitsch (2016); Cheskin and March (2015).
23. For a brilliant discussion of Russia's identity crisis in the late 1990s, see Morozov (2009).
24. Hesli and Reisinger (2003).
25. Colton and McFaul (2003); Balzer (2003); Lipman and McFaul (2001).
26. Colton and McFaul (2002).
27. The social group theory of voting behavior was one of the first systematic attempts to study such influence in the context of voting outcomes. See Paul Felix Lazarsfeld, Bernard Berelson, and Hazel Gaudet, "The People's Choice," (1944).
28. Bonikowski (2016); Bonikowski and DiMaggio (2016).
29. Bonikowski and DiMaggio (2016), 950.
30. Laruelle (2008, 2009a, 2009b).
31. Vujacic (2007).
32. Alexseev and Hale (2015); Chaisty and Whitefield (2015); Gerber (2014); Toal (2017).
33. Chaisty and Whitefield (2015).
34. Alexseev and Hale (2015), 202–203.
35. Ibid., 204.
36. Alexseev (2016), 166–168.
37. Ibid.
38. Ibid., 187.
39. Zhanna Nemtsova's interview with Gleb Pavlovsky, November 27, 2018.
40. *Короче, я тебе сейчас ситуацию просто объясню, на пальцах,—сказал Вовчик.— Наш национальный бизнес выходит на международную арену. А там крутятся всякие бабки—чеченские, американские, колумбийские, ну ты понял. И если на*

них смотреть просто как на бабки, то они все одинаковые. Но за каждыми бабками на самом деле стоит какая-то национальная идея. У нас раньше было православие, самодержавие и народность. Потом был этот коммунизм. А теперь, когда он кончился, никакой такой идеи нет вообще, кроме бабок. Но ведь не могут за бабками стоять просто бабки, верно? Потому что тогда чисто непонятно—почему одни впереди, а другие сзади?—Во как,—сказал Ханин.—Учись, Ваван.—И когда наши русские доллары крутятся где-нибудь в Карибском бассейне,—продолжал Вовчик,—даже на самом деле не въедешь, почему это именно русские доллары. Нам не хватает национальной и-ден-тич-ности. . . Последнее слово Вовчик выговорил по складам.—Понял? У чеченов она есть, а у нас нет. Поэтому на нас как на говно и смотрят. А надо) чтобы была четкая и простая русская идея, чтобы можно было любой суке из любого Гарварда просто объяснить: тыр-пыр-восемь-дыр, и нефига так глядеть. Да и сами мы знать должны, откуда родом.—Ты давай задачу ставь,—сказал Ханин и подмигнул Татарскому в зеркальце.—Это ж мой главный криэйтор. У него минута времени больше стоит, чем мы с тобой вместе в неделю зарабатываем.—Задача простая,—сказал Вовчик.—Напиши мне русскую идею размером примерно страниц на пять. И короткую версию на страницу. Чтоб чисто реально было изложено, без зауми. И чтобы я любого импортного пидора—бизнесмена там, певицу или кого угодно—мог по ней развести. Чтоб они не думали, что мы тут в России просто денег украли и стальную дверь поставили. Чтобы такую духовность чувствовали, бляди, как в сорок пятом под Сталинградом, понял? Victor Pelevin, *Generation P* (1999).

41. Clowes (2011).

42. Ibid., 4.

43. For an insightful discussion about the Russian concept *pravda*, see Roudakova (2017).

44. For a perceptive discussion of *Brat 2* and various other films that relate to Russia's national identity, see Hashamova (2007).

45. Treisman (2011).

46. https://www.levada.ru/2019/02/22/chetvertyj-krizis-rejtingov-putina-za-20-let-chto-delat-vlasti/

47. Frye et al. (2017). See also: https://www.washingtonpost.com/world/europe/how-to-understand-putins-jaw-droppingly-high-approval-ratings/2016/03/05/17f5d8f2-d5ba-11e5-a65b-587e721fb231_story.html?utm_term=.b54c7f9ef44d

48. Putin divorced his first wife, Lyudmila, in 2013.

49. https://www.obozrevatel.com/crime/19602-kobzon-rasskazal-na-kom-putin-zhenilsya-vo-vtoroj-raz.htm

50. "No Putin, no Russia," October 23, 2014, https://themoscowtimes.com/articles/no-putin-no-russia-says-kremlin-deputy-chief-of-staff-40702

51. https://www.novayagazeta.ru/news/2019/07/30/153785-levada-tsentr-38-rossiyan-ne-hoteli-by-videt-putina-na-postu-prezidenta-posle-2024-goda

52. Smyth (2020).

53. I've even experienced this anecdotally when the border control officers (at passport check points) expressed admiration for Vladimir Putin.

54. Lucan Way and Adam Casey, "Russia Has Been Meddling in Foreign Elections for Decades" (2018) (https://www.washingtonpost.com/news/monkey-cage/wp/2018/01/05/russia-has-been-meddling-in-foreign-elections-for-decades-has-it-made-a-difference/?utm_term=.6218c35c6af4)

55. Burkhardt (2017), 126.

56. Keating (2017).

57. *Dvadsat' let reform glazami rossian* (2011), 219; also, on contradictions in public opinion, see Levinson at: http://www.levada.ru/2016/02/16/mneniya-na-raznye-sluchai/

58. Burkhardt (2017), 126.

59. Gostev (2018) (https://www.svoboda.org/a/29230553.html)

60. The reopening of the EUSPb in 2018 does appear to be an exception that proves the more general trend.

61. Khapaeva (2009), 361.

62. Nougayrede (2015). See also Levinson at: http://www.levada.ru/2016/02/16/mneniya-na-raznye-sluchai/

63. Byzov (2018).

64. Rogov et al. (2018).

65. Treisman's (2016) study of presidential popularity is perhaps the strongest statement of this view.

66. See, for example, the framing of the radio debate on Echo Moskvy: http://echo.msk.ru/programs/klinch/1713818-echo/ Also, the editorial column for *Novaya gazeta*: https://www.novayagazeta.ru/articles/2016/04/15/68213-praymeriz-dlya-partii-holodilnika

67. Abizadeh (2005).

68. "Эпохи, особенно те, которые мы лично чувственно проживали, нельзя ни реабилитировать, ни обвинить. Единственно адекватное восприятие любой эпохи—это восприятие посредством двойной оптики. Это восприятие одновременно объективное и субъективное. Мои родители, например, чья молодость пришлась на 30-е годы, вспоминали эти годы как одновременно страшные и счастливые. Страшные, понятно почему. А счастливые, потому что именно в те годы они встретились и полюбили друг друга, потому что в те годы родился мой старший брат, потому что в те годы были театр Таирова, кинокомедия «Веселые ребята» и мороженое на Всесоюзной сельскохозяйственной выставке. Да, им повезло: никто из них и их близких не оказался в те годы стертым в лагерную пыль. И если они искренне говорили, что были счастливы тогда, это вовсе не значит, что они прославляли или хотя бы оправдывали «культ личности». Никогда я не слышал от них, что «при

Сталине порядок был». Я всего лишь слышал от них, что для них, лично для них, те годы оказались счастливыми. И я им верю. Если я говорю о том, что 70-е годы были для меня и для многих моих друзей-сверстников годами наивысшего творческого подъема, головокружительных художественных идей, годами любви, дружбы и счастливых полунищих застолий, то это вовсе не значит, что я горячо одобряю и поддерживаю решения партийных съездов и оказание интернациональной помощи братскому афганскому народу, что я выражаю свое восхищение высокими художественными достоинствами выда ющегося произведения «Малая земля» и что мне безразличны преследования диссидентов. [И если я говорю, что 90-е годы были для меня важны как годы надежд, как годы повышенной социальной и культурной активности, это вовсе не значит, что мне так уж нравились стрелки-перестрелки, бандитские «крыши», душераздирающий вид старушек, продававших сигареты и белые батоны около станций метро, полугодовые задержки пенсий и обнищание и без того не сильно жирующих масс.] Дело в том, что история, живая история—это прежде всего сумма и сложное взаимодействие конкретных, реальных человеческих судеб—счастливых, трагических, всяких. История страны и человечества—это история людей. Разных людей. Отдельных" (Lev Rubinstein's page on Facebook, September 20, 2015). Found at: https://www.face-book.com/nvrostova/posts/10214568023941953

69. On how the discourses on Russia's national identity made the annexation of Crimea conceivable, see Hopf (2016).
70. https://rus.lsm.lv/statja/novosti/politika/dejatelnost-putina-polozhitelno-ocenivayut-60-russkogovorjaschih-zhiteley-latvii.a128983/
71. The 2018 pension reform did damage somewhat Putin's symbolic authority, return-ing the salience of economic issues.
72. Under public pressure, the Kremlin later reduced the increase from eight to five years for women.
73. Sharafutdinova (2010).
74. Lev Gudkov shared in an interview that sociologists saw that trend already in 1996 (http://www.yeltsinmedia.com/interviews/gudkov/?fbclid=IwAR2Wo JIie27AuCCNej9xm4-YIg_BUD9SL6BgsWnYRERK1t6fR8IcYiSfQ1c).
75. The analogy with the "hot knife going through butter" in connection to Putin's access to power is borrowed from Vitaly Mansky's documentary *Putin's Witnessess* (2018).
76. Norris (2012).
77. Putin's meeting in Krasnodar with public representatives on patriotic education for young people (September 12, 2012) (http://en.kremlin.ru/events/president/news/16470).
78. The concept used by Emile Durkheim, and applied to post-Crimea Russia by Greene and Robertson (2019), 111.

79. Tajfel and Turner (1979).

80. Haslam et al. (2010), 50.

81. Ibid.; Turner and Oakes (1986).

82. I thank Venelin Ganev for his insightful comments in relation to the applicability of Taylor's "politics of recognition" in the international sphere.

83. Ringmar (2002).

84. Morozov (2009), 579–580.

85. Huysmans (1998); Mitzen (2006); Zarakol (2010).

86. Tajfel and Turner (1979); Duckitt (1989).

87. Brubaker (1994), 69.

88. Moscovici (1984).

89. Hopf (2013).

90. On the sociopsychological concept of collective identity, see David and Bar-Tal (2009).

91. Ilf and Petrov (2011).

CHAPTER 2

1. Elena Milchanovska, "Iosif Kobzon: Putin uzhe zhenilsia vtoroj raz," *Sobesednik. ru*, January 7, 2015 (https://sobesednik.ru/obshchestvo/20150107-iosif-kobzon-putin-uzhe-zhenilsya-vtoroy-raz).

2. For a related interpretation of Putin as a father and Russia as a daughter, see Engström (2018) (https://www.ridl.io/ru/rodina-doch-jeroticheskij-patriotizm-i/).

3. For how Russians understand democracy, see Volkov and Goncharov (2015).

4. Volkov and Goncharov (2015), 4 (http://www.levada.ru/sites/default/files/report_fin.pdf).

5. https://www.rbc.ru/society/07/10/2011/5703ed1f9a79477633d38989; Bryanski (2012) (https://uk.reuters.com/article/uk-russia-putin-religion/russian-patriarch-calls-putin- era-miracle-of-god-idUKTRE81722Y20120208)

6. https://www.vesti.ru/doc.html?id=141807&cid=1

7. "Net Putina – net Rossii: president v otsenkakh chinovnikov i biznesmenov," *Rbc.ru*, October 23, 2014 (https://www.rbc.ru/photoreport/23/10/2014/54491408cbb20f72ecea58db).

8. Greene and Robertson (2019).

9. Ibid.

10. "Самое главное, что сделал Путин,—вернул россиянам чувство гордости. Путин—живой, настоящий, былинный богатырь для общественного сознания. Он покарал злодея—Шамиль Басаев мертв. Он поставил америк анцев на место—сказал им в лицо все, что думает. И он выиграл Олимпиаду 2014-го! Путин за время своего правления сделал все, что обещал. И вообще все его проблемы оказались разом решены—он ведь расправился с

олигархами! Между прочим, ни один из предыдущих политических деятелей до него—ни Горбачев, ни Ельцин—ничем подобным похвастаться не могли. Более того, тот же Ельцин оставил страну с унизительным Хасавюртовским миром, который для русского человека не что иное, как наглая пощечина. Горбачев и вовсе развалил страну. Путин же войну выиг- рал и переломил отношение к России, жестко изменив внутреннюю конфигурацию власти и заставив международное сообщество вновь рассматривать нашу страну как независимого и сильного партнера. У Путина есть это понимание—кто ты и зачем ты. И оно, конечно же, немаловажно" (p. 41).

11. Sharafutdinova (2020).
12. Solovyev (2008), 35. Путин, в отличие от Ельцина, ведет себя как истинный государственник. Правление Ельцина про-шло под девизом "Бери каждый, что может!". Это было время, когда Россию раздирали, когда рассеивали земли, – Путин земли собирает. Ельцин терял союзников – Путин этих союзников вновь находит. В определенном смысле Путин – политический антагонист Ель-цина. Тут уже действует иной исторический фактор. Путин обладает иным пониманием, иным личным и жизненным опытом: он гораздо лучше знает жизнь, чем знал ее Ельцин, и благодаря этому гораздо острее чувствует идею. Кроме всего прочего, по прошествии вре- мени выяснилось, что в определенные моменты Ельцин оказывался откровенно слаб как политический деятель. Несомненно, ему не было равных в уничтожении ко нкурентов, но в вопросах поиска по-настоящему сильных людей для своей команды он ощутимо "не дотяги- вал". Путин, наверное, самый национальный из всех президентов, которые у нас когда-либо были. Но не в том плане, что он русский по национальности, а по ощущению себя гражданином именно этой страны и ответственности за могилы предков. Он не мыслит себя в отрыве от России.
13. On informal instruments of power used in relations between the Russian state and media, see Naoumova et al. (2012).
14. Mickiewicz (1990).
15. Mickiewicz (2005).
16. Ibid.
17. Goscilo (2013).
18. Gessen (2013); Hill and Gaddy (2013); Shevtsova (2007); Zygar (2016); Myers (2015).
19. Gessen (2013); Soldatov and Borogan (2010).
20. Morozov (2009).
21. Zarakol (2010).
22. Haslam et al. (2010).
23. Haslam et al. (2010), 18.
24. Hogg (2001), 186.
25. NPL, ixx.

26. Ibid.
27. For philosophical foundations of this approach, see Molchanov (2013).
28. https://www.themoscowtimes.com/2019/04/13/putins-melody-is-no-longer-music-to-russians-ears-a65221
29. Reicher (2004).
30. Gessen (2012).
31. "Почему народ так любит Путина? Потому что это абсолютно сказочный персонаж. Все у него плохо: вот его не берут на службу, вот он идет учиться с трудом, вот он мальчик из небогатой семьи, вот он во дворе, вот он с мальчишками, и ничего в нем особенного нет, и роста он невысокого, и на службу его с большим трудом принимают, но и то – не туда куда- то послали, и генералом он не стал, и на службе не закрепился, и в Питере его с трудом взяли куда-то работать, и в университете он никому особо и не нужен. . . . Обычный русский парень, ничем не блистал, очень спокойный, от службы не отлынивал, но особого рвения не про- являл. И вдруг в его жизни происходит некое превращение, абсолютно сказочное построе- ние: Родина сказала, человек встал и – смог. Это такое объединение сказки про Ивана-сол- дата и Ивана-дурачка. Встал и смог, когда его заметили и назначили на пост директора ФСБ. И потом, когда уже стал Президентом, – все, точка. Здесь уже все разговоры закончились. Взялся, впрягся, и вдруг выясняется, что 'гигант' Ельцин, 'мыслитель' Горбачев – никто по сравнению с Путиным. Потому что Путин – не номенклатурный. Он первый не номенклатурный Президент России. Вдруг выяснилось, что парень из народа лучше, чем номенклатура. И вот этот факт, что он один из нас, обеспечил ему такую колоссальную поддержку. Именно поэтому Путину все прощают; именно поэтому его все так любят и боятся, что он уйдет. Путин совершенно архетипичен, как березка, и в то же самое время это воплощение солдата, вышедшего из огня" (p. 39).
32. Zhanna Nemtsova's interview with Gleb Pavlovsky, November 27, 2018 (22nd min), https://www.youtube.com/watch?v=JgqFuPtBuAc&fbclid=IwAR1Dv5B09VlJlI1hvhKEZVLWyh_LgTWasrm9SjBpIemEzQEpIrEKcwfIABg
33. Cassiday and Johnson (2013), 58.
34. https://www.youtube.com/watch?v=7J6Xwr0l090
35. Ibid.
36. Arutunyan (2014), 4.
37. Sharkov (2016).
38. Myers (2015).
39. Ahrend (2006); Aleksashenko (2018).
40. Aleksashenko (2018).
41. Treisman (2011).
42. Gudkov (2006).
43. "Bei Chechniu, spasai Rossiu," *Komsomol'skaia Pravda* (October 2, 1999).
44. Even cruder in Russian: "v tualete poimaem, my i v sortire ih zamochim."

45. http://bd.fom.ru/report/cat/power/pow_gov/government_putin/ifp00477

46. See opinion polls at: http://bd.fom.ru/cat/power/pow_gov/government_putin.

47. Rutland (2000).

48. Haslam et al. (2009), 45.

49. Oushakine (2009).

50. Oushakine (2000).

51. For criticism of arguments presenting Putin's Russia as fascist, see Laruelle (2018).

52. Brandenberger and Dubrovsky (1998).

53. Brandenberger (2004, 2010).

54. Laruelle (2009).

55. Chaisty and Whitefield (2015, 2012).

56. Laruelle (2016a).

57. For an analysis of the role of the "external other" in self-perceptions, see Webster and Sobieszek (1974); Andersen et al. (2002).

58. Studies have long shown that the presence of a subject with highly desirable characteristics results in a decrease of self-esteem. See, for example, Morse and Gergen (1970).

59. Toal (2017), 86.

60. Stent (2015), 135–141.

61. Kolesnikov (2017).

62. Morozov (2009), 582.

63. Indeed, on December 5, 2017, the IOC banned Russian athletes from the 2018 Winter Olympics; https://www.bbc.co.uk/sport/winter-sports/42242007

64. The real pool of candidates participating in 2018 presidential elections has changed as the Communist Party of the Russian Federation advanced Pavel Grudinin's candidacy instead of Gennady Ziuganov; Gordon and Mironov did not participate; and two other candidates, Baburin and Suraykin, joined the race later.

65. Sharafutdinova (2019a).

66. Tajfel and Turner (1979); Duckitt (1989); Jackson and Smith (1999); Jackson (2002).

67. Kolstø and Blakkisrud (2016).

68. Herrera and Butkovich Kraus (2016).

69. Sharafutdinova (2019a).

70. Ibid.

71. Vitaly Mansky, *Putin's Witnesses* (2018).

CHAPTER 3

1. Karl Marx, *The Eighteenth Brumaire of Louis Bonaparte* (1852).

2. The most recent analysis by Kirill Rogov, for example, suggests that the Kremlin created more of an appearance of consolidated support, and it was done through strengthening authoritarian institutions. "Putin's Reelection: Capturing

Russia's Electoral Patterns," *Point & Counterpoint,* June 7, 2018 (http://www. ponarseurasia.org/point-counter/article/putins-reelection-capturing-russias-electoral-patterns-discussion-kirill-rogov)

3. David and Bar-Tal (2009), 367.

4. It would be an overstatement to say that all observers agree on the issue of Putinism's stability. For a recent discussion of the systemic fragility, see, for example, Greene and Robertson (2019), 10.

5. https://sobesednik.ru/obshchestvo/20160614-lyudmila-ulickaya-rossiya-prekrasnaya-strana-a-zhit-v-ney

6. Prokhorova (2018); Gudkov and Hartog (2017).

7. Fanailova (2018).

8. *Economist,* December 10, 2011.

9. Sharafutdinova (2019b).

10. Parsons (1961).

11. Theodore Adorno's study of authoritarian personality being the most classic expression.

12. Greenstein (1992); Bandura (1999, 1995).

13. Lev Gudkov promotes this version of the argument in his *Abortivnaia Modernizatsiia* (2012).

14. (translated by the author) Разносятся песни все шире, И слава повсюду везде О нашей единственной в мире Великой Советсткой стране По полюсу гордо шагает, Меняет движение рек, Высокие горы сдвигает—Советский простой человек.

15. See, for example, Paretskaya (2012) (in Klumbyte and Sharafutdinova 2012); Siegelbaum (2008); Tsipursky (2016).

16. Breslauer (1978).

17. Brandenberger and Dubrovsky (1998), 873; Brandenberger (2002).

18. Brandenberger (2002), 6.

19. Ibid., 8.

20. Ibid., 5.

21. Although Soviet pedagogy is a massive discipline developed throughout Soviet history, Nadezhda Krupskaya and Anton Makarenko are frequently credited as the founders of the Soviet pedagogical school.

22. I can even attest to this based on my own experience, reading as a Soviet child.

23. Jones and Grupp (1982); Taylor (2003).

24. Zinoviev (1985); Ashwin (1998).

25. The relevant body of literature both on the formative years of the Soviet Union (the 1930s) and the late Soviet period (1960s–1980s) has been growing exponentially recently. See Rolf (2009); Roth-Ey (2011); Hoffmann (2003); Yurchak (2013); Kaganovsky (2009).

26. Bloch and Reddaway (1977).

27. Following the title of the Young Researchers' conference—"The Dreamfactory of Communism"—organized by the Havighurst Center, Miami University of Ohio (September 2007).
28. Dimke (2014).
29. Yurchak (2005).
30. On the debate about Soviet "alternative" modernity, see David-Fox (2006); Kotkin (1997); Kozlova (2005).
31. For discussion of Soviet nostalgia, see Abramov (2012); Oushakine (2007); Kalinina (2014); Boele (2011).
32. Stryker and Burke (2000).
33. For a similar conceptualization, see Hopf (2002).
34. Markus (1977), 64.
35. Strauss and Quinn (1997).
36. Ibid.
37. Baiburin (2012).
38. Faulkner, *Requiem for a Nun*, Act 1, Sc. 3 (1951).
39. Bassin and Kelly (2012), 22.
40. Misiunas and Taagepera (1993); Shtromas (1996); Risch (2011).
41. Levada (2001c).
42. Among the more recent studies, see Hopf (2002); Bassin and Kelly (2012); Tsipursky (2016).
43. Kotkin (1997), 358.
44. Ibid., 14.
45. Brandenberger (2004), quoting Slezkine's *Arctic Mirrors: Russia and the Small Peoples of the North* (Ithaca, NY: Cornell University Press, 1994), 248.
46. Mitchell (2014).
47. Lipset (1997).
48. Ponomarev (2009); Brandenderger (2002).
49. On Soviet propaganda, especially in the 1930s, see Brandenberger (2012); Westerman (2012). On how culture in the USSR was Sovietized, see Rolf (2009).
50. On the political pressures on Dmitry Shostakovich, the Soviet composer, see Mitchell (2014); Volkov (1991).
51. https://tass.ru/obschestvo/4676408
52. Tolczyk and Williams (1999).
53. Entitled *Belomorsko-Baltiiskii kanal imeni Stalina: Istoriia storitel'stva, 1931–1934* gg.
54. Я знаю: мне нужно учиться,– писателю у чекистов, — Искусству быть инженером, строителем новых людей.
55. See Pinsky (2017).
56. Author's translation.

   Если вы есть—будьте первыми, Первыми, кем бы вы ни были. Из песен—лучшими песнями, Из книг—настоящими книгами.

   I am grateful to Serguei Ooshakine for bringing this poem to my attention.

57. Author's translation. Над головой мой триколор. Хладнокровных ни одного. Быть первыми это наш рок. Это мой круг, это мой дом. Timati, "The Best Friend" (2015).
58. On Soviet dissent, see Alexeeva (1987).
59. Orlova (2007).
60. Ibid.
61. The poem was written by Lev Oshanin and the music composed by Arkady Ostrovski in 1962. Both were very prominent creators of Soviet official culture in the postwar decades.
62. Kelly (2008), 733.
63. Ibid., 715.
64. Зато, говорю, мы делаем ракеты И перекрыли Енисей, А также в области балета Мы впереди, говорю, планеты всей, Мы впереди планеты всей!
65. Klumbytė (2011).
66. Yurchak (2013).
67. Ibid.
68. Kozlov et al. (2011).
69. Steinbeck (2017), 139.
70. I faced the traces of this phenomenon myself, anecdotally, when I saw the reaction of my family member who was offended by the suggestion that Russia looked a bit like Brazil, made by an Ecuadorian friend visiting Russia in the summer of 2003.
71. Orlov and Popov (2016).
72. Sukhanov (1992). (Когда Ельцин немного пришел в себя, он дал волю чувствам: "До чего довели наш бедный народ,—сокрушался он.—Всю жизнь рассказывали сказки, всю жизнь чего-то изобретали. А ведь в мире все уже изобретено, так нет же—не для людей, видно, это . . .")
73. Strictly speaking, this was not the first spacebridge that connected American and Soviet audiences. The first one was held in September 1982; it connected youth audiences in Moscow and Los Angeles. There were a few others before the one discussed here. But the initial attempts were more local in nature and did not receive such a big response. For history of early spacebridges, see http://gorbymedia.com/post/05-07-1985-2
74. "Spacebridge 2013"—Phil Donahue and Vladimir Pozner. *The Nuntucket Project*, https://www.youtube.com/watch?v=32wQ6bVvnBw
75. http://gorbymedia.com/post/02-19-1986
76. Shirvindt (2014).
77. Oushakine (2010); Abramov and Chistyakova (2012); Gorbachev (2015).
78. Abramov and Chistyakova (2012).
79. Oushakine (2010), 667.
80. Ibid., 669.
81. Ibid., 653.
82. Abramov and Chistyakova (2012), 56.

83. Ibid., 56.
84. Ibid., 58.
85. Ibid., 58.
86. Levada (2001c).
87. I myself was about seven or eight when I realized who Ronald Reagan was. For a little Soviet girl, he was the main "evil" to be confronted. I remember asking my parents about him. I also remember that Reagan was perceived (arguably by many more of the Soviet children) with the pictures of the atomic "mushroom clouds"—a frequent occurrence in Soviet learning materials designed for a specific course we knew under the title "NVP" (primary military education). Undoubtedly, similar images, learning, and questions must have bothered the American families and kids growing up during the Cold War.
88. Evans (1993).
89. For a post-structuralist perspective of the necessity of antagonistic representation for identity construction, see Morozov (2009).
90. Smolkin (2018).
91. Magnúsdóttir (2018).
92. Samuel Huntington (2004) discussed the role of external enemies as a force for national consolidation in the United States, too.
93. Volkan (1988).
94. Korostelina (2007), 206.
95. Reicher (2004), 921.
96. Avramov (2012).
97. Ibid., 21.
98. Ibid., 43; Magnúsdóttir (2018).
99. Magnúsdóttir (2018).
100. Chernykh, "Segodnia parmezanom ugostilsia . . . ," *Komsomol'skaia Pravda*, August 18, 2015.
101. Magnúsdóttir (2018).
102. Ibid., 19.
103. Avramov (2012); Peacock (2008).
104. As a Soviet child who grew up when the United States was under the Reagan administration, I remember asking my parents about "the evil Reagan." The images of the "mushroom" from the atomic bomb explosion were also unforgettable.

CHAPTER 4

1. https://www.levada.ru/2019/07/02/dolgo-li-proderzhitsya-edinstvo-za-schet-vneshnej-ugrozy/
2. Ibid.
3. Berend (1996); Morozov (2009).
4. Velmet (2011); Kuzio (2002); Holy (1996).

5. Morozov (2009), 581.

6. 73% of Soviet citizens (within the RSFSR) voted to preserve the USSR in a March 1991 referendum on the future of the Soviet Union. Some of the republics (Armenia, Georgia, Moldova, and the three Baltic republics) did not participate at all in this referendum and, instead, had their own referenda on independence.

7. The question of reformability of the Soviet system became a subject of heated debates in academia. See, for example, the exchange in *Slavic Review* 63, no. 3 (2004).

8. Malinova (2012).

9. On "market bolshevism," see Reddaway and Glinski (2001).

10. See Tismaneanu (1988); Budrytė (2016, 2005); Korostelina (2011).

11. *Foreign Affairs*, Sept./Oct. 1997, https://www.foreignaffairs.com/articles/russia-fsu/1997-09-01/russia-still-enemy

12. Budrytė (2017).

13. Urban (1994), 733–734.

14. Yurchak (2013).

15. On memory wars, see Rutten et al. (2013); Kattago (2009).

16. Budrytė (2017); Gruzina (2011).

17. Adams (2010); Suny (1993).

18. Hale (2004).

19. Cheskin and March (2016).

20. Aron (2012).

21. The literature on Russia's crony capitalism is massive. For some examples, see Klebnikov (2001); Hoffman (2002); Goldman (2003).

22. Sharafutdinova (2010).

23. Pipes (1997).

24. This asymmetry is clearly felt in the private conversations between Boris Yeltsin and Bill Clinton, the transcripts of which were released in August 2018 by the Clinton presidential library (https://clinton.presidentiallibraries.us/solr-search?q=Yeltsin &facet=tag%3A%22Declassified%22).

25. Kortunov's presentation at a conference "A Wasted 25 Years? Russia, the United States and the EU: Patterns of Confrontation and Cooperation," Oxford University, February 26–27, 2016.

26. Sharafutdinova and Dawisha (2017).

27. https://meduza.io/short/2016/03/18/gde-rabotayut-deti-vysokopostavlennyh-chinovnikov-v-odnoy-kartinke   https://republic.ru/russia/vysokopostavlennye_nasledniki-397312.xhtml

28. Morozov (2009), 296.

29. Ibid.

30. Haslam et al. (2010).

31. Yeltsin's reaction to the return of the Soviet anthem music early in Putin's presidency, shown in Vitaly Mansky's documentary, *Putin's Witnesses* (2018), is very telling of Yeltsin's personal attitude toward Soviet symbols.

32. Smith (2002).
33. Ibid., 89, 99.
34. http://www.yeltsinmedia.com/events/oct-20-1992/
35. Ibid.
36. Ibid.
37. Reddaway and Glinski (2001).
38. http://www.yeltsinmedia.com/events/oct-20-1992/
39. Hellman (1998).
40. In his seminal analysis of the role of short-term reform winners in blocking further reforms, Joel Hellman argues for political inclusion as a way out of the partial reform equilibrium impasse (1998).
41. On 1996 presidential elections, see McFaul (1996); Mikhailov, Bazhanov, and Farukshin (2002).
42. Smith (2002).
43. Ibid., 63.
44. Ibid., 65.
45. Ibid., 67.
46. Ibid., 76–77.
47. Urban (1994), 738.
48. Ibid., 739.
49. Ethnographic work by anthropologists described these outcomes best. See, for example, Burawoy et al. (2000); Round and Williams (2010); White (2004).
50. Oslon (1997), 117.
51. The best expression of this strategy is the newspaper *Ne dai bog*, published as part of the 1996 electoral campaign for Boris Yeltsin and distributed for free among millions of Russian citizens.
52. http://www.yeltsinmedia.com/articles/press-and-opposition/
53. http://www.yeltsinmedia.com/articles/october-1993/
54. http://www.yeltsinmedia.com/articles/new_administration/
55. http://www.yeltsinmedia.com/interviews/slonim
56. Anderson (2006), 141.
57. Ibid., 50.
58. Trubina (2010), 67.
59. Levada (2011b), 284.
60. Parkinson et al. (2004), 121.
61. Kushkova (2012).
62. In fact, the latent nature of these predispositions might explain even better their emotional significance. As I discussed in the previous chapter, the emotional arousal that is associated with acquiring such cultural models is a big factor in their durability (Strauss and Quinn 1997).
63. Pinkus (1990).
64. Reddaway (2019).

65. Hopf (2002), 60.

66. Alexeeva 1987.

67. Yurchak (2013).

68. Ibid., 2.

69. Burke and Stets (1999), 349.

70. Oushakine (2007).

71. Gudkov (2011), 71.

72. Ibid.

73. Oslon (1997), 112.

74. Burawoy, Krotov, and Lytkina (2000).

75. Alexievich (2016), 48.

76. Ibid, 50.

77. Oushakine (2000).

78. Ibid.

79. Olson (1997), 116.

80. Alexievich (2016), 68.

81. Shevchenko (2008).

82. Levada (2011), 469.

83. Ibid., 242.

84. Menzel (2007); Dubin (1998).

85. Umland (2010); Livers (2010).

86. Menzel (2007).

87. Oushakine (2009).

88. *From opinion towards understanding* (2016), 46.

89. Ibid., 49 (http://www.levada.ru/cp/wp-content/uploads/2016/01/2013-2015-Eng1.pdf).

90. "Operation Provide Hope"; Borenstein (2017) (http://plotsagainstrussia.org/eb7nyuedu/2017/5/19/operation-provide-leftovers-or-more-wrongs-about-buildings-and-food-part-2).

91. Kuran (1997); King and Bruner (2000).

92. Hashamova (2007), 15.

93. Ibid., 43.

94. Dolin (2017); Khots (2017).

95. Gudkov (2004), 271.

96. Ibid.

97. Levada (2001a), 2.

98. Urban (1994).

99. Admittedly, some political forces such as the "national patriots" from "NPF Pamyat" blamed the Communist past on Russia's "internal others" such as the Jews.

100. On this distinction, see Ignatieff (2013).

101. From Nicholas Dirks's quote used as an epigraph to his seminal 2000 article on symbolic development in contemporary Russia; Oushakine (2000), 991.

102. Ibid., 995.
103. Naumova (2004).
104. Meštrović (1987), 570.
105. Sztompka (2000b).

CHAPTER 5

1. For the conception of emotions as the "residue of lived experience," see Petersen (2017).
2. Kahneman (2011).
3. Horwitz (2018).
4. Volkan (2009), 211–212.
5. Volkan (2001), 1997.
6. Walker (2017); Carleton (2017, 2011); Malinova (2017); Bernstein (2016); Wood (2011); Hutchings and Rulyova (2008); Trubina (2010).
7. Compare this to 43% of respondents selecting Crimea annexation as the historical event that elicits national pride in the same poll. https://www.kommersant.ru/doc/3229504
8. https://www.interfax.ru/russia/551815
9. On the victory parade, see Wood (2011), 191. On "immortal regiment," see Fedor (2017).
10. Gudkov (2005).
11. Wood (2011), 198.
12. Carleton (2011), 615–616.
13. Khapaeva (2009), 365, 367.
14. The latest study by Olga Malinova appears as an exception at this moment (2018). See also Belmonte and Rochlitz (2019).
15. Kasamara et al. (2018); Etkind (2013); Kalashnikov (2018); Toymentsev (2011); Adler (2005). For notable exceptions, see works by sociologists and anthropologists undertaken with reference to the 1990s (Oushakine 2009; Shevchenko 2008; Sztompka 2000).
16. Etkind (2013).
17. Ibid.
18. Schreck and Volchek (2016); Volchek and Coalson (2016).
19. The Yeltsin Center in Yekaterinburg that was opened in 2015 spearheads such effort. See also Aven (2018).
20. Greene (2018).
21. Gudkov (2005).
22. There is recently a growing concern with trivializing the term, which appears overused in modern discourse.
23. Alexander et al. (2004), 10.
24. Ibid., 11.

25. Oushakine (2009).
26. Gudkov (2005).
27. It is interesting to compare, in this regard, how social and economic dislocation was viewed differently in Eastern European post-communist countries that viewed their newfound nationhood and liberal economic and political reforms through the prism of the "return to Europe."
28. Simon and Klandermans (2001).
29. See Petersen (2017) on emotions as a residue of experience.
30. Abramov (2012).
31. Ibid.
32. Oushakine (2007); Kalinina (2014); Boele (2011).
33. Boym (2008); Davis (2011).
34. Abramov (2012).
35. Gorbachev (2015), 187.
36. Such nostalgia for the "exciting times" (*veselye vremena*) was conveyed by one of the members of the focus group I interviewed in Samara in 2016.
37. Pavlovsky 2018 (https://www.colta.ru/articles/society/18517) (https://aillarionov.livejournal.com/1073623.html#%2F1073623.html).
38. Ibid.
39. Ibid.
40. Ibid.
41. There are no big reasons to distrust his story as it relates to the framing of the 1990s. Pavlovsky might, understandably, have exaggerated his personal role as a "king-maker"; but the specific point about the 1990s seems very plausible.
42. The critics later noted ironically the literal usage of this term—"time of troubles"—constructed by historians long after that era has passed.
43. Wijermars (2018).
44. http://kremlin.ru/events/president/news/57416
45. Radio show transcript, January 18, 2012.
46. The 1993 Constitutional crisis.
47. The vote statistics have been widely criticized by commentators, and the selection bias of the main viewers of these programs should of course be kept in mind.
48. http://www.kurginyan.ru
49. http://osutivremeni.ru/
50. Kurginyan (2012), Vol. 1.
51. Ibid., 23.
52. Ibid., 25.
53. Ibid., 53.
54. https://kprf.ru/opponents/103981.html
55. For a great overview of the textbook, see Solonari (2009).
56. Ibid., 837.
57. Ibid., 839.

58. Ibid., 839–840.

59. Tsyrlina-Spady and Stoskopf (2017).

60. https://moiarussia.ru/lihie-90-e-vremya-kogda-zabivali-strelku-i-rubili-kapustu/

61. Ibid.

62. Belmonte and Rochlitz (2018).

63. Lipman (2015); Duncan (2015); Laqueur (2014); Laruelle (2013); Prozorov (2005).

64. Pomerantsev (2013) (https://www.li.com/docs/default-source/publications/pomeransev1_russia_imr_web_final.pdf).

65. One can plausibly suggest that his KGB training was very helpful in this regard.

66. "Vy tut ne v Amerike . . ." Found at: https://lenta.ru/articles/2018/05/02/love-hate/. See also: "Putin perezhival iz za frazy mochit' v sortire." Found at: https://www.bbc.com/russian/russia/2011/07/110715_putin_toilet_aforism

67. On Putin's use of masculinity for political aims, see Sperling (2014).

68. Baradat and Phillips (2019).

69. Oushakine (2009).

70. kremlin.ru

71. Focus-group interviews (November 2016).

72. Focus-group interview (Samara, November 2016).

73. *"В начале 90х когда произошел развал Советского союза и когда страна фактически . . . и не было даже страны как таковой, она вся разбилась на маленькие группки . . . и люди не понимали что делать.. когда у них фактически вот только все было . . . когда у них была стабильность, люди точно знали у них есть квартира, дети там ходят бесплатно в школу, садик и все такое.. вот это все закончилось . . . это др. эпоха началась.. тогда началось разделение на богатых и бедных . . .тогда люди начали понимать . . . тогда многих сократили . . . родители работали на заводе Масленникова.. и просто не стало работы . . . ты видел как кто то там челночит, много зарабатывает . . . это вызывало некоторую долю зависти; потому что это деньги. а ты не мог это сделать . . . у кого то там смекалки не было; у кого то не было возможности . . . И то что сейчас происходит; сейчас конечно пропасть между богатыми и бедными она стала гораздо больше. И сейчас это др. страна конечно."*

74. https://wciom.ru/index.php?id=236&uid=115565

75. https://wciom.ru/index.php?id=236&uid=115565

76. http://old.wciom.ru/zh/print_q.php?s_id=289&q_id=23092&date=15.12.2002

77. http://old.wciom.ru/zh/print_q.php?s_id=289&q_id=23094&date=15.12.2002

78. https://wciom.ru/zh/print_q.php?s_id=1067&q_id=74102&date=31.01.2016

79. https://wciom.ru/zh/print_q.php?s_id=1067&q_id=74102&date=31.01.2016

80. For the changing political attitudes in Moscow and among the middle classes, see Dmitriev (2015). For a further elaboration of the political effects of depending on the state, however, see Rosenfeld (2017).

81. Zubarevich (2011).

82. Levinson (2011); Medvedev (2015). (https://www.vedomosti.ru/opinion/articles/2011/06/14/nastoyaschie_lihie#ixzz1PRnrKTbq)
83. https://www.ridl.io/en/monetochka-the-manifesto-of-metamodernism/. For a different interpretation of the song about the 1990s as a satire, see https://meduza.io/en/shapito/2018/08/21/monetochka-s-new-music-video-about-russia-s-crime-addled-1990s-is-modeled-on-a-classic-cult-film
84. Engström (2018).
85. эта дезавуация формулы "лихие 90-е" произошла в определенный момент и по определённой политической причине и представляет собой не художественную образность, а точный, выверенный политический ход, ибо вся идеология ставилась на том, что это спасение от "лихих 90-х" есть следующий период. Если это не "лихие," а "святые 90-е," то им надо противопоставить следующий период, и мы видим, что именно делает Центр Ельцина: главный бренд—"Ельцин приди, Путина забери" (June 8, 2017) https://regnum.ru/news/2285752.html

CHAPTER 6

1. Written in November 1917, this work was published in 1920.
2. Somers (1994), 626.
3. "Ведь и эксперименты Кремля с медиаполитикой развернулись поначалу не от избытка коварства, а от нищеты государственного инструментария—у федерального центра не было денег и авторитета. Указам президента даже губернаторы подчинялись изредка и с неохотой, зато центральную прессу и телевидение потребляла вся страна. Так слабый Кремль нащупывал новую силу, постоянно импровизируя с коммуникативностью." Found at: https://aillarionov.livejournal.com/1073623.html#%2F1073623.html
4. See yeltsinmedia.org interviews; also Aven's book (2018). See also Enikopolov, Petrova, and Zhuravskaya (2011).
5. Bekbulatova (2018) (https://meduza.io/feature/2018/07/09/dissident-kotoryy-stal-ideologom-putina)
6. Inkeles (1958).
7. On Pavlovsky's conspirology, see Yablokov (2018).
8. https://meduza.io/feature/2018/07/09/dissident-kotoryy-stal-ideologom-putina
9. https://meduza.io/feature/2018/07/09/dissident-kotoryy-stal-ideologom-putina
10. Presidential decree #646, December 5, 2016. Found at: http://kremlin.ru/acts/bank/41460
11. Gatov (2015).
12. Rubin, Zholobova, and Badanin (2019).
13. Zakem et al. (2017).
14. https://compromat.group/dossier/583-gromov-aleksey-alekseevich.html

15. Laruelle (2016).

16. The Kremlin's control over ORT and NTV was established already in 2000–2001, as the previous owners, Boris Berezovsky and Vladimir Gusinsky, were pressured to sell their stakes to Gazprom or Gazprom-affiliated structures.

17. Gehlbach (2010).

18. Ibid., 79.

19. Mickiewicz (1990).

20. Russian journalist Natalya Rostova wrote a series of articles about *temniki* in *Novaya Gazeta* in February 2005 (Rostova 2005a, 2005b).

21. Gelman (2005).

22. Ibid.

23. Lipman (2005), 320.

24. https://euvsdisinfo.eu/temnik-the-kremlins-route-to-media-control/

25. http://2005.novayagazeta.ru/nomer/2005/14n/n14n-s03-2.shtml

26. On censorship and self-censorship in the 2010s, see Schimpfossl and Yablokov (2014).

27. Ponomareva (2016).

28. https://cpj.org/2017/04/russian-journalist-dies-after-severe-beating.php

29. https://cpj.org/reports/2004/05/worlds-worst-places-to-be-a-journalist.php

30. Gehlbach (2010), 78.

31. Morozov (2011).

32. Ibid.; http://os.colta.ru/media/projects/18065/details/19871/?expand=yes#expand

33. Hemment (2015).

34. https://www.rferl.org/a/1062670.html

35. Morozov (2011).

36. Zelenskiy (2017) (https://meduza.io/en/feature/2017/12/01/meet-bishop-tikhon-vladimir-putin-s-rumored-confessor)

37. Morozov (2018).

38. Putin's meeting in Krasnodar with public representatives on patriotic education for young people (September 12, 2012) (http://en.kremlin.ru/events/president/news/16470).

39. Freedom House (2015), 12–13. (https://freedomhouse.org/report/freedom-press/2016/russia)

40. Rutenberg (2017).

41. Ibid.

42. Ibid.

43. Waller (2018).

44. Irisova (2017), 203–218.

45. Ibid., 207.

46. "Discourse in Danger" (https://pen.org//sites/default/files/PEN_Discourse_In_Danger_Russia_web.pdf).

47. Rogov (2018).

48. https://themoscowtimes.com/articles/like-share-convict-russian-authorities-target-social-media-users-52114; https://www.rbc.ru/society/23/01/2018/5a673f129a794712579d7dbe?from=main

49. Ibid.

50. Ibid.

51. Dubrovsky (2019).

52. https://themoscowtimes.com/articles/vkontakte-founder-pavel-durov-learns-hes-been-fired-through-media-34425

53. https://www.bbc.com/news/world-europe-26543464; Piper (2014).

54. Lipman (2016).

55. https://themoscowtimes.com/news/russias-brain-drain-on-the-rise-over-economic-woes-report-60263

56. Surkov (2007).

57. Surkov (2006).

58. Ibid.

59. Morozov (2018), 41.

60. *Pro suverennuiu demokratiiu*, 253.

61. Dmitry Medvedev, "Rossia vpered" (https://rg.ru/sujet/3917/).

62. See, for example, Yurgens and Gontmakher, "President dolzhen zaiavit- o sebe," *Vedomosti*, July 27, 2011. https://www.vedomosti.ru/opinion/articles/2011/07/27/medvedevu_pora_perejti_rubikon

63. Zygar (2016), 175.

64. Sharafutdinova (2014).

65. Sharafutdinova (2017, 2014).

66. Medvedev (2014).

67. Petlyanova (2014).

68. Morozov (2018).

69. Wesolowsky (2018).

70. Kelly (2014).

71. Gessen (2018).

CHAPTER 7

1. Но в центре просторов есть место
   Где светло и туда все глядят.
   И там на совесть и честь всех научат как есть:
   Детей, стариков и ребят.
   Вечерний мудозвон!
   Вечерний мудозвон!
   Подлинный труженик наших времен. (Борис Гребенщиков, «Вечерний М», 2019)

2. Wengle and Evans (2018).

3. "Istochniki informatsii: predpochteniia" (2019).

4. "V Rossii televidenie ostaetsia osnovnym istochnikom informatsii."

5. Oates (2016), 402.

6. "Istochniki informatsii: predpochteniia" (2019).

7. "Istochniki informatsii: predpochteniia" (2019).

8. Much of the Russian programming represents copycat versions of their Western counterparts.

9. Walker and Orttung (2014); Oates (2016).

10. https://www.colta.ru/news/21719-glavnym-razvlecheniem-rossiyan-ostaetsya-televizor

11. Oates (2016).

12. Tolz and Teper (2018), 216.

13. Personal communication.

14. Tolz and Teper (2018), 215.

15. Ibid., 217.

16. Ibid., 223. See also Schimpfossl and Yablokov (2014).

17. Tolz and Teper (2018) argue that this trend started with the Pussy Riot campaign in 2012.

18. Tolz and Teper (2018).

19. Rogov (2016).

20. Toal (2017) illustrates very persuasively the centrality of affective sensibilities in Ukraine.

21. Levinson (2018) (neprik zapas).

22. https://www.rbc.ru/politics/01/08/2019/5d418f489a79470e1276cebe

23. Ibid.

24. Bargh et al. (2012), 594.

25. Reber (1989).

26. This observation about "embodied reasoning" is in accord with other studies that highlight the importance of biopolitics in Putin's Russia. See, for example, Medvedev (2018).

27. https://sobesednik.ru/politika/20170303-bityy-politolog-zachem-rossiyskomu-tv-vyacheslav-kovtun

28. https://meduza.io/feature/2017/04/27/greg-vayner-on-zhe-grigoriy-vinnikov

29. On this incident, read here: https://www.gazeta.ru/politics/photo/get-ot-of-here.shtml

30. https://topwar.ru/135830-nichtozhnye-gosti-vladimira-soloveva.html

31. Mikhail Shakhov reviewed a few more of these personalities: https://ruposters.ru/news/03-03-2017/rossiskie-tv-show.

32. Berry and Sobieraj (2013).

33. The only independent TV channel in Russia, which was banned from the cable TV networks in Russia.

34. https://www.levada.ru/2018/09/07/vybor-mezhdu-putinym-i-pensiej/

35. For an exemplary analysis, see the Safonova interview: Tatiana Stanovaya, https://daily.afisha.ru/relationship/9987-sverhchelovek-putin-politolog-obyasnyaet-chto-ne-tak-s-novym-shou-o-prezidente/

36. https://daily.afisha.ru/relationship/9987-sverhchelovek-putin-politolog-obyasnyaet-chto-ne-tak-s-novym-shou-o-prezidente/

37. *Sunday Evening with Solovyev*, January 29, 2014. https://russia.tv/video/show/brand_id/21385/episode_id/962739/video_id/965530/viewtype/picture/

38. Sobieraj, Berry, and Connors (2013).

39. Oates and Steiner (2018); Burret (2018).

40. Garret (2009).

41. Sobieraj, Berry, and Connors (2013).

42. This is associated especially with the anchor Kirill Kleimenov's new style.

43. Poluekhtova (2010).

44. Ibid.

45. Barker (2002), 5.

46. Taylor (2018); Zygar (2016).

CHAPTER 8

1. https://mineconom74.ru/news/zarplata-chelyabincev-prodolzhaet-rasti

2. For an opinion about the Wagner group from an anonymous professional in the sphere of legal private military formations, see: "Golovorezy s tesakami napererez," Lenta.ru, February 21, 2018. Found at: https://lenta.ru/articles/2018/02/21/chvk_interview/. For more on the Wagner group and the use of semi-state security forces in Russia, see Marten 2019.

3. For problematizing the concept of "plausible deniability," see Cormac and Aldrich (2018).

4. https://www.bbc.com/russian/news-44621427

5. The case of Pskov paratroopers who died in Ukraine in the summer of 2014, were buried, and had their names removed from their graves is yet another such case.

6. Worldbank data: https://data.worldbank.org/indicator/SP.DYN.LE00.FE.IN?locations=RU

7. Worldbank data: https://data.worldbank.org/indicator/SP.DYN.LE00.MA.IN?locations=RU

8. https://fom.ru/politika/10946

9. https://www.svoboda.org/a/29524899.html

10. https://www.hrw.org/news/2018/11/29/russian-rap-under-fire#

11. Khachaturov and Polovinko (2018).

12. Rogov (2018).

13. Paneyakh (2018) (https://www.inliberty.ru/article/modern-paneyakh/).

14. https://www.gazeta.ru/culture/news/2018/11/27/n_12340909.shtml

15. https://meduza.io/en/feature/2018/11/13/five-reasons-why-russians-just-donated-25-4-million-rubles-to-save-an-independent-news-magazine

16. https://themoscowtimes.com/news/russian-activists-launch-database-to-profile-police-brutality-62947

17. https://www.mk.ru/politics/2018/12/08/zaveshhanie-lyudmily-alekseevoynam-nuzhny-dva-neporotykh-pokoleniya.html

18. Zavadskaya (2018).

19. Ibid.

EPILOGUE

1. Putin (2010).
2. Illustrated by the popularity of fidget spinners among Russian boys in the spring and summer of 2017 as the most recent example.
3. Чекисты бывшими не бывают.
4. The story did not look good in the Soviet period given my father's party career.

Bibliography

Abizadeh, Arash. "Does Collective Identity Presuppose an Other? On the Alleged Incoherence of Global Solidarity." *American Political Science Review* 99, no. 1 (2005): 45–60.

Abramov, Roman. "Muzeefikatsiia sovetskogo: istoricheskaia travma ili nostal'giia," January 2014. Gefter.ru

Abramov, Roman. "Vremia i prostranstvo nostal'gii," *Sotsiologicheskii zhurnal* 4 (2012): 5.

Abramov, Roman, and Anna Chistyakova. "Nostal'gicheskie reprezentatsii pozdnego sovetskogo perioda v mediaproektakh L. Parfenova: po volnam kollektivnoi pamiati." *Mezhdunarodnyi zhurnal issledovanii kul'tury* 1, no. 6 (2012): 52–58.

Adams, Laura L. *The Spectacular State: Culture and National Identity in Uzbekistan.* Durham, NC: Duke University Press, 2010.

Adler, Nanci. "The Future of the Soviet Past Remains Unpredictable: The Resurrection of Stalinist Symbols amidst the Exhumation of Mass Graves." *Europe–Asia Studies* 57, no. 8 (2005): 1093–1119.

Adler, Nanci. "In Search of Identity: The Collapse of the Soviet Union and the Recreation of Russia." In *The Politics of Memory: Transitional Justice in Democratizing Societies*, edited by De Brito, Alexandra Barahona, Carmen González Enríquez, and Paloma Aguilar. Oxford: Oxford University Press, 2001.

Ahrend, Rudiger. "Russia's Post-Crisis Growth: Its Sources and Prospects for Continuation." *Europe–Asia Studies* 58, no. 1 (2006): 1–24.

Aleksashenko, Sergey. *Putin's Counterrevolution.* Washington, DC: Brookings Institution Press, 2018.

Alexander, Jeffrey C., Ron Eyerman, Bernard Giesen, Neil J. Smelser, and Piotr Sztompka. *Cultural Trauma and Collective Identity.* Berkeley: University of California Press, 2004.

Alexeeva, Lyudmila. *Soviet Dissent: Contemporary Movements for National Religious and Human Rights.* Middletown, CT: Wesleyan University Press, 1987.

Alexievich, Svetlana. *Secondhand Time: The Last of the Soviets*. Text Publishing, 2016.

Alexseev, Mikhail A. "Backing the USSR 2.0: Russia's Ethnic Minorities and Expansionist Ethnic Russian Nationalism." *The New Russian Nationalism* (2016): 160.

Alexseev, Mikhail A., and Henry E. Hale. "Rallying 'Round the Leader More than the Flag: Changes in Russian Nationalist Public Opinion 2013–14." *The New Russian Nationalism* 2015 (2000): 192–220.

Aminzade, Ron, and Doug McAdam. "Emotions and Contentious Politics." *Mobilization: An International Quarterly* 7, no. 2 (2002): 107–109.

Andersen, Susan M., Serena Chen, and Regina Miranda. "Significant Others and the Self." *Self and Identity* 1, no. 2 (2002): 159–168.

Anderson, Benedict. *Imagined Communities: Reflections on the Origin and Spread of Nationalism*. London: Verso Books, 2006.

Aron, Leon. *Roads to the Temple: Truth, Memory, Ideas, and Ideals in the Making of the Russian Revolution, 1987–1991*. New Haven, CT: Yale University Press, 2012.

Arutunyan, Anna. *The Putin Mystique: Inside Russia's Power Cult*. Interlink Publishing, 2014.

Asch, Solomon E. *Social Psychology*. New York: Prentice-Hall, 1952.

Ashwin, Sarah. "Endless Patience: Explaining Soviet and Post-Soviet Social Stability." *Communist and Post–Communist Studies* 31, no. 2 (1998): 187–198.

Aven, Petr. *Vremya Berezovskogo*. Moskva: Corpus, 2018.

Avramov, Konstantin. *Soviet America: Popular Responses to the United States in Post–World War II Soviet Union*. PhD dissertation, University of Kansas, 2012.

Baiburin, Albert. "Rituals of Identity: The Soviet Passport." In *Soviet and Post-Soviet Identities*, edited by Mark Bassin and Catriona Kelly, 91–110. Cambridge: Cambridge University Press, 2012.

Balzer, Harley. "Managed Pluralism: Vladimir Putin's Emerging Regime." *Post-Soviet Affairs* 19, no. 3 (2003): 189–227.

Bandura, Albert. *Self-efficacy in Changing Societies*. Cambridge: Cambridge University Press, 1995.

Bandura, Albert. "Social Cognitive Theory of Personality." *Handbook of Personality* 2 (1999): 154–196.

Baradat, Leon P., and John A. Phillips. *Political Ideologies: Their Origins and Impact*. Routledge, 2019.

Bargh, John A., Kay L. Schwader, Sarah E. Hailey, Rebecca L. Dyer, and Erica J. Boothby. "Automaticity in Social-Cognitive Processes." *Trends in Cognitive Sciences* 16, no. 12 (2012): 593–605.

Barker, David. *Rushed to Judgment: Talk Radio, Persuasion, and American Political Behavior*. New York: Columbia University Press, 2002.

Bar-Tal, Daniel. *Group Beliefs: A Conception for Analyzing Group Structure, Processes, and Behavior*. New York: Springer Science & Business Media, 2012.

Bar-Tal, Daniel. *Shared Beliefs in a Society: Social Psychological Analysis*. Thousand Oaks, CA: Sage Publications, 2000.

Bassin, Mark, and Catriona Kelly, eds. *Soviet and Post-Soviet Identities*. Cambridge: Cambridge University Press, 2012.

Batson, C. Daniel, R. J. R. Blair, Jerold D. Bozarth, Anne Buysse, Susan F. Butler, Michael Carlin, C. Sue Carter, et al. *The Social Neuroscience of Empathy*. MIT Press, 2011.

Bekbulatova, Taisia. "Dissident kotoryi stal ideologom Putina." 2018. https://meduza.io/feature/2018/07/09/dissident–kotoryy–stal–ideologom–putina.

Belmonte, Alessandro, and Michael Rochlitz. "The Political Economy of Collective Memories: Evidence from Russian Politics." *Journal of Economic Behavior & Organization* 168 (2019): 229–250.

Berdiaev, Nikolai. *Filosofiia Svobody: Istoki i Smysl Russkogo Kommunizma*. Moskva: Svarog i K, 1997.

Berdiaev, Nikolai. "Sud′ba Rossii. Sostavlenie i posleslovie: K.P. Kovalev." Moskva: Sovetskii pisatel, 1990.

Berend, Tibor Iván. *Central and Eastern Europe, 1944–1993: Detour from the Periphery to the Periphery*. Vol. 1. Cambridge: Cambridge University Press, 1996.

Bernstein, Seth. "Remembering War, Remaining Soviet: Digital Commemoration of World War II in Putin's Russia." *Memory Studies* 9, no. 4 (2016): 422–436.

Berry, Jeffrey M., and Sarah Sobieraj. *The Outrage Industry: Political Opinion Media and the New Incivility*. Oxford: Oxford University Press, 2013.

Bloch, Sidney, and Peter Reddaway. *Psychiatric Terror: How Soviet Psychiatry Is Used to Suppress Dissent*. New York: Basic Books, 1977.

Bode, Veronika. "Kakie cherty sovetskogo cheloveka unasledoval sovremennyi rossiianin. Proekt Levada tsentra pod nazvaniem "Sovetskii prostoi chelovek," *Radio Svoboda*. September 25, 2011.

Boele, Otto. "Remembering Brezhnev in the New Millennium: Post-Soviet Nostalgia and Local Identity in the City of Novorossiisk." *The Soviet and Post-Soviet Review* 38, no. 1 (2011): 3–29.

Bonikowski, Bart, and Paul DiMaggio. "Varieties of American Popular Nationalism." *American Sociological Review* 81, no. 5 (2016): 949–980.

Bonikowski, Bart. "Nationalism in Settled Times." *Annual Review of Sociology* 42 (2016): 427–449.

Borenstein, Eliot. *Overkill: Sex and Violence in Contemporary Russian Popular Culture*. Ithaca, NY: Cornell University Press, 2008.

Borenstein, Eliot. "Operation Provide Leftovers, or, More Wrongs about Building and Food" (Part 2). *Plots Against Russia Blog*. May 19, 2017. http://plots-againstrussia.org/eb7nyuedu/2017/5/19/operation-provide-leftovers-or-more-wrongs-about-buildings-and-food-part-2.

Boym, Svetlana. *The Future of Nostalgia*. New York: Basic Books, 2008.

Brandenberger, David. *National Bolshevism: Stalinist Mass Culture and the Formation of Modern Russian National Identity, 1931–1956*. Russian Research Center Studies 93. Cambridge, MA: Harvard University Press, 2002.

Brandenberger, David. "A New Short Course?: AV Filippov and the Russian State's Search for a 'Usable Past.'" *Kritika: Explorations in Russian and Eurasian History* 10, no. 4 (2009): 825–833.

Brandenberger, David. *Propaganda State in Crisis: Soviet Ideology, Indoctrination, and Terror under Stalin, 1927–1941.* New Haven, CT: Yale University Press, 2012.

Brandenberger, David. "Stalin, the Leningrad affair, and the Limits of Postwar Soviet Russocentrism." *The Russian Review* 63, no. 2 (2004): 241–255.

Brandenberger, David L., and A. M. Dubrovsky. "'The People Need a Tsar': The Emergence of National Bolshevism as Stalinist Ideology, 1931–1941." *Europe–Asia Studies* 50, no. 5 (1998): 873–892.

Breslauer, George W. "On the Adaptability of Soviet Welfare-State Authoritarianism." *Soviet Society and the Communist Party* (1978) : 3–25.

Brown, Kate. *Plutopia: Nuclear Families, Atomic Cities, and the Great Soviet and American Plutonium Disasters.* New York: Oxford University Press, 2013.

Brubaker, Rogers. "Nationhood and the National Question in the Soviet Union and Post-Soviet Eurasia: An Institutionalist Account." *Theory and Society* 23, no. 1 (1994): 47–78.

Brudny, Yitzhak M. *Reinventing Russia.* Russian Research Center Studies, 91. Cambridge, MA: Harvard University Press, 2000.

Bryanski, Gleb. "Russian Patriarch Kirill Calls Putin's Era 'Miracle of God,'" *Reuters*, February 12, 2012 (https://uk.reuters.com/article/uk–russia–putin–religion/russian–patriarch–calls–putin–era–miracle–of–god–idUKTRE81722Y20120208).

Budnitsky, O. V., and L. G. Novikova. *Garvardskii proekt: rassekrechennye svidetel'stva o Velikoi Otechestvennoi voine.* Moskva: Politicheskaia entsiklopediia, 2018.

Budrytė, Dovilė. "Decolonization of Trauma and Memory Politics: Insights from Eastern Europe." *Humanities* 5, no. 1 (2016): 7.

Budrytė, Dovilė. *Taming Nationalism? Political Community Building in the Post-Soviet Baltic States.* London: Routledge, 2017.

Budrytė, Dovilė. "Lithuania's New (In) Security: Transatlantic Tensions and the Dilemma of Dual Loyalty." *The Baltic States and Their Region: New Europe Or Old?* 3 (2005): 41.

Bukowski, M. "The Specter of Orientalism in Europe: From Exotic Other to Stigmatized Brother." *Anthropological Quarterly* 79, no. 3 (2006): 463–482.

Burawoy, Michael, Pavel Krotov, and Tatyana Lytkina. "Involution and Destitution in Capitalist Russia." *Ethnography* 1, no. 1 (2000): 43–65.

Burke, Peter J., and Jan E. Stets. "Trust and Commitment through Self-verification." *Social Psychology Quarterly* 62, no. 4 (1999): 347–366.

Burkhardt, Fabian. "Presidential Power in Putin's Third Term: Was Crimea a Critical Juncture in Domestic Politics? In *A Successful Failure: Russia after Crime(a)*, edited by Olga Irisova, Anton Barbashin, Fabian Burkhardt, and Ernest Wyciszkiewicz, 119–141. Warsaw: Centre for Polish–Russian Dialogue and Understanding, 2017.

Burret, Tina. "China and the United States on Russian TV: Russia First." *Russian Analytical Digest*, No. 229, December 17, 2018.

Byzov, Leotii. "Rossiiskoe obshchestvo v post–mobilizatsionnoi lomke," November 25, 2018. http://rueuro.ru/item/54–rossijskoe–obshchestvo–v–postmobilizatsionnoj–lomke

Camerer, Colin, George Loewenstein, and Drazen Prelec. "Neuroeconomics: How Neuroscience Can Inform Economics." *Journal of Economic Literature* 43, no. 1 (2005): 9–64.

Carleton, Gregory. "History Done Right: War and the Dynamics of Triumphalism in Contemporary Russian Culture." *Slavic Review* 70, no. 3 (2011): 615–636.

Carleton, Gregory. *Russia: The Story of War*. Cambridge, MA: Harvard University Press, 2017.

Cassiday, Julie A., and Emily D. Johnson. "A Personality Cult for the Postmodern Age." In *Putin as Celebrity and Cultural Icon*, edited by Helena Goscilo, 37–64. 2013.

Chaisty, Paul, and Stephen Whitefield. "The Effects of the Global Financial Crisis on Russian Political Attitudes." *Post–Soviet Affairs* 28, no. 2 (2012): 187–208.

Chaisty, Paul, and Stephen Whitefield. "Putin's Nationalism Problem," *E–International Relations*, April 20, 2015. https://www.e–ir.info/2015/04/20/putins–nationalism–problem/

Chandra, Kanchan. "What Is Ethnic Identity and Does It Matter?" *Annual Review of Political Science* 9 (2006): 397–424.

Cheskin, Ammon, and Luke March. "Latvia's 'Russian Left': Trapped between Ethnic, Socialist, and Social-Democratic Identities." In *Europe's Radical Left: From Marginality to the Mainstream?* edited by L. March and D. Keith, 231–252. London: Rowman & Littlefield, 2016.

Cheskin, Ammon, and Luke March. "State–Society Relations in Contemporary Russia: New Forms of Political and Social Contention." *East European Politics* 31, no. 3 (2015): 261–273.

Clément, Karine. "V chem problema s avtoritarizmom." *Neprikosnovennyi zapas* 5, no. 121 (2018): 76–88.

Clément, Karine. "Social Mobilizations and the Question of Social Justice in Contemporary Russia." *Globalizations* 16, no. 2 (2019): 155–169.

Clowes, Edith W. *Russia on the Edge: Imagined Geographies and Post-Soviet Identity*. Ithaca, NY: Cornell University Press, 2011.

Colton, Timothy J., and Michael McFaul. "Are Russians Undemocratic?" *Post-Soviet Affairs* 18, no. 2 (2002): 91–121.

Colton, Timothy J., and Michael McFaul. *Popular Choice and Managed Democracy: The Russian Elections of 1999 and 2000*. Washington, DC: Brookings Institution Press, 2003.

Coplan, Amy, and Peter Goldie. *Empathy: Philosophical and Psychological Perspectives*. Oxford: Oxford University Press, 2011.

Cormac, Rory, and Richard J. Aldrich. "Grey is the New Black: Covert Action and Implausible Deniability." *International Affairs* 94, no. 3 (2018): 477–494.

Cote, James E., and Charles G. Levine. *Identity, Formation, Agency, and Culture: A Social Psychological Synthesis.* New York: Psychology Press, 2014.

Craib, Ian. *Experiencing Identity.* Thousand Oaks, CA: Sage, 1998.

Crimea: The Way Home. Documentary television film. 2015.

Croissant, Aurel, and Stefan Wurster. "Performance and Persistence of Autocracies in Comparison: Introducing Issues and Perspectives." *Contemporary Politics* 19, no. 1 (2013): 1–18.

David, Ohad, and Daniel Bar-Tal. "A Sociopsychological Conception of Collective Identity: The Case of National Identity as an Example." *Personality and Social Psychology Review* 13, no. 4 (2009): 354–379.

David-Fox, Michael. "Multiple Modernities vs. Neo-traditionalism: On Recent Debates in Russian and Soviet History." *Jahrbücher für Geschichte Osteuropas* 54, no. 4 (2006): 535–555.

Davis, Fred. "Yearning for Yesterday: A Sociology of Nostalgia." In *The Collective Memory Reader*, edited by Jeffrey K. Olick, Vered Vinitzky-Seroussi, and Daniel Levy, 446–451. Oxford: Oxford University Press, 2011.

De Mesquita, Bruce Bueno, and Rose McDermott. "Crossing No Man's Land: Cooperation from the Trenches." *Political Psychology* 25, no. 2 (2004): 271–287.

Denzau, Arthur T., and Douglass C. North. "Shared Mental Models: Ideologies and Institutions." *Kyklos* 47, no. 1 (1994): 3–31.

Deyermond, Ruth. "Assessing the Reset: Successes and Failures in the Obama Administration's Russia Policy, 2009–2012." *European Security* 22, no. 4 (2013): 500–523.

Dickson, Eric S. "Rational Choice Epistemology and Belief Formation in Mass Politics." *Journal of Theoretical Politics* 18, no. 4 (2006): 454–497.

DiMaggio, Paul. "Culture and Cognition." *Annual Review of Sociology* 23, no. 1 (1997): 263–287.

Dimke, Daria. "'Pamiati pavshikh bud'te dostoiny': praktiki postroeniia lichnosti v utopicheskikh soobschestvakh." *Sotsiologiia vlasti* no. 4 (2014).

Dmitriev, Mikhail. "Lost in Transition? The Geography of Protests and Attitude Change in Russia." *Europe–Asia Studies* 67, no. 2 (2015): 224–243.

Dolin, Anton. "Brat 20. Anton Dolin o Danile Bagrove, glavnom geroe postsovetskogo kino." 2017. Found at: https://meduza.io/feature/2017/06/17/brat-20

Dubin, Boris. "Kul'turnaia reproduktsiia i kul'turnaia dinamika v segodniashnei Rossii." *Monitoring obshchestvennogo mneniia* 4 (1998): 22–32.

Dubin, Boris. "Simuliativnaia vlast' i tseremonial'naia politika. O politicheskoi kul'ture sovremennoi Rossii." *Vestnik obshchestvennogo mneniia* 1, no. 81 (2006): 14–25.

Dubrovsky, Dmitry. "Ideologichesky donos pod vidom 'nauchnogo znania.'" *Ridl.io.* March 25, 2019. https://www.ridl.io/ru/ideologicheskij-donos-pod-vidom-nauchnogo-znanija/

Duckitt, John. "Authoritarianism and Group Identification: A New View of an Old Construct." *Political Psychology* 10, no. 1 (1989): 63–84.

Duncan, Peter J. S. "Ideology and Interests in Putin's Construction of Eurasia." In *The Eurasian Project and Europe*, pp. 102–116. London: Palgrave Macmillan, 2015.

Durkheim, Emile. *De la division du travail social: étude sur l'organisation des sociétés supérieures.* Paris: F. Alcan, 1893.

Durkheim, Emile. *Le suicide: étude de sociologie.* Paris: F. Alcan, 1897.

Durkheim, Emile. *Suicide: A Study in Sociology.* London: Routledge, 2005.

Eifert, Benn, Edward Miguel, and Daniel N. Posner. "Political Competition and Ethnic Identification in Africa." *American Journal of Political Science* 54, no. 2 (2010): 494–510.

Engström, Maria. "Monetochka: The Manifesto of Metamodernism." *Riddle.* 2018. https://www.ridl.io/ru/monetochka-manifest-metamodernizma/

Engström, Maria. "Rodina-doch: eroticheskii patriotism i budushchee Rossii," *Riddle.* 2018. https://www.ridl.io/ru/rodina-doch-jeroticheskij-patriotizm-i/

Enikolopov, Ruben, Maria Petrova, and Ekaterina Zhuravskaya. "Media and Political Persuasion: Evidence from Russia." *American Economic Review* 101, no. 7 (2011): 3253–3285.

Etkind, Aleksandr. "Soviet Subjectivity: Torture for the Sake of Salvation?" *Kritika: Explorations in Russian and Eurasian History* 6, no. 1 (2005): 171–186.

Etkind, Alexander. *Warped Mourning: Stories of the Undead in the Land of the Unburied.* Stanford, CA: Stanford University Press, 2013.

Evans, Alfred B. *Soviet Marxism–Leninism: The Decline of an Ideology.* Santa Barbara, CA: ABC–CLIO, 1993.

Fanailova, Elena. "Rabstvo kak intellectual'noe nasledie i kul'turnaia pamiat.'" 2014. https://www.svoboda.org/a/25320219.html

Fedor, Julie. "Memory, Kinship, and the Mobilization of the Dead: The Russian State and the 'Immortal Regiment' Movement." In *War and Memory in Russia, Ukraine and Belarus*, pp. 307–345. Cham: Palgrave Macmillan, 2017.

Fedor, Julie, and Rolf Fredheim. "'We need more clips about Putin, and lots of them': Russia's State-Commissioned Online Visual Culture." *Nationalities Papers* 45, no. 2 (2017): 161–181.

Femenia, Nora. *National Identity in Times of Crises: The Scripts of the Falklands–Malvinas War.* New York: Nova, 1996.

Fitzpatrick, Sheila. "Revisionism in Soviet History." *History and Theory* 46, no. 4 (2007): 77–91.

Fossato, Floriana. "Discussion: Is Runet the Last Adaptation Tool?" *The Russian Cyberspace Journal* 1, no. 1 (2009).

Fossato, Floriana. "Virtual'naya politika i rossiiskoe TV." *Pro et Contra* 10, no. 4 (2006): 13–28.

Friedenberg, Jay, and Gordon Silverman. *Cognitive Science: An Introduction to the Study of Mind.* Thousand Oaks, CA: Sage, 2011.

Friedrich, Carl J., and Zbigniew K. Brzezinski. *Totalitarian Dictatorship*. Cambridge, MA: Harvard University Press, 1965.

Frye, Timothy, Scott Gehlbach, Kyle L. Marquardt, and Ora John Reuter. "Is Putin's Popularity Real?" *Post-Soviet Affairs* 33, no. 1 (2017): 1–15.

Fukuyama, Francis. "Against Identity Politics," *Foreign Affairs* 97, no. 5 (2018): 90–115.

Gabowitsch, Mikhail. "K diskussii o teoreticheskom nasledii Yuriia Levady." *Vestnik obshchestvennogo mneniia: Dannye. Analiz. Diskussii*. 96, no. 4 (2008): 50–61.

Gabowitsch, Mischa. *Protest in Putin's Russia*. New York: John Wiley & Sons, 2016.

Garrett, R. K. "Politically Motivated Reinforcement Seeking: Reframing the Selective Exposure Debate." *Journal of Communication* 59 (2009): 676–699.

Gatov, Vasily. "How the Kremlin and the Media Ended Up in Bed Together." *The Moscow Times* 11 (2015).

Gatov, Vasily. "Kratky kurs istorii Fake News." *New Times*, December 24, 2018. https://newtimes.ru/articles/detail/175021

Gatskova, Kseniia, and Maxim Gatskov. "Third Sector in Ukraine: Civic Engagement before and after the 'Euromaidan.'" *VOLUNTAS: International Journal of Voluntary and Nonprofit Organizations* 27, no. 2 (2016): 673–694.

Gehlbach, Scott. "Reflections on Putin and the Media." *Post-Soviet Affairs* 26, no. 1 (2010): 77–87.

Gelman, Marat. "Tsenzury net, est' redaktsionnaia politika," *Novaia gazeta*, February 24, 2005. http://2005.novayagazeta.ru/nomer/2005/14n/n14n-s02.shtml

Gerber, Theodore P. "Beyond Putin? Nationalism and Xenophobia in Russian Public Opinion." *The Washington Quarterly* 37, no. 3 (2014): 113–134.

Gerschewski, Johannes. "The Three Pillars of Stability: Legitimation, Repression, and Co-optation in Autocratic Regimes." *Democratization* 20, no. 1 (2013): 13–38.

Gessen, Masha. *The Future Is History: How Totalitarianism Reclaimed Russia*. London: Granta Books, 2017.

Gessen, Masha. *The Man without a Face: The Unlikely Rise of Vladimir Putin*. New York: Riverhead, 2012.

Gessen, Masha. "Putin Lied about His Nuclear Doctrine and Promised Russians That They Would Go to Heaven." *New Yorker*, October 19, 2018. https://www.newyorker.com/news/our-columnists/putin-lied-about-his-nuclear-doctrine-and-promised-russians-that-they-would-go-to-heaven

Goldenberg, Amit, Eran Halperin, Martijn van Zomeren, and James J. Gross. "The Process Model of Group-Based Emotion: Integrating Intergroup Emotion and Emotion Regulation Perspectives." *Personality and Social Psychology Review* 20, no. 2 (2016): 118–141.

Goldman, Marshall I. *The Piratization of Russia: Russian Reform Goes Awry*. New York: Routledge, 2003.

Gorbachev, Oleg. "The Namedni Project and the Evolution of Nostalgia in Post-Soviet Russia." *Canadian Slavonic Papers* 57, no. 3–4 (2015): 180–194.

Gordeev, Vladislav. "Chislo toskuiushchikh po SSSR rossiian vozroslo do maski-muma." *rbc.ru*, December 19, 2018. https://www.rbc.ru/society/19/12/2018/5c197ede9a79475481d5e3ef?utm_source=fb_rbc&fbclid=IwAR0C8Wj-je70iNh43vzGcRrsyaStJjceAhW4uV5dLvMER6RdZCKxTxtnEWM

Gorshkov, M. K., R. Krumm, and V. V. Petukhov. *Dvadsat' let reform glazami rossian.* Moskva: Ves mir, 2011.

Goscilo, Helena, ed. *Putin as Celebrity and Cultural Icon.* Vol. 80. New York: Routledge, 2013.

Gostev, Aleksandr. "Syria, strakh i Zapad. Rossiiane vse sil'nee boiatsia bol'shoi voiny," *Radio Svoboda*, May 17, 2018. https://www.svoboda.org/a/29230553.html

Govorukhin, Stanislav, Maya Ganina, Kirill Lavrov, and Vladimir Dudintsev. "Homo Sovieticus." *World Affairs* 152, no. 2 (1989): 104–108.

Greene, Samuel A. "Running to Stand Still: Aggressive Immobility and the Limits of Power in Russia." *Post-Soviet Affairs* 34, no. 5 (2018): 333–347.

Greene, Samuel, and Graeme Robertson. *Putin v. the People.* New Haven, CT: Yale University Press, 2019.

Greene, Samuel, and Graeme Robertson. "Agreeable Authoritarians: Personality and Politics in Contemporary Russia." *Comparative Political Studies*, January 2017. http://journals.sagepub.com/doi/10.1177/0010414016688005

Greenstein, Fred I. "Can Personality and Politics Be Studied Systematically?" *Political Psychology* 13 (1992): 105–128.

Gruzina, Ieva. "Relationship between History and a Sense of Belonging: Russian Speaking Minority Integration in Latvia." *CEU Political Science Journal* 6, no. 3 (2011): 397–432.

Gudkov, Lev. *Abortivnaia modernizatsiia.* Moskva: ROSSPEN, 2011.

Gudkov, Lev. *Negativnaia identichnost: Stat'i 1997–2002 godov.* Moskva: NLO, 2004.

Gudkov, Lev. *'Pamiat' o voine i massovaia identichnost' rossiian'.* Moskva: NLO, 2005.

Gudkov, Lev. "Xenophobia: Past and Present,=." *Russia in Global Affairs*, February 7, 2006. https://eng.globalaffairs.ru/number/n_6185

Gudkov, Lev and Eva Hartog. "The Evolution of Homo Sovieticus to Putin's Man," *The Moscow Times*, October 13, 2017. https://www.themoscowtimes.com/2017/10/13/the-evolution-of-homo-sovieticus-to-putins-man-a59189

Gunnell, John G. "Are We Losing Our Minds? Cognitive Science and the Study of Politics." *Political Theory* 35, no. 6 (2007): 704–731.

Haidt, Jonathan. "The Emotional Dog and Its Rational Tail: A Social Intuitionist Approach to Moral Judgment." *Psychological Review* 108, no. 4 (2001): 814.

Hale, Henry E. "Explaining Ethnicity." *Comparative Political Studies* 37, no. 4 (2004): 458–485.

Halfin, Igal. *From Darkness to Light: Class, Consciousness, and Salvation in Revolutionary Russia.* Pittsburgh: University of Pittsburgh Press, 2000.

Halfin, Igal, and Jochen Hellbeck. "Rethinking the Stalinist Subject: Stephen Kotkin's 'Magnetic Mountain' and the State of Soviet Historical Studies." *Jahrbücher für Geschichte Osteuropas* 44, no. 3 (1996): 456.

Hashamova, Yana. *Pride and Panic: Russian Imagination of the West in Post-Soviet Film.* Chicago: Intellect Books, 2007.

Haslam, S. Alexander, Stephen D. Reicher, and Michael J. Platow. *The New Psychology of Leadership: Identity, Influence and Power.* New York: Psychology Press, 2010.

Havel, Vaclav. "The Power of the Powerless." In *Living in Truth.* London: Faber and Faber, 1986.

Hellbeck, Jochen. *Revolution on My Mind: Writing a Diary under Stalin.* Cambridge, MA: Harvard University Press, 2009.

Hellbeck, Jochen. "Working, Struggling, Becoming: Stalin-Era Autobiographical Texts." *The Russian Review* 60, no. 3 (2001): 340–359.

Hellman, Joel S. "Winners Take All: The Politics of Partial Reform in Postcommunist Transitions." *World Politics* 50, no. 2 (1998): 203–234.

Hemment, Julie. *Youth Politics in Putin's Russia: Producing Patriots and Entrepreneurs.* Bloomington: Indiana University Press, 2015.

Herbst, John E., and Sergei Erofeev. "The Putin Exodus: The New Russian Brain-Drain." Atlantic Council Report, February 21, 2019. https://www.atlanticcouncil.org/in-depth-research-reports/report/the-putin-exodus-the-new-russian-brain-drain-3/, accessed May 12, 2020.

Herrera, Yoshiko M., and Nicole M. Butkovich Kraus. "Pride versus Prejudice: Ethnicity, National Identity, and Xenophobia in Russia." *Comparative Politics* 48, no. 3 (2016): 293–315.

Hesli, Vicki L., and William M. Reisinger, eds. *The 1999–2000–Elections in Russia: Their Impact and Legacy.* Cambridge University Press, 2003.

Hill, F., and C. Gaddy. "Operative in the Kremlin." Washington, DC: Brookings Focus, 2013.

Hochschild, Arlie Russell. *Strangers in Their Own Land: A Journey to the Heart of Our Political Divide.* New York: The New Press, 2016.

Hoffman, David. "Oligarchs: Power and Wealth in the New Russia." (2002).

Hoffmann, David Lloyd. *Stalinist Values: The Cultural Norms of Soviet Modernity, 1917–1941.* Ithaca, NY: Cornell University Press, 2003.

Hofstede, Geert H., and Geert Hofstede. *Culture's Consequences: Comparing Values, Behaviors, Institutions and Organizations across Nations.* Thousand Oaks, CA: Sage, 2001.

Hogg, Michael A. 2001. "A Social Identity Theory of Leadership." *Personality and Social Psychology Review* 5, no. 3 (2001): 184–200.

Holmes, Larry. 2008. *How Ordinary Russians Experience Their Lives and World: A Report of a Participant–Observer.* Lewiston: Edwin Mellen Press.

Holy, Ladislav. *The Little Czech and the Great Czech Nation: National Identity and the Post-Communist Social Transformation.* Cambridge Studies in Social and Cultural Anthropology 103. Cambridge: Cambridge University Press, 1996.

Honey, Larisa. "Pluralizing Practices in Late-Socialist Moscow: Russian Alternative Practitioners Reclaim and Redefine Individualism." *Soviet Society in the Era of Late Socialism, 1964–1985.* Lanham: Lexington Books (2012): 117–142.

Honneth, Axel. *The Struggle for Recognition: The Moral Grammar of Social Conflicts.* MIT Press, 1996.

Hopf, Ted. "'Crimea Is Ours': A Discursive History." *International Relations* 30, no. 2 (2016): 227–255.

Hopf, Ted. "Common-Sense Constructivism and Hegemony in World Politics." *International Organization* 67, no. 2 (2013): 317–354.

Hopf, Ted. *Social Construction of International Politics: Identities and Foreign Policies, Moscow, 1955 and 1999.* Ithaca, NY: Cornell University Press, 2002.

Horwitz, Robert B. "Politics as Victimhood, Victimhood as Politics." *Journal of Policy History* 30, no. 3 (2018): 552–574.

Hutchings, Stephen, and Natalia Rulyova. "Commemorating the Past/Performing the Present: Television Coverage of the Second World War Victory Celebrations and the (De)construction of Russian Nationhood." In *The Post-Soviet Russian Media: Conflicting Signals*, edited by Birgit Beumers, Stephen C. Hutchings, and Natalya Rulyova, 153–172. New York: Routledge, 2009.

Huysmans, Jef. "Security! What Do You Mean? From Concept to Thick Signifier." *European Journal of International Relations* 4, no. 2 (1998): 226–255.

Ilf, Ilya, and Evgeny Petrov. *The Twelve Chairs: A Novel.* Northwestern University Press, 2011.

Ignatieff, Michael. "Enemies vs. Adversaries." *New York Times*, Op-ed, October 16, 2013. https://www.nytimes.com/2013/10/17/opinion/enemies–vs–adversaries.html

Inkeles, Alex. *Public Opinion in Soviet Russia: A Study in Mass Persuasion.* Vol. 1. Cambridge, MA: Harvard University Press, 1958.

Inkeles, A., and R. A. Bauer. *The Soviet Citizen: Daily Life in a Totalitarian.* Cambridge: Harvard University Press, 1959.

Irisova, Olga. "Of Chiefs and Men." April 18, 2018. https://www.ridl.io/en/of–chiefs–and–men/

Irisova, Olga. "Who Gets to Speak in 'Post-Crimean' Russia?" in *A Successful Failure: Russia after Crime(a)*, edited by Olga Irisova, Anton Barbashin, Fabian Burkhardt, and Ernest Wyciszkiewicz. Warsaw: Center for Polish–Russian Dialogue and Understanding, 2017.

"Istochniki informatsii: predpochteniia." September 14, 2019. https://fom.ru/SMI–i–internet/14256

Ivanova, Anna. "Socialist Consumption and Brezhnev's Stagnation: A Reappraisal of Late Communist Everyday Life," *Kritika: Explorations in Russian and Eurasian History* 17, no. 3 (Summer 2016): 665–678.

Jackson, Jay W. "Intergroup Attitudes as a Function of Different Intergroup Conflict." *Self and Identity* 1, no. 1 (2002): 11–33.

Jackson, Jay W., and Eliot R. Smith. "Conceptualizing Social Identity: A New Framework and Evidence for the Impact of Different Dimensions." *Personality and Social Psychology Bulletin* 25, no. 1 (1999): 120–135.

Johnston, Timothy. *Being Soviet: Identity, Rumour, and Everyday Life under Stalin 1939–1953.* Oxford: Oxford University Press, 2011.

Jones, Ellen, and Fred W. Grupp. "Political Socialization in the Soviet Military." *Armed Forces & Society* 8, no. 3 (1982): 355–387.

Kaganovsky, Lilya. "The Cultural Logic of Late Socialism." *Studies in Russian and Soviet Cinema* 3, no. 2 (2009): 185–199.

Kaganovsky, Lilya. *How the Soviet man Was Unmade: Cultural Fantasy and Male Subjectivity under Stalin.* Pittsburgh: University of Pittsburgh Press, 2008.

Kahneman, Daniel. *Thinking, Fast and Slow.* New York: Macmillan, 2011.

Kalashnikov, Antony. "Stalinist Crimes and the Ethics of Memory." *Kritika: Explorations in Russian and Eurasian History* 19, no. 3 (2018): 599–626.

Kalinina, Ekaterina. "Mediated Post-Soviet Nostalgia." PhD dissertation, Södertörn University, 2014.

Kasamara, Valeria, Anna Sorokina, and Marina Maximenkova. "Pride and Shame in Collective Memory of Russian and American Youths." *Nationalities Papers* 46, no. 5 (2018) : 1–21.

Kattago, Siobhan. "Agreeing to Disagree on the Legacies of Recent History: Memory, Pluralism and Europe after 1989." *European Journal of Social Theory* 12, no. 3 (2009): 375–395.

Kattago, Siobhan. "War Memorials and the Politics of Memory: The Soviet War Memorial in Tallinn." *Constellations* 16, no. 1 (2009): 150–166.

Katz, Elihu, Paul F. Lazarsfeld, and Elmo Roper. *Personal Influence: The Part Played by People in the Flow of Mass Communications.* New York: Routledge, 2017.

Kaylan, Melik. "Kremlin Values: Putin's Strategic Conservatism." *World Affairs* 177, no. 1 (2014): 9–17.

Keating, Joshua. "Russia Resurgent." January 2, 2017. http://www.slate.com/articles/news_and_politics/cover_story/2017/01/how_vladimir_putin_engineered_russia_s_return_to_global_power.html

Kelly, Catriona. "Defending Children's Rights, "In Defense of Peace": Children and Soviet Cultural Diplomacy." *Kritika: Explorations in Russian and Eurasian History* 9, no. 4 (2008): 711–746.

Kelly, Lidia. "Russia Can Turn US to Radioactive Ash: Kremlin-Backed Journalist." March 16, 2014. https://www.reuters.com/article/ukraine–crisis–russia–kiselyov/russia–can–turn–us–to–radioactive–ash–kremlin–backed–journalist–idUSL6N0MD0P920140316

Khachaturov, Arnold, and Vacheslav Polovinko. "Strana napugannykh atomov," *Novaya gazeta*, December 18, 2018. https://www.novayagazeta.ru/articles/2018/12/18/78978–strana–raspavshayasya–na–atomy?fbclid=IwAR1NbA63pO_7EPe7y3z4NZegGGU08TDTVPVCosL–PmWDjUudZJkPgeEXg48

Khapaeva, Dina. "Historical Memory in Post-Soviet Gothic Society." *Social Research* 76, no. 1 (2009): 359–394.

Kharkhordin, Oleg. *The Collective and the Individual in Russia: A Study of Practices.* Studies on the History of Society and Culture 32. Berkeley: University of California Press, 1999.

Kharkhordin, Oleg. "What Is the State? The Russian Concept of Gosudarstvo in the European Context." *History and Theory* 40, no. 2 (2001): 206–240.

Khots, ALeksandr. "'Brat–2' kak proobraz Putina ili mifologia 'pravdy.'" 2017. Found at: https://inforesist.org/brat–2–kak–proobraz–putina–ili–mifologiya–pravdyi/

King, Maryon F., and Gordon C. Bruner. "Social Desirability Bias: A Neglected Aspect of Validity Testing." *Psychology & Marketing* 17, no. 2 (2000): 79–103.

Kinnvall, Catarina. "Globalization and Religious Nationalism: Self, Identity, and the Search for Ontological Security." *Political Psychology* 25, no. 5 (2004): 741–767.

Klebnikov, Paul. *Godfather of the Kremlin: The Decline of Russia in the Age of Gangster Capitalism.* New York: Houghton Mifflin Harcourt, 2001.

Klicperová, Martina, I. K. Feierabend, and C. R. Hofstetter. "In the Search for a Post-Communist Syndrome. A Theoretical Framework and Empirical Assessment." *Journal of Community and Applied Social Psychology* 7, no. 1 (1997): 39–52.

Klumbytė, Neringa. "Political Intimacy: Power, Laughter, and Coexistence in Late Soviet Lithuania." *East European Politics and Societies* 25, no. 4 (2011): 658–677.

Klumbytė, Neringa, and Gulnaz Sharafutdinova, eds. *Soviet Society in the Era of Late Socialism, 1964–1985.* Lanham, MD: Rowman & Littlefield, 2012.

Kobzon, Iosif. *Ia Sam Sebe Sudia.* Moskva: ACT, 2018.

Kolesnikov, Andrei. "Ego Fulton: K desiatiletiiu Miunkhenskoi rechi Vladimira Putina." *rbc.ru*, February 10, 2017. https://www.rbc.ru/opinions/politics/10/02/2017/589d716d9a79476fb72a221a?from=newsfeed

Kolstø, Pal, and Helge Blakkisrud. *The New Russian nationalism.* Edinburgh University Press, 2016.

Kondrashov Andrei. *Putin.* Documentary television film. 2018.

Korostelina, Karina. "Shaping Unpredictable Past: National Identity and History Education in Ukraine." *National Identities* 13, no. 1 (2011): 1–16.

Korostelina, Karina. *Social Identity and Conflict: Structures, Dynamics, and Implications.* New York: Springer, 2007.

Kotkin, Stephen. *Armageddon Averted: The Soviet Collapse, 1970–2000.* Oxford: Oxford University Press, 2008.

Kotkin, Stephen. *Magnetic Mountain: Stalinism as a Civilization.* Berkeley: University of California Press, 1997.

Kozlov, Vladimir Aleksandrovich, Sheila Fitzpatrick, and Sergeĭ Vladimirovich Mironenko, eds. *Sedition: Everyday Resistance in the Soviet Union under Khrushchev and Brezhnev.* New Haven, CT: Yale University Press, 2011.

Kozlova, Natalia. "Stseny iz chastnoi zhizni perioda 'zastoia': semeinaia perepiska." *Zhurnal sotsiologii i sotsial'noi antropologii* 3 (1999): 120–133.

Kozlova, Olesya, and Dmitry Bondarev. "Natsional'nye osobennosti razvitiia zhanra obshchestvenno–politicheskogo tok–shou na rossiiskom televidenii." *Vestnik Volgogradskogo gosudarstvennogo universiteta. Seria 8: Literaturovedenie. Zhurnalistika* 10 (2011): 119–125.

Kozlova, Natalia. *Sovetskie liudi: Stseny iz istori.* Moskva: Evropa, 2005.

Krylova, Anna. "Soviet Modernity: Stephen and the Bolshevik Predicament." *Contemporary European History* 23, no. 02 (2014): 167–192.

Krylova, Anna. "The Tenacious Liberal Subject in Soviet Studies." *Kritika: Explorations in Russian and Eurasian History* 1, no. 1 (2000): 119–146.

Kukhterin, Sergei. "Fathers and Patriarchs in Communist and Post-Communist Russia." In *Gender, State and Society in Soviet and PostSoviet Russia*, edited by S. Ashwin, 71–89. London: Routledge, 2000.

Kuran, Timur. *Private Truths, Public Lies: The Social Consequences of Preference Falsification.* Cambridge, MA: Harvard University Press, 1997.

Kurginyan, Sergei. *Sut' Vremeni*, Volumes 1–4. Moskva: MOF-ETS, 2012.

Kushkova, Anna. "Surviving in the Time of Deficit: The Narrative Construction of a 'Soviet Identity.'" In *Soviet and Post Soviet Identities*, edited by Mark Bassin and Catriona Kelly, 55–72. Cambridge: Cambridge University Press, 2012.

Kuzio, Taras. "History, Memory and Nation Building in the Post-Soviet Colonial Space." *Nationalities Papers* 30, no. 2 (2002): 241–264.

Laird, Roy. "The Soviet Legacy 1994: Homo Sovieticus Is Alive if Not Well." *European Security* 4, no. 2 (1995): 225–240. doi: 10.1080/09662839508407216

Laqueur, Walter. "After the Fall: Russia in Search of a New Ideology." *World Affairs* 176, no. 6 (2014): 71–77.

Laruelle, Marlene. "Conservatism as the Kremlin's new toolkit: An ideology at the lowest cost." *Russian analytical digest* 138, no. 8 (2013).

Laruelle, Marlene. *In the name of the nation: Nationalism and politics in contemporary Russia.* Springer, 2009a.

Laruelle, Marlene. "Is Russia Really "Fascist"? A Comment on Timothy Snyder." *PONARS Eurasia Policy Memo* 539 (2018).

Laruelle, Marlene. "Misinterpreting Nationalism: Why Russkii Is Not a Sign of Ethnonationalism." *PONARS Eurasia Policy Memo* 416 (2016a).

Laruelle, Marlene. "The Izborsky Club, or the New Conservative Avant-Garde in Russia." *The Russian Review* 75, no. 4 (2016b): 626–644.

Laruelle, Marlène, ed. *Russian Nationalism and the National Reassertion of Russia.* New York: Routledge, 2009b.

Laruelle, Marlene. *Russian Eurasianism: An Ideology of an Empire.* Washington, D.C: Woodrow Wilson Press/The John Hopkins University Press, 2008.

Lazarsfeld, Paul Felix, Bernard Berelson, and Hazel Gaudet. "The people's choice." (1944).

Lenin, Vladimir. "Sovety postoronnego." *Pravda* No. 250, November 7, 1920.

Levada, Yurii A. "Homo post-sovieticus." *Russian Social Science Review* 44, no. 1 (2003): 32–67.

Levada, Yurii. "Koordinaty cheloveka k itogam izucheniia 'cheloveka sovetskogo.'" *Monitoring Obshchestvennogo Mneniia: Ekonomicheskie i Sotsial'nye Peremeny* 1, no. 51 (2001a).

Levada, Yurii. "Homo Praevaricatus: Russian Doublethink.'" In *Contemporary Russian Politics: A Reader*, edited by A. Brown, pp. 312–322. Oxford: Oxford University Press, 2001b.

Levada, Yurii. "Chelovek Sovetskij: problema rekonstruktsii iskhodnykh form." *Monitoring obshchestvennogo mnenia* no. 2 (March–April, 2001c): 7–16.

Levada, Yurii. *Sotsiologicheskie ocherki 1993–2000.* Moskva: Karpovcow, (2011a).

Levada, Yurii. *Sovetskii prostoi chelovek: opyt sotsialnogo portreta na rubezhe 90–kh.* Moscow: Mirovoy Okean, 1993.Levada, Yurii "Sochineniia: Problema cheloveka." (prepared by T.V. Levada), Moskva: Karpov, 2011b.

Levinson, Alexei. "Nastupili 'likhie' 2010–e," June 14, 2011. https://www.vedomosti.ru/opinion/articles/2011/06/14/nastoyaschie_lihie#ixzz1PRnrKTbq

Levinson, Alexei. "Post-Krym, post-futbol." *Neprikosnovennyi zapas* 5 (2018): 194–199. https://magazines.gorky.media/nz/2018/5/post-krym-post-futbol.html

Lipman, Maria. "Constrained or Irrelevant: The Media in Putin's Russia." *Current History* 104, no. 684 (2005): 319–324.

Lipman, Maria. "The Demise of RBC and Investigative Reporting in Russia." *The New Yorker*, May 18, 2016. Found at: https://www.newyorker.com/news/news–desk/the–demise–of–rbc–and–investigative–reporting–in–russia

Lipman, Maria. "Putin's 'Besieged Fortress' and Its Ideological Arms." In *The State of Russia: What Comes Next?*, edited by Maria Lipman and Nikolay Petrov, pp. 110–136. Basingstoke, UK: Palgrave Macmillan, 2015.

Lipman, Masha, and Michael McFaul. "'Managed Democracy' in Russia: Putin and the Press." *Harvard International Journal of Press/Politics* 6, no. 3 (2001): 116–127.

Lipset, Seymour Martin. *American Exceptionalism: A Double-Edged Sword.* New York: W. W. Norton, 1997.

Livers, Keith. "The Tower or the Labyrinth: Conspiracy, Occult, and Empire-Nostalgia in the Work of Viktor Pelevin and Aleksandr Prokhanov." *The Russian Review* 69, no. 3 (2010): 477–503.

Loewenstein, George, Scott Rick, and Jonathan D. Cohen. "Neuroeconomics." *Annual Review of Psychology* 59 (2008): 647–672.

"The Long Life of Homo sovieticus." *The Economist*, December 10, 2011. http://www.economist.com/node/21541444

Lukin, Alexander. "Russia's New Authoritarianism and the Post-Soviet Political Ideal." *Post-Soviet Affairs* 25, no. 1 (2009): 66–92.

Lutyński, Jan. *Nauka i polskie problemy: komentarz socjologa.* Warsaw: Państwowy Instytut Wydawn., 1990.

Magaloni, Beatriz. *Voting for Autocracy: Hegemonic Party Survival and Its Demise in Mexico*. Cambridge: Cambridge University Press, 2006.

Magnúsdóttir, Rósa. *Enemy Number One: The United States of America in Soviet Ideology and Propaganda, 1945–1959*. New York: Oxford University Press, 2018.

Malinova, Olga. "In Search of a 'Usable Past': Discourse about National Identity in Post-Soviet Russia." Paper presented at the 22nd IPSA World Congress of Political Science, Madrid, July 2012.

Malinova, Olga. "Obsession with Status and Ressentiment: Historical Backgrounds of the Russian Discursive Identity Construction." *Communist and Post-Communist Studies* 47, no. 3 (2014): 291–303.

Malinova, Olga. "Political Uses of the Great Patriotic War in Post-Soviet Russia from Yeltsin to Putin." In *War and Memory in Russia, Ukraine and Belarus*, edited by Julie Fedor, Markku Kangaspuro, Jussi Lassila, and Tatiana Zhurzhenko, 43–70. Cham: Palgrave Macmillan, 2017.

Mannheim, Karl. *Ideology and Utopia*. New York: Routledge, 2013 (first published in 1929).

Mansky, Vitalii. *Putin's Witnesses*. Documentary Television Film, 2018.

Mantzavinos, Chrysostomos, Douglass C. North, and Syed Shariq. "Learning, Institutions, and Economic Performance." *Perspectives on Politics* 2, no. 01 (2004): 75–84.

Maor, Moshe, and James Gross. "Emotion Regulation by Emotional Entrepreneurs: Implications for Political Science and International Relations." In *73rd Annual Conference of the Midwest Political Science Association*, Chicago. 2015.

Markus, Hazel. "Self-schemata and Processing Information about the Self." *Journal of Personality and Social Psychology* 35, no. 2 (1977): 63.

Marody, Mira. "Homo Sovieticus and the Change of Values: The Case of Poland." *Landmark 1989: Central and Eastern European Societies Twenty Years after the System Change* 32 (2010): 80.

Marody, Mirosława. "Antynomie zbiorowej podświadomości." *Studia socjologiczne* 2 (1987): 89–99.

Marten, Kimberly. "Russia's Use of Semi-State Security Forces: The Case of the Wagner Group." *Post-Soviet Affairs* 35, no. 3 (2019): 181–204.

Maslovskiy, Mikhail. "Social and Cultural Obstacles to Russian Modernisation." *Europe-Asia Studies* 65, no. 10 (2013): 2014–2022.

Matravers, Derek. "Empathy as a Route to Knowledge." In *Empathy: Philosophical and Psychological Perspectives*, edited by Amy Coplan and Peter Goldie, 19–30. Oxford, New York: Oxfird University Press, 2011.

Matza, Tomas. "Moscow's Echo: Technologies of the Self, Publics, and Politics on the Russian Talk Show." *Cultural Anthropology* 24, no. 3 (2009): 489–522.

McDermott, Rose. "The Feeling of Rationality: The Meaning of Neuroscientific Advances for Political Science." *Perspectives on Politics* 2, no. 04 (2004): 691–706.

McFaul, Michael. "Russia as It Is: A Grand Strategy for Confronting Putin." *Foreign Affairs* 97, no. 4 (2018): 82–91.

Medvedev, Sergei. "Biopolitika avtoritarnogo tranzita." *Colta.ru*, December 14, 2018. https://www.colta.ru/articles/society/20042

Medvedev, Sergei. "Likhie devyanostye kak opyt svobody." *Radio svoboda*, September 16, 2015. https://www.svoboda.org/a/27252441.html

Medvedev, Sergei. "Russkii ressentiment." *Otechestvennye zapiski* 6, no. 63 (2014).

Menzel, Birgit. "The Occult Revival in Russia Today and Its Impact on Literature." *The Harriman Review* 16, no. 1 (2007): 1–14.

Meštrović, Stjepan G. "Durkheim's Concept of Anomie Considered as a 'Total' Social Fact." *British Journal of Sociology* (1987): 567–583.

Mickiewicz, Ellen. "Excavating Concealed Tradeoffs: How Russians Watch the News." *Political Communication* 22, no. 3 (2005): 355–380.

Mickiewicz, Ellen P. *Split Signals: Television and Politics in the Soviet Union*. Oxford: Oxford University Press on Demand, 1990.

Mikhailov, V., V. Bazhanov, and M. Farukshin. *Osobaia zona: vybory v Tatarstane*. Ulianovsk, 2002.

Mikhalkov, Nikita. *55*. Documentary television film. 2007.

Misiunas, Romuald J., and Rein Taagepera. *The Baltic States, Years of Dependence, 1940–1990*. Berkeley: University of California Press, 1993.

Mitchell, Rebecca. Review of *Music and Soviet Power: 1917–1932*, by Marina Frolova-Walker and Jonathan Walker. Woodbridge: Boydell Press, 2012 (in *Revolutionary Russia* 27, no. 1 (2014): 79–81.

Mitzen, Jennifer. "Ontological Security in World Politics: State Identity and the Security Dilemma." *European Journal of International Relations* 12, no. 3 (2006): 341–370.

Moisi, Dominique. *The Geopolitics of Emotion: How Cultures of Fear, Humiliation, and Hope Are Reshaping the World*. New York: Anchor, 2010.

Molchanov, Mikhail A. "Classical Eastern and Western Traditions of Political Leadership." In *The Ashgate Research Companion to Political Leadership*, edited by Joseph Masciulli, Mikhail A. Molchanov, and W. Andy Knight, 31–50. London: Routledge, 2013.

Moon, David. *The Russian Peasantry 1600–1930: The World the Peasants Made*. New York: Routledge, 2014.

Morozov, Aleksandr. "Ot zamorozhennykh konfliktov – k doktrine 'Rossiia bez granits.'" *Colta.ru*, August 7, 2018. https://www.colta.ru/articles/society/18767-ot-zamorozhennyh-konfliktov-k-doktrine-rossiya-bez-granits

Morozov, Aleksandr. "Tak nazyvaemye partnery: . . ." *Colta.ru*, March 14, 2017. http://www.colta.ru/articles/society/14209

Morozov, Aleksandr. "'Kazus Nemtsova' i spetspropagandony" (The Nemtsov Case and the Special Propagandists), January 17, 2011. www.openspace.ru/media/projects/18065/details/19871/?expand=yes, accessed November 6, 2018.

Morozov, Aleksandr. *Konets fabriki obrazov.* http://www.russ.ru/pole/Konec–fabriki–obrazov

Morozov, V. "Identity and Hegemony in EU-Russia Relations: Making Sense of the Asymmetrical Entanglement." *EU-Russia Relations in Crisis: Understanding Diverging Perceptions,* edited by Tom Casier and Joan DeBardeleben, 30–49. Abingdon: Routledge, 2018.

Morozov, Viacheslav. *Rossia i drugie: identichnost' i granitsy politcheskogo soobshchestva.* Moskva: Novoe Literaturnoe Obozrenie, 2009.

Morse, Stan, and Kenneth J. Gergen. "Social Comparison, Self-Consistency, and the Concept of Self." *Journal of Personality and Social Psychology* 16, no. 1 (1970): 148.

Moscovici, Serge. "The Phenomenon of Social Representations." In *Social Representations,* edited by R. M. Farr and S. Moscovici, 3–69. Cambridge: Cambridge University Press, 1984.

Myers, Steven Lee. *The New Tsar: The Rise and Reign of Vladimir Putin.* New York: Simon & Schuster, 2015.

Naiman, Eric. "On Soviet Subjects and the Scholars Who Make Them." *The Russian Review* 60, no. 3 (2001): 307–315.

Naoumova, Irina, Anna Kachkaeva, Ilia Kiria, and Annette Rogers. "Informal Instruments of Formal Power: Case of Russian Mass Media." *International Business: Research, Teaching and Practice* 6, no. 1 (2012): 96–116.

Naumova, Nina. "Retsidiviruyushchaya modernizatsiya v Rossii: beda, vina ili resurs chelovechestva." Edited by V. N. Sadovsky and V. A. Yadov. Moscow: RGB, 2004.

Nikonova, Olga. "Soviet Patriotism in a Comparative Perspective: A Passion for Oxymora." *Studies in East European Thought* 62, no. 3–4 (2010): 353–376.

Norris, Stephen M. *Blockbuster History in the New Russia: Movies, Memory, and Patriotism.* Bloomington: Indiana University Press, 2012.

Nougayrede, Natalie. "The Putin Paradox: Distrusted, Feared, and Yet Revered." *The Guardian,* May 21, 2015. https://www.theguardian.com/commentisfree/2015/may/21/russia–vladimir–putin–propaganda

Nowak, Stefan. "System wartości społeczeństwa polskiego." *Studia socjologiczne* 4, no. 75 (1979): 155–173.

Oates, Sarah. "Russian Media in the Digital Age: Propaganda Rewired." *Russian Politics* 1, no. 4 (2016): 398–417.

Oates, Sarah, and Sean Steiner. "Projecting Power: Understanding Russian Strategic Narrative." *Russian Analytical Digest,* No. 229, December 17, 2018: 2–5.

Orlov, I. B., and A. D. Popov. *Russo Turisto. Sovetskii vyezdnoi turizm, 1955–1991.* Moskva: Higher School of Economics Press, 2016.

Orlova, Galina. "Apologiia strannoi veshchi: 'malen'kie khitrosti' sovetskogo cheloveka." *Neprikosnovennyi zapas* 34, no. 2 (2004).

Orlova, Galina. "Modal'nost' ili ideologicheskaia vozgonka dushi: dvizhenie za kommunistecheskij trud v 1960–e gody." *Neprikosnovennyi zapas* 108, no. 4 (2016).

Orlova, Galina. "'Traktor v pole dyr–dyr–dyr/Vse my boremsia za mir': sovetskoe miroliubie v brezhnevskuiu epokhu." *Neprikosnovennyi zapas* 54, no. 4 (2007).

Oslon, Aleksandr. *Khronika pikiruiushchego obshchestva (Obshchestvennoe mnenie iiul' 1996–mart 1997). Sotsiologicheskie issledovaniia* no. 8 (1997): 109–125.

Ost, David. *The Defeat of Solidarity: Anger and Politics in Postcommunist Europe.* Ithaca, NY: Cornell University Press, 2006.

Oushakine, Serguei. "In the State of Post-Soviet Aphasia: Symbolic Development in Contemporary Russia." *Europe-Asia Studies* 52, no. 6 (2000): 991–1016.

Oushakine, Serguei Alex. *The Patriotism of Despair: Nation, War, and Loss in Russia.* Ithaca, NY: Cornell University Press, 2009.

Oushakine, Serguei Alex. "Remembering in Public: On the Affective Management of History." *Ab Imperio* 2013, no. 1 (2013): 269–302.

Oushakine, Serguei Alex. "Totality Decomposed: Objectalizing Late Socialism in Post-Soviet Biochronicles." *The Russian Review* 69, no. 4 (2010): 638–669.

Oushakine, Serguei. "Translating Communism for Children: Fables and Posters of the Revolution." *Boundary* 243, no. 3 (2016): 159–219.

Oushakine, Serguei Alex. "'We're nostalgic but we're not crazy': Retrofitting the Past in Russia." *The Russian Review* 66, no. 3 (2007): 451–482.

Paneyakh, Ella. "Otmiranie gosudarstva. Rossiiskoe obshchestvo mezhdu postmodernom and arkhaikoi." *InLiberty*, November 30, 2018. https://www.inliberty.ru/article/modern–paneyakh/

Paperno, Irina. *Stories of the Soviet Experience: Memoirs, Diaries, Dreams.* Ithaca, NY: Cornell University Press, 2009.

Paretskaya, Anna. "A Middle Class without Capitalism? Socialist Ideology and Post-Collectivist." *Soviet Society in the Era of Late Socialism, 1964–1985* (2012): 43.

Parkinson, Brian, Agneta H. Fischer, and Antony S. R. Manstead. *Emotion in Social Relations: Cultural, Group, and Interpersonal Processes.* New York: Psychology Press, 2004.

Parsons, Talcott. "An Outline of the Social System." In *Theories of Society*, edited by Talcott Parsons, E. Shils, K. Naegele, and J. Pitts. New York: Free Press, 1961.

Pavlovsky, Gleb. *Ironicheskaia imperiia.* Moskva: Evropa, 2019.

Peacock, Margaret. "Contested Innocence: Image of the Child in the Cold War." PhD dissertation, University of Texas, 2008.

Petersen, Roger. "Emotions as the Residue of Lived Experience." *PS, Political Science & Politics* 50, no. 4 (2017): 932.

Petersen, Roger D. *Understanding Ethnic Violence: Fear, Hatred, and Resentment in Twentieth-Century Eastern Europe.* Cambridge: Cambridge University Press, 2002.

Petlyanova, Nina. "Desant: Desyatki boitsov." *Novaya gazeta*, August 26, 2014. https://www.novayagazeta.ru/articles/2014/08/26/60865–desant

Pinkus, Benjamin. *The Jews of the Soviet Union: The History of a National Minority.* Cambridge Russia, Soviet and Post-Soviet Studies 62. Cambridge: Cambridge University Press, 1990.

Pinsky, Anatoly. "The Origins of Post-Stalin Individuality: Aleksandr Tvardovskii and the Evolution of 1930s Soviet Romanticism." *The Russian Review* 76, no. 3 (2017): 458–483.

Piper, Elizabeth. "Media Squeeze Tightens as Russia Harks Back to WW2." *Chicago Tribune*, March 14, 2014. https://www.chicagotribune.com/news/ct-xpm-2014-03-14-sns-rt-us-ukraine-crisis-russia-media-insight-20140313-story.html

Pipes, Richard. "Is Russia Still an Enemy?" *Foreign Affairs* 76, no. 5 (1997): 65–78.

Pipes, Richard. *Russia under the Old Regime*. London: Weidenfeld and Nicolson, 1974.

Poluekhtova, Irina. "Dinamika rossiiskoi teleauditorii." *Sotsiologicheskie issledovaniia* 1 (2010): 66–77.

Pomerantsev, Peter. "Russia: A Postmodern Dictatorship?" Legatum Institute, Global Transitions Lecture Series, 2013. https://www.li.com/docs/default-source/publications/pomeransev1_russia_imr_web_final.pdf

Ponomarev, E. R. "Uchebnik patriotizma (literatura v sovetskoi shkole v 1940-50e gody)." *Novoe literaturnoe obozrenie* 97 (2009): 37–57.

Ponomareva, Alya. "Dlia zhurnalistov proveli 'sploshnuiu dvoinuiu.'" *Radio Svoboda*, July 11, 2016. https://www.svoboda.org/a/27851576.html

Pop-Eleches, Grigore, and Joshua A. Tucker. *Communism's Shadow: Historical Legacies and Contemporary Political Attitudes*. Princeton, NJ: Princeton University Press, 2017.

Prokhorova, Irina. "Totalitarnoe soznanie i missia intellektuala." *The NewTimes*, May 28, 2018. https://newtimes.ru/articles/detail/165063

Prozorov, Sergei. "Russian Conservatism in the Putin Presidency: The Dispersion of a Hegemonic Discourse." *Journal of Political Ideologies* 10, no. 2 (2005): 121–143.

Putin, Vladimir, Nataliia Gevorkian, Nataliya Gevorkyan, Natalya Timakova, and Andrei Kolesnikov. *First Person: An Astonishingly Frank Self-portrait by Russia's President Vladimir Putin*. New York: Public Affairs, 2000.

Putin, Vladimir. "Razgovor s Vladimirom Putinym. Prodolzhenie." December 16, 2010. https://www.vesti.ru/doc.html?id=414412

Reber, A. S. "Implicit Learning and Tacit Knowledge." *Journal of Experimental Psychology: General* 118, no. 3 (1989): 219–235.

Reddaway, Peter. *The Dissidents: A Memoir of Working with the Resistance in Russia, 1960–1990*. Washington, DC: Brooking Institution Press, 2019.

Reddaway, Peter, and Dmitri Glinski. *The Tragedy of Russia's Reforms: Market Bolshevism against Democracy*. Washington, DC: US Institute of Peace Press, 2001.

Reicher, Stephen. "The Context of Social Identity: Domination, Resistance, and Change." *Political Psychology* 25, no. 6 (2004): 921–945.

Ringmar, Erik. "The Recognition Game: Soviet Russia against the West." *Cooperation and Conflict: Journal of the Nordic International Studies Association* 37, no. 2 (2002): 115–36.

Risch, William Jay. *The Ukrainian West: Culture and the Fate of Empire in Soviet Lviv*. Harvard Historical Studies 173. Cambridge, MA: Harvard University Press, 2011.

Rogachevskii, Andrei. "Homo Sovieticus in the Library." *Europe-Asia Studies* 54, no. 6 (2002): 975–988.

Roginsky, Arseny. "Pamiat o stalinizme." Polit.ru December 11, 2008. https://polit.ru/article/2008/12/11/memory/

Rogov, Kirill. "The Art of Coercion: Repressions and Repressiveness in Putin's Russia." *Russian Politics* 3, no. 2 (2018): 151–174.

Rogov, Kirill. "'Crimean Syndrome' Mechanisms of Authoritarian Mobilization." *Russian Politics & Law* 54, no. 1 (2016): 28–54.

Rolf, Malte. "A Hall of Mirrors: Sovietizing Culture under Stalinism." *Slavic Review* 68, no. 3 (2009): 601–630.

Rosenfeld, Bryn. "Reevaluating The Middle-Class Protest Paradigm: A Case-Control Study of Democratic Protest Coalitions in Russia." *American Political Science Review* 111, no. 4 (2017): 637–652.

Rosenfeld, Gavriel D. *Munich and Memory: Architecture, Monuments, and the Legacy of the Third Reich*. Vol. 22. Berkeley: University of California Press, 2000.

Ross, Andrew A. G. *Mixed Emotions: Beyond Fear and Hatred in International Conflict*. Chicago: University of Chicago Press, 2014.

"V Rossii televidenie ostaetsia osnovnym istochnikom informatsii." Found at: https://ria.ru/20190801/1557077080.html

Rostova, Nataliya. "Posobie dlia bednykh mysliu." *Novaia gazeta*, February 24, 2005. http://2005.novayagazeta.ru/nomer/2005/14n/n14n-s00.shtml

Rostova, Nataliya. "V 'shporakh' rozhdaetsia istina." *Novaia gazeta*, February 24, 2005. http://2005.novayagazeta.ru/nomer/2005/14n/n14n-s01.shtml

Roth-Ey, Kristin. *Moscow Prime Time: How the Soviet Union Built the Media Empire That Lost the Cultural Cold War*. Ithaca, NY: Cornell University Press, 2011.

Roudakova, Natalia. *Losing Pravda: Ethics and the Press in Post-Truth Russia*. Cambridge: Cambridge University Press, 2017.

Round, John, and Colin Williams. "Coping with the Social Costs of 'Transition': Everyday Life in Post-Soviet Russia and Ukraine." *European Urban and Regional Studies* 17, no. 2 (2010): 183–196.

Rubin, Mikhail, Maria Zholobova, and Roman Badanin. "'Povelitel' kukol. Portret Alekseia Gromova, rukovoditelia rossiiskoi gosudarstvennoi propagandy," January 23, 2019. *ProektMedia* https://www.proekt.media/portrait/alexey–gromov/

Rutenberg, Jim. "RT, Sputnik and Russia's New Theory of War." *New York Times Magazine*, September 13, 2017. https://www.nytimes.com/2017/09/13/magazine/rt–sputnik–and–russias–new–theory–of–war.html

Rutland, Peter. "Putin and the Oligarchs." In *Putin's Russia. Past Imperfect, Future Uncertain*, edited by Stephen A. Wegren, 133–152. Lanham, MD: Rowman & Littlefield, 2003.

Rutland, Peter. "Putin's Path to Power," *Post-Soviet Affairs* 16 no. 4 (2000): 313–354.

Rutten, Ellen, Julie Fedor, and Vera Zvereva, eds. *Memory, Conflict and New Media: Web Wars in Post-Socialist States*. New York: Routledge, 2013.

Sakwa, Richard. "Putin and the Oligarchs." *New Political Economy* 13, no. 2 (2008): 185–191.

Sanfey, Alan G., George Loewenstein, Samuel M. McClure, and Jonathan D. Cohen. "Neuroeconomics: Cross-Currents in Research on Decision-Making." *Trends in Cognitive Sciences* 10, no. 3 (2006): 108–116.

Satter, David. *It Was a Long Time Ago, and It Never Happened Anyway: Russia and the Communist Past.* New Haven, CT: Yale University Press, 2011.

Sauve, Guillaume. "In Memory of the Divided Self: The Tenacious Assumptions of Soviet Morality during Perestroika." Paper presented at the ASN World Convention, Columbia University, April 18–20, 2013.

Schimpfossl, Elisabeth, and Ilya Yablokov. "Coercion or Conformism? Censorship and Self-Censorship among Russian Media Personalities and Reporters in the 2010s." *Demokratizatsiya: The Journal of Post-Soviet Democratization* 22, no. 2 (2014): 295–311.

Schreck, Carl, and Dmitry Volchek. "One Russian's Search for His Great-Grandfather's Soviet Police Killers," June 23, 2016. https://www.rferl.org/a/russia–search–for–great–grandfathers–soviet–executioners/27816261.html

Sharafutdinova, Gulnaz. "American Lessons: On the Path Toward Russian 'Progressivism.'" *PONARS Policy Memo* 195, 2012.

Sharafutdinova, Gulnaz. "Public Opinion Formation and Group Identity: The Politics of National Identity Salience in Putin's Russia." *Problems of Post-Communism*, forthcoming.

Sharafutdinova, Gulnaz. "Authoritarian Legitimation and Insecure Collective Identity: Lessons From Putin's Russia," unpublished manuscript, 2019a.

Sharafutdinova, Gulnaz. "Was There a "Simple Soviet" Person? Debating the Politics and Sociology of *Homo Sovieticus*" *Slavic Review* 78, no. 1, (2019b): 173–195.

Sharafutdinova, Gulnaz. "Managing National Ressentiment: Morality Politics in Putin's Russia." *Vocabularies of International Relations after the Crisis in Ukraine.* Routledge (2017): 130–151.

Sharafutdinova, Gulnaz. *Political Consequences of Crony Capitalism Inside Russia.* Notre Dame, IN: University of Notre Dame Press, 2010.

Sharafutdinova, Gulnaz. "The Pussy Riot Affair and Putin's Démarche from Sovereign Democracy to Sovereign Morality." *Nationalities Papers* 42, no. 4 (2014): 615–621.

Sharafutdinova, Gulnaz, and Karen Dawisha. "The Escape from Institution-Building in a Globalized World: Lessons from Russia." *Perspectives on Politics* 15, no. 2 (2017): 361–378.

Sharkov, Damien. "Russians Go Wild For Song About Loving 'Someone Like Putin.'" *Newsweek.com* April 21, 2016. https://www.newsweek.com/russians-go-wild-hit-about-loving-someone-putin-450578

Shevchenko, Olga. *Crisis and the Everyday in Postsocialist Moscow.* Bloomington: Indiana University Press, 2008.

Shevtsova, Lilĩa. *Russia lost in transition: the Yeltsin and Putin legacies*. Carnegie Endowment, 2007.

Shiller, Robert J., Maxim Boycko, Vladimir Korobov, Sidney G. Winter, and Thomas Schelling. "Hunting for Homo Sovieticus: Situational versus Attitudinal Factors in Economic Behavior." *Brookings Papers on Economic Activity* 1992, no. 1 (1992): 127–194.

Shirvindt, Alexandr. *Skleroz rasseianny po zhizni*. Moskva: KoLibri, 2014.

Shtromas, Aleksandras. "The Baltic States as Soviet Republics: Tensions and Contradictions." In *The Baltic States: The National Self-Determination of Estonia, Latvia and Lithuania*, edited by Graham Smith, 86–117. London: Palgrave Macmillan, 1996.

Siegelbaum, Lewis H. *Cars for Comrades: The Life of the Soviet Automobile*. Ithaca, NY: Cornell University Press, 2008.

Simon, Bernd, and Bert Klandermans. "Politicized Collective Identity: A Social Psychological Analysis." *American Psychologist* 56, no. 4 (2001): 319.

Smith, Kathleen E. *Mythmaking in the New Russia: Politics and Memory during the Yeltsin Era*. Ithaca, NY: Cornell University Press, 2002.

Smolkin, Victoria. *A Sacred Space Is Never Empty: A History of Soviet Atheism*. Princeton, NJ: Princeton University Press, 2018.

Sobieraj, Sarah, Jeffrey M. Berry, and Amy Connors. "Outrageous Political Opinion and Political Anxiety in the US." *Poetics* 41 (2013): 407–432.

Sokolon, Marlene K. *Political Emotions: Aristotle and the Symphony of Reason and Emotion*. DeKalb: Northern Illinois University Press, 2006.

Soldatov, Andrei, and Irina Borogan. *The New Nobility: The Restoration of Russia's Security State and the Enduring Legacy of the KGB*. New York: Public Affairs, 2010.

Solonari, Vladimir. "Creating a 'People': A Case Study in Post-Soviet History-Writing." *Kritika: Explorations in Russian and Eurasian History* 4, no. 2 (2003): 411–438.

Solonari, Vladimir. "Normalizing Russia, Legitimizing Putin." *Kritika: Explorations in Russian and Eurasian History* 10, no. 4 (2009): 835–846.

Solovyev, Vladimir. *Putin. Putevoditel' dlia neravnodushnykh*. Moskva: Eksmo, 2008.

Somers, Margaret R. "The Narrative Constitution of Identity: A Relational and Network Approach." *Theory and Society* 23, no. 5 (1994): 605–649.

Sorokin, Vladimir. "Postsovetskii chelovek razocharoval bol'she chem sovetskii." *Kommersant.ru*, August 17, 2015. https://www.kommersant.ru/doc/2786007

Sperling, Valerie. *Sex, Politics, and Putin: Political Legitimacy in Russia*. Oxford: Oxford University Press, 2014.

Steinbeck, John. *Russkii dnevnik*. EKSMO, 2017.

Stent, Angela E. *The Limits of Partnership: US–Russian Relations in the Twenty-First Century—Updated Edition*. Princeton, NJ: Princeton University Press, 2015.

Stets, Jan E., and Peter J. Burke. "Identity Theory and Social Identity Theory." *Social Psychology Quarterly* 63, no. 3 (2000): 224–237.

Strauss, Claudia, and Naomi Quinn. *A Cognitive Theory of Cultural Meaning.* Publications of the Society for Psychological Anthropology, 9. Cambridge: Cambridge University Press, 1997.

Stryker, Sheldon, and Peter J. Burke. "The Past, the Present, and the Future of an Identity Theory." *Social Psychology Quarterly* 63, no. 4 (2000): 284–297.

Sukhanov, L. E. *Tri goda s Yeltsinym. Zapiski pervogo pomoshchnika.* Riga: Vaga, 1992.

Suny, Ronald Grigor. "On Ideology, Subjectivity, and Modernity: Disparate Thoughts about Doing Soviet History." *Russian History* 35, no. 1–2 (2008): 251–258.

Suny, Ronald. *The Revenge of the Past: Nationalism, Revolution, and the Collapse of the Soviet Union.* Stanford, CA: Stanford University Press, 1993.

Surkov, Vladislav. "Suverenitet eto politicheskii sinomim konkurentosposobnosti," presentation at the United Russia Party School, February 7, 2006.

Surkov, Vladislav. *Russkaia politicheskaia kultura: vzglyad iz utopii.* Moskva: B.C.G. Press, 2007.

Sztompka, Piotr. "Civilisational Competence: A Prerequisite of Post-Communist Transition." *Centre for European Studies* (2000a).

Sztompka, Piotr. "Cultural Trauma: The Other Face of Social Change." *European Journal of Social Theory* 3, no. 4 (2000b): 449–466.

Sztompka, Piotr. *Trauma Wielkiej Zmiany Spolczne Koszty Transformacji.* Warsaw: PAN ISP, 2000c.

Tajfel, Henri. "Social Identity and Intergroup Behaviour." *Information (International Social Science Council)* 13, no. 2 (1974): 65–93.

Tajfel, Henri, and John C. Turner. "An Integrative Theory of Intergroup Conflict." *The Social Psychology of Intergroup Relations* 33, no. 47 (1979): 74.

Taylor, Brian D. *The Code of Putinism.* Oxford: Oxford University Press, 2018.

Taylor, Brian D. *Politics and the Russian Army: Civil-Military Relations, 1689–2000.* Cambridge: Cambridge University Press, 2003.

Thomas, Geoff, Robin Martin, Olga Epitropaki, Yves Guillaume, and Allan Lee. "Social Cognition in Leader–Follower Relationships: Applying Insights from Relationship Science to Understanding Relationship-Based Approaches to Leadership." *Journal of Organizational Behavior* 34, no. S1 (2013): S63–S81.

Tismaneanu, Vladimir. "Lenin's Troubled Legacies: Bolshevism, Marxism and the Russian Traditions." Lecture delivered at the Havighurst Center for Russian and Eurasian Studies (2001). Found at: http://www.cas.miamioh.edu/havighurstcenter/papers/Tismaneanu.pdf

Tismaneanu, Vladimir. *The Crisis of Marxist Ideology in Eastern Europe: The Poverty of Utopia.* Taylor & Francis, 1988.

Tismaneanu, Vladimir. "The Leninist Debris or Waiting for Perón." *East European Politics and Societies* 10, no. 3 (1996): 504–535.

Tismaneanu, Vladimir. "Democracy and Memory: Romania Confronts its Communist Past." *The Annals of the American Academy of Political and Social Science* 617, no. 1 (2008): 166–180.

Toal, Gerard. *Near Abroad: Putin, the West and the Contest over Ukraine and the Caucasus*. Oxford: Oxford University Press, 2017.

Tolczyk, Dariusz, and Glyndwr Williams. *See No Evil: Literary Cover-ups and Discoveries of the Soviet Camp Experience*. New Haven, CT: Yale University Press, 1999.

Tolz, Vera, and Yuri Teper. "Broadcasting Agitainment: A New Media Strategy of Putin's Third Presidency." *Post-Soviet Affairs* 34, no. 4 (2018): 213–227.

Toymentsev, Sergey. "Legal but Criminal: The Failure of the "Russian Nuremberg" and the Paradoxes of Post-Soviet Memory." *Comparative Literature Studies* 48, no. 3 (2011): 296–319.

Treisman, Daniel. "Presidential Popularity in a Hybrid Regime: Russia under Yeltsin and Putin." *American Journal of Political Science* 55, no. 3 (2011): 590–609.

Trubina, Elena. "Past Wars in the Russian Blogosphere: On the Emergence of Cosmopolitan Memory." *Digital Icons: Studies in Russian, Eurasian and Central European New Media* 4 (2010): 63–85.

Trudoliubov, Maxim. "Stalin as Superman and Dangers of Polling in an Autocracy." *The Russia File*, Kennan Institute, April 19, 2019. https://www.wilsoncenter.org/blog-post/stalin-superman-and-the-dangers-polling-autocracy, accessed May 12, 2020.

Tsipursky, Gleb. *Socialist Fun: Youth, Consumption, and State-Sponsored Popular Culture in the Soviet Union, 1945–1970*. Pittsburgh: University of Pittsburgh Press, 2016.

Tsyrlina-Spady, Tatyana, and Alan Stoskopf. "Russian History Textbooks in the Putin Era: Heroic Leaders Demand Loyal Citizens." In *Globalisation and Historiography of National Leaders*, edited by Joseph Zajda, Tatyana Tsyrlina-Spady and Michael Lovorn, 15–33. Dordrecht: Springer, 2017.

Tumarkin, Maria M. "The Long Life of Stalinism: Reflections on the Aftermath of Totalitarianism and Social Memory." *Journal of Social History* 4, no. 44 (2011): 1047–1061.

Turner, John C., and Penelope J. Oakes. "The Significance of the Social Identity Concept for Social Psychology with Reference to Individualism, Interactionism and Social Influence." *British Journal of Social Psychology* 25, no. 3 (1986): 237–252.

Tyszka, Krzysztof. "*Homo Sovieticus* Two Decades Later." *Polish Sociological Review* 4, no. 168 (2009): 507–522.

Umland, Andreas. "Aleksandr Dugin's Transformation from a Lunatic Fringe Figure into a Mainstream Political Publicist, 1980–1998: A Case Study in the Rise of Late and Post-Soviet Russian Fascism." *Journal of Eurasian Studies* 1, no. 2 (2010): 144–152.

Umland, Andreas. "Varieties of Russian Exceptionalism in Putin's Russia: Guest Editor's Introduction." *Russian Politics & Law* 50, no. 6 (2012): 3–6.

Urban, Michael. "The Politics of Identity in Russia's Postcommunist Transition: The Nation against Itself." *Slavic Review* 53, no. 3 (1994): 733–765.

Vainshtein, Grigory. "Totalitarian Public Consciousness in a Post-Totalitarian Society: The Russian Case in the General Context of Post-Communist Developments." *Communist and Post–Communist Studies* 27, no. 3 (1994): 247–259.

Van Lange, Paul A. M., Arie W. Kruglanski, and E. Tory Higgins. *Handbook of Theories of Social Psychology Two*. Vol. 2. Thousand Oaks, CA: Sage, 2011.

Van Zon, Hans. "Neo-patrimonialism as an Impediment to Economic Development: The Case of Ukraine." *The Journal of Communist Studies and Transition Politics* 17, no. 3 (2001): 71–95.

Velmet, Aro. "Occupied Identities: National Narratives in Baltic Museums of Occupations." *Journal of Baltic Studies* 42, no. 2 (2011): 189–211.

Vogler, Carolyn. "Social Identity and Emotion: The Meeting of Psychoanalysis and Sociology." *The Sociological Review* 48, no. 1 (2000): 19–42.

Volchek, Dmitry, and Robert Coalson. "Discovery of a Relative's Executioners Leads to a Surprising Reconciliation." *RFE/RL*, November 21, 2016. https://www.rferl.org/a/stalin-great-terror-search-for-great-grandfather-executioners-reconciliation-russia/28131158.html

Volkan, Vamik D. "Large-Group Identity, International Relations and Psychoanalysis." *International Forum of Psychoanalysis* 18, no. 4 (2009): 206–213, Taylor & Francis Group.

Volkan, Vamik D. "Large-Group Psychodynamics and Massive Violence." *Ciência & Saúde Coletiva* 11 (2006): 1199–1210.

Volkan, Vamik D. *The Need to Have Enemies and Allies: From Clinical Practice to International Relationships*. London: Jason Aronson, 1988.

Volkov, Denis, and Stepan Goncharov. *Demokratiia v Rossii: Ustanovki naseleniia*. 2015. http://www.levada.ru/sites/default/files/report_fin.pdf

Volkov, Solomon. *Testimony: The Memoirs of Dmitri Shostakovich*. London: Limelight Editions, 1991.

Von Soest, Christian, and Julia Grauvogel. "How do Non-Democratic Regimes Claim Legitimacy? Comparative Insights from Post-Soviet Countries." S/srn.com 2015.

Vujacic, Veljko. "Stalinism and Russian Nationalism: A Reconceptualization." *Post-Soviet Affairs* 23, no. 2 (2007): 156–183.

Walker, Christopher, and Robert W. Orttung. "Breaking the news: The role of state-run media." *Journal of Democracy* 25, no. 1 (2014): 71–85.

Walker, Shaun. *The Long Hangover: Putin's New Russia and the Ghosts of the Past*. Oxford: Oxford University Press, 2017.

Waller, Julian G. "Mimicking the Mad Printer: Legislating Homophobia in the Post-Soviet Space," Working paper. November 2018.

Webster, Murray, and Barbara Sobieszek. *Sources of Self-Evaluation: A Formal Theory of Significant Others and Social Influence*. New York: John Wiley & Sons, 1974.

Wengle, Susanne, and Christine Evans. "Symbolic State-Building in Contemporary Russia." *Post-Soviet Affairs* 34, no. 6 (2018): 384–411.

Wesolowsky, Tony. "'Listen to Us Now': Putin Unveils Weapons, Vows to Raise Living Standards in Fiery Annual Address." *RFE/RL.org* March 1, 2018. https://www.rferl.org/a/putin-set-give-annual-address-amid-presidential-election-campaign/29069948.html

Westerman, Frank. *Engineers of the Soul: The Grandiose Propaganda of Stalin's Russia.* New York: Abrams, 2012.

White, Anne. *Small-Town Russia: Postcommunist Livelihoods and Identities: A Portrait of the Intelligentsia in Achit, Bednodemyanovsk and Zubtsov, 1999–2000.* New York: Routledge, 2004.

Wijermars, Mariëlle. *Memory Politics in Contemporary Russia.* Taylor & Francis, 2018.

Winerman, Lea. "The Mind's Mirror." *American Psychological Association* 36, no. 9 (October 2005). https://www.apa.org/monitor/oct05/mirror.aspx

Wood, Elizabeth A. "Performing Memory: Vladimir Putin and the Celebration of World War II in Russia." *The Soviet and Post-Soviet Review* 38, no. 2 (2011): 172–200.

Yablokov, Ilya. *Fortress Russia: Conspiracy theories in the post-Soviet world.* John Wiley & Sons, 2018.

Yadov, Vladimir A. "Razmyshleniia o predmete sotsiologii." *Sotsiologicheskie issledovaniia* 2 (1990): 3–16.

Yudin, Grigory. "Kollektivnoe i individual'noe v filosofskoi antropologii E. Durkheim," *Sotsiologicheskoe obozrenie* 12, no. 2, (2013): 122–132.

Yurchak, Alexei. *Everything Was Forever, Until It Was No More: The Last Soviet Generation.* Princeton, NJ: Princeton University Press, 2006.

Yurchak, Alexei. *Everything Was Forever, Until It Was No More: The Last Soviet Generation.* Princeton, NJ: Princeton University Press, 2013.

Yurgens, Igor', and Evgeny Gontmakher. "President dolzhen zaiavit– o sebe." *Vedomosti,* July 27, 2011. https://www.vedomosti.ru/opinion/articles/2011/07/27/medvedevu_pora_perejti_rubikon

Zakem, Vera, Paul Saunders, Umida Hashimova, and P. Kathleen Frier. *Mapping Russian Media Network: Media's Role in Russian Foreign Policy and Decision–Making.* No. DRM–2017–U–015367–1Rev. Arlington, VA: CNA Analysis and Solutions, 2017.

Zarakol, Ayse. *After Defeat: How the East Learned to Live with the West.* Cambridge Studies in International Relations 118. Cambridge: Cambridge University Press, 2010.

Zaslavsky, Victor. *The Neo-Stalinist State: Class Ethnicity and Consensus in Soviet Society.* New York: Routledge, 2016.

Zavadskaya, Margarita. "The New Norms of Protest Politics in Russia," September 27, 2018. (2018a). https://www.ridl.io/en/the–new–norms–of–protest–politics–in–russia/

Zavadskaya, Margarita. "Rossiiskaia molodezh: flagman politicheskoi aktivnosti ili iakor' avtoritarizma," December 13, 2018. (2018b). (www.ridl.io)

Zelenskyi, Mikhail (translated by Kevin Rothrock) "Meet Bishop Tikhon, Vladimir Putin's Rumored Confessor." *Meduza.io.* December 1, 2017. https://meduza.io/en/feature/2017/12/01/meet-bishop-tikhon-vladimir-putin-s-rumored-confessor

Zerubavel, Eviatar. *Social Mindscapes: An Invitation to Cognitive Sociology.* Cambridge, MA: Harvard University Press, 2009.

Zhegulev, Ilya. 2017. "Greg Veiner, on zhe Grigory Vinnikov." *medusa.io,* April 27, 2017. https://meduza.io/feature/2017/04/27/greg–vayner–on–zhe–grigoriy–vinnikov

Zinoviev, Alexander. "Homo Sovieticus," trans. *Charles Janson*, Boston, 1985.

Zubarevich, Natal'ia. "Chetyre Rossii." *Vedomosti.ru* 30 (2011).

Zygar, Mikhail. *All the Kremlin's Men: Inside the Court of Vladimir Putin*. New York: Public Affairs, 2016.

Zygar, Mikhail. *Vsia kremlevskaia rat': Kratkaia istoriia sovremennoi Rossii*. Moscow: Intellektual'naia literatura, 2016.

Index

For the benefit of digital users, indexed terms that span two pages (e.g., 52–53) may, on occasion, appear on only one of those pages.

CPSIA information can be obtained
at www.ICGtesting.com
Printed in the USA
BVHW031710170922
646931BV00004B/14